Reporting on Latino/a/x Communities

This book offers a critical and practical guide for journalists reporting on issues affecting the Latinx community.

Reporting on Latino/a/x Communities emphasizes skills and best practices for covering topics such as economics, immigration and gender. The authors share honest stories about challenges Latino/a/x journalists face in newsrooms, including imposter syndrome and lack of representation in news, along with strategies to face and tackle systematic barriers. Stories from leaders in the media industry are also featured, including journalists and media professionals from ABC News, *Los Angeles Times*, Alt.Latino at NPR and mitú. Additionally highlighted are experimental and non-traditional new initiatives and outlets leading the future of news media for Latino/a/x audiences.

This book is an invaluable guide for any student or journalist interested or involved in the news media and questions of Latino/a/x representation.

Teresa Puente has spent her career reporting on immigration and Latino issues in the United States and has also reported extensively from Mexico. Previously, she was a staff reporter at the *Chicago Tribune* and was on the editorial board at the *Chicago Sun-Times*. Early in her career, she worked as a reporter for the *Press-Telegram* in Long Beach and *The Orange County Register*. Her recent journalistic work has been published in *TIME*, *The Guardian*, *Newsweek*, *The Daily Beast*, *The Hill*, *The Miami Herald*, and *In These Times*. Puente received the Studs Terkel Award from Public Narrative for her coverage of Chicago's diverse communities. Puente, an assistant professor at CSULB, teaches News Reporting and Ethics, Social Media Communication and Bilingual Magazine Reporting & Production, which publishes the Spanish-language magazine *Dig En Español*. Puente holds an MFA in creative writing from Columbia College Chicago and a bachelor's degree with a double major in journalism and political science from Indiana University-Bloomington. She previously taught journalism at Columbia College Chicago, was also a visiting assistant professor in the Graduate School of Journalism at Columbia University and taught journalism at the Tecnológico de Monterrey campus in Guadalajara, Mexico.

Jessica Retis, Ph.D. is Professor in the School of Journalism, Director of the Bilingual Journalism M.A. and Center for University Education Scholarship (CUES) Fellow at the University of Arizona. She holds a Major in Communications (University of Lima, Peru), a Masters in Latin American Studies (Universidad Nacional Autónoma de México) and a Ph.D. in Contemporary Latin America (Complutense University of Madrid, Spain). Retis has three decades of experience as a college educator in Mexico, Spain and the United States, and two decades as a journalist in Peru, Mexico and Spain. She is co-author of *Narratives of Migration, Relocation and Belonging: Latin Americans in London* and co-editor of *The Handbook of Diasporas, Media and Culture.* Her areas of research include: Latin America, migration, diasporas and transnational communities; Latino media in Europe, North America and Asia; journalism studies, bilingual journalism, and journalism education. At the University of Arizona, Dr. Retis teaches Latinxs and News Media in the United States, Global Latinxs, Journalism Theory, and Journalism Research Methods. She serves as the Academic Officer At-Large at the National Association of Hispanic Journalists (NAHJ), co-chair of the Latino/a Studies Section at the Latin American Studies Association, and co-chair of the Diaspora and the Media Working Group at the International Association for Media and Communication Research (IAMCR). She also serves in the board of the *Journalism and Mass Communication Quarterly* (NMCQ), the flagship journal of the Association of Education in Journalism and Mass Communication (AEJMC).

Amara Aguilar is a professor of journalism at University of Southern California Annenberg School for Communication and Journalism. She teaches journalism for mobile/emerging platforms, social media storytelling for Latinx audiences, visual journalism, engaging diverse communities, public relations strategy and interactive design, among other courses. At USC, she co-founded Annenberg Media's award-winning bilingual outlet, Dímelo, focused on serving Latinx audiences. Amara has written for the *Los Angeles Times*, CNN, Nieman Lab and other outlets. She has worked as a designer, visual journalist, reporter, social media engagement producer and consultant. Amara was honored with the SPJ Distinguished Teaching Award in 2021, earned an Online News Association Challenge Fund grant for Innovation in Education in 2020, was named a TOW Knight Disruptive Educator for innovation in 2018, MediaShift's top innovative journalism educator in 2018, a Scripps Howard Foundation-AEJMC visiting social media fellow in 2017 and an Apple Distinguished Educator in 2015. Her collaborations at USC include work with ABC7, L.A. TACO, NBC Latino, Snap Inc., mitú, Fusion, KPCC, NPR Next Generation Radio, Las Fotos Project, Azteca America and others. She earned her doctorate at USC's Rossier School of Education in Organizational Change and Leadership, where her research focused on converged newsrooms.

Jesús Ayala Rico is one of the most respected and decorated broadcast journalism professors in the country, bringing 20 years of professional journalism experience into the classroom. As a veteran award-winning news producer, Ayala has won four national Emmys and seven Edward R. Murrow Awards and has trained and mentored ten Emmy winners and nine Murrow Award winners. Prof. Ayala teaches courses in both English and Spanish at California State University, Fullerton where he oversees the nationally recognized newscast Al Día – under Ayala's leadership Al Día has won over 40 national collegiate journalism awards and became CSUF's first-ever Emmy award-winning broadcast. The newscast has also won a Hearst Award, a Pacemaker Award and the prestigious Edward R. Murrow Award for Best TV newscast. Prior to joining CSUF, Mr. Ayala covered breaking news stories from around the world as a Producer for all ABC News broadcasts including World News Tonight, Good Morning America, Nightline and 20/20. He excelled as an expert covering Latin America and South America and covered the devastating earthquake in Haiti, the Pope's visits to Cuba, civil disturbances in Venezuela and the rescue of 33 trapped miners in Chile. In 2008, he covered Barack Obama's historic presidential campaign and worked as a White House pool producer. While at ABC News, he worked with news icons like Barbara Walters, Diane Sawyer, Ted Koppel and the late Peter Jennings. He is a graduate of UC Berkeley and USC's Annenberg School of Journalism, and he obtained his journalism teaching certification from the Walter Cronkite School of Journalism. Prof. Ayala serves as a judge for the Golden Mike Awards, The News & Documentary Emmy Awards and the Edward R. Murrow Awards.

Reporting on Latino/a/x Communities

A Guide for Journalists

Edited by Teresa Puente, Jessica Retis, Amara Aguilar, and Jesús Ayala Rico

NEW YORK AND LONDON

Cover image: Authors and Getty Image 1280596472

First published 2022
by Routledge
605 Third Avenue, New York, NY 10158

and by Routledge
4 Park Square, Milton Park, Abingdon, Oxon, OX14 4RN

Routledge is an imprint of the Taylor & Francis Group, an informa business

Library of Congress Cataloging-in-Publication Data
A catalog record for this title has been requested

ISBN: 978-1-032-07975-2 (hbk)
ISBN: 978-1-032-07973-8 (pbk)
ISBN: 978-1-003-21233-1 (ebk)

DOI: 10.4324/9781003212331

Typeset in Bembo
by KnowledgeWorks Global Ltd.

Dedication

This book is dedicated to our families, colleagues, educators, students and the Latina/o/x journalists who have paved the way for future generations.

Contents

List of Contributors

Alejandro Alvarado Bremer, Ph.D. Dr. Alvarado is the Director of the Spanish-Language Journalism Master's program. He is an Associate Professor of Journalism and Communication, and functions as the Spanish-language editor of the South Florida Media Network. An Emmy award-winning TV writer, he served as business news reporter and producer at CBS Telenoticias and later was editor-in-chief for ZDNet Latin America, as well as producer and copy editor at Univision. Dr. Alvarado is a published author of several books including *Evolving Realities of US Hispanic Media*, and *Mexicanos al Grito de Guerra. Undocumented immigrants in the US Armed Forces*. A prolific writer on global and regional affairs, he has been published by U.S. Spanish-language most important publications, including El Nuevo Herald, La Prensa de Nueva York, La Raza, La Voz de Phoenix, among others. Dr. Alvarado holds a Ph.D. and a Master's on International Studies from the University of Miami, and a Bachelors in Political Science from the Universidad Nacional Autónoma de México.

Laura Castañeda, Ed.D., is a Professor of Professional Practice and Associate Dean of Diversity, Inclusion, Equity and Access at the USC Annenberg School for Communication and Journalism. She has worked as a staff writer and columnist for The San Francisco Chronicle and The Dallas Morning News, and a staff writer and editor at The Associated Press in San Francisco, New York and Mexico. She earned undergraduate degrees in journalism and international relations from USC, a master's degree in international political economy from Columbia University, and a doctorate from USC's Rossier School of Education.

Lourdes M. Cueva Chacón, Ph.D., is an Assistant Professor in the School of Journalism & Media Studies at San Diego State University. She earned her Ph.D. from The University of Texas at Austin and also holds a M.S. in Information Science from UNC Chapel Hill. Cueva Chacón has more than seven years of experience reporting the U.S.-Mexico border and Latinx communities. Her research areas include coverage of minoritized and marginalized communities in the United States and digital journalism in the Americas.

Claudia E. Cruz is the director of internships and managing editor of Noticiero Móvil at the Reynolds School of Journalism at the University of Nevada, Reno. Formerly, she was a technology reporter for *CNET en Español* and served as the local editor of *Mountain View Patch*. Claudia was editor of *El Correo de Queens* and freelancer for *The Manhattan Times*. She's a past president of the Bay Area chapter of the National Association of Hispanic Journalists. Claudia has a M.A. from the Graduate School of Journalism at CUNY, a J.D. from The Ohio State University and a B.A. in Government and Latin American Studies from Wesleyan University.

Dr. Melita M. Garza is an American journalism historian who studies news as an agent of democracy, specializing in English- and Spanish-language news, the immigrant press and coverage of underrepresented groups. As an associate professor at TCU's Bob Schieffer College of Communication, Garza teaches journalism history, business journalism, media literacy and diversity and the media. She earned a Ph.D. from the University of North Carolina at Chapel Hill in 2012 after two decades reporting for the *Chicago Tribune*, *Bloomberg News* and *the Los Angeles Times*. Garza also holds an MBA from the University of Chicago and an A.B. from Harvard University.

Edna Negrón is a professor of journalism at Ramapo College of New Jersey, where she teaches reporting, writing and producing digital news. She is a veteran journalist with more than 25 years in print and online journalism. She has worked as a reporter, assistant editor and digital news producer for newspapers and websites in New York and Florida, including *Newsday* in New York City and on Long Island, *The Sun-Sentinel* in South Florida and *The Record* in North Jersey. Her research focuses on Latino issues and community journalism.

Dr. Nathian Shae Rodriguez is an Associate Professor of Digital Media in the School of Journalism & Media Studies at San Diego State University and core faculty in the Area of Excellence: Digital Humanities and Global Diversity. He specializes in critical-cultural and digital media studies. His research focuses on minority representation in media, specifically LGBTQ and Latinx portrayals and identity negotiation, as well as pop culture, identity, critical communication pedagogy and issues of masculinity/mascing. Dr. Rodriguez also has ten years of professional radio experience in on-air talent, sales, promotions and social media marketing.

Mercedes Vigón, Ph.D. associate director of the International Media Center, and associate professor at Florida International University for 20 years. Her research focuses on analyzing the challenges that journalists face when confronting inequalities, human rights violations and other threats to democracy. A native of Spain, she launched the FIU Journalism Master's Program with "Tec de Monterrey," Mexico and trained journalists all over Latin America, the Caribbean and Europe. She also worked as a TV news director for Net Financial News, as executive producer and international writer for CBS Telenoticias and as a journalist with UPI.

Vanessa Vancour has made a career out of working to improve diversity of coverage in newsrooms through mentorship and leadership. One of her largest initiatives is the creation of Noticiero Móvil, a bilingual news program aimed at improving coverage of Latinx issues in northern Nevada. Vanessa is passionate about bilingual storytelling and community engagement. She is known for her TEDx talk titled "I'm Mexican, Does that Change Your Assumptions about Me?" In the talk, she provides tactical tips on managing your own biases and preconceived notions. She is also a speaker coach and avid community volunteer.

Preface

A couple years ago a group of Latinx journalism professors got together to present their research and projects at the Broadcast Education Association Latin America conference in Mérida, Mexico. We talked about our work, our students, challenges and triumphs – but we knew something was missing. We didn't have a textbook that was focused on the specific work we were doing with our Latinx students to serve our community. We decided then that we needed to write a book for journalists, together. We are blessed that we have been able to bring this book, *Reporting on Latino/a/x Communities: A Guide for Journalists*, to life as colleagues, educators and always as amigos. See Figure 0.1

FIGURE 0.1 Preface

Prologue

Early on in my career, after I had been working at Spanish-language station channel 34 in Los Angeles for a couple of years, I found out that a Network affiliate was looking for a reporter to cover the growing Latino community. Even though I was enamored with the work I was doing and realized that in Spanish-language media we were making a difference in people's lives through our reporting, I was intrigued by the prospect that a local station that broadcast in English would finally be looking to cover the Latino community.

Not too many Latino reporters wanted to do that kind of reporting, called at the time "the taco beat." But for me, it was an exciting proposition. It would be unique - no one else was doing that.

After preparing my demo reel and meeting a few times with the news director, I got the impression that I was in. This was an opportunity to report about a community I knew well and that I was a part of. Then came the call from my lawyer. The station general manager felt I did not look "ethnic enough" and sounded "too ethnic" and that it could be "insulting" to their audience. Instead, he hired a young Latina with long beautiful black hair who didn't speak Spanish. I don't mean to imply that you have to speak Spanish to cover the Latino community, but in the early 1980's in Los Angeles it would have helped.

Sure, I was disappointed that I didn't get the job. More than that, it was a revelation on how we were viewed in the huge metropolis of Los Angeles in the early 1980's. We were 25% of the population, yet we were invisible, even though we had such deep roots in California and all of the Southwest.

That experience turned out to be a blessing in disguise. I spent the next three and a half decades working in Spanish-language media. I went from the local station to the network as co-anchor of Noticias Univision and then co-host of news magazine show Aquí y Ahora. During that time, I traveled the world. I was a witness to some of the most important history-making events - from superpower summits, to elections in the U.S. and Latin America, natural disasters, armed conflicts and papal trips. I interviewed dozens of presidents and heads of state in the U.S. and Latin America.

I seriously doubt that I would have been able to have those experiences as a journalist had I gotten the reporter's position in that English-language station in Los Angeles. To this day, you can count on one hand all the Latinas or Latinos who have anchored network newscasts.

I worked at Univision for 37 years. Some would consider that a lifetime. Actually, it was a lifetime. There came a point when I was honored with a lifetime achievement award, then another and another and another. Of course, I was flattered and humbled to think that someone would consider recognizing the work I had done up to that point in my career. But part of me wondered: Is this a hint? What are they trying to tell me? Is it time for me to move on? Do I need a new lifetime? So I put that on the long list of reasons why it was time for me to leave Univision and reinvent myself.

As part of that "reinvention" in my new "lifetime," I was determined to continue to tell the Latino story - but this time, to new audiences on other platforms, no matter how big or how small.

Many things have changed since I started my career on Spanish-language television back in 1981. At that time, there were 14 million Latinos in the U.S. Now there are over 62 million. Spanish-language television was small, considered by many as low power, low quality stations that no one watched except for recently arrived immigrants who didn't speak English. Now it's a powerhouse that competes with so-called mainstream media not just in quality but in ratings. Some journalists would go to work at Univision or its local affiliates as a stepping stone to learn the trade and move on to bigger and better things. Now journalists and media executives from mainstream media move over to Spanish language media.

Another thing that has changed is the Latino community itself. It has not only grown in numbers, but the majority are now bilingual, much more sophisticated, more demanding, more educated, more diverse, socially conscious, business savvy and more politically active.

One thing that has not changed is my unwavering desire to report to and about the Latino community. Early on in my career, I realized how much they depended on us to - not just to be informed about what is going on in their communities, their state, even their countries of origin - but to get by in what to so many was their newly adopted country. It was evident that there needed to be a social component to the journalism we practiced in Spanish-language media. Empowering the Latino community through information became my passion, and I made it my mission.

I remember, at the beginning of my career, people would tell me to try to crossover to English language media because Latinos would assimilate and there was no future in Spanish-language media. That was one of the reasons why I applied for that reporter's job in the English-language affiliate. I now see that they were right in one sense - Latinos have assimilated and acculturated. But they were wrong in thinking that meant leaving behind their language and their culture. On the contrary, Latinos are more proud than ever of their cultural heritage.

Mainstream media has been losing out on the opportunity to attract a new audience that is culturally rich and contributes so much to our country, including trillions to our economy. Latinos do not see or hear their stories being told on mainstream media news programs or major publications in proportion to what they represent in our society. As a result, many continue to turn to Spanish-language media - not so much for the language, but because of the content.

To be fair, now more than ever before, you can turn on the morning shows or evening news on the three major networks and see a Latino correspondent reporting or maybe even anchoring. You can pick up a major newspaper (or read it on an app) and see Latino names on the byline. However, it's not enough to have a Latino name and face on your staff. To feel represented, Latinos need to hear their stories. They need to see themselves portrayed for who they are: Americans, Latino Americans. They are professionals, doctors, lawyers, engineers, economists, politicians, judges, entertainers, caretakers, professors, business owners and yes, some of them, not most of them, are immigrants.

Reporting on the Latino community cannot be limited to covering the border, DREAMers or farmworkers. Their stories must be told. Every immigrant has a story and a whole set of circumstances that lead them to make decisions that others might not agree with. But immigration should not be the main or only coverage you see, hear and read about in mainstream media. You do a disservice to our community and the country as a whole because you create the wrong perception in parts of mainstream America where people end up viewing Latinos as "invaders" who are coming to take away our way of life. That could not be further from the truth.

Latinos are Americans, too. The Latino story is an American story. They are your neighbors, your kids' teachers, your parents' nurses. They are your colleagues. They are the artists your kids listen to and the workers - and often owners - of that restaurant you like to frequent. They have triumphs and many face adversity.

Latinos are the largest ethnic group in the United States and the second largest voting bloc in the country after white Americans. The great majority, around 80 percent, are U.S. citizens. Yet, they, we, are still perceived as foreigners in our own country. As journalists, we have the power and the responsibility to change that perception.

The scholars and journalists writing this book will help guide you in that direction. They will introduce you to all the new technologies and the insane number of outlets out there to feature your storytelling. The stories you tell will be up to you, and it will be up to you to convince your editors, news directors and producers that they are stories worth telling. That will be your contribution to our democracy and perhaps your biggest challenge.

As for me, I continue with my own mission to tell Latino stories but now on mainstream media. This time around, no one has complained about me not looking "ethnic enough" and sounding "too ethnic."

Maria Elena Salinas

1

Reporting on Latin/a/x Communities

Lessons to Learn

Jessica Retis and Teresa Puente

As we embark into the new decade to report about the demographic changes of this country, it becomes imperative to provide journalists as well as journalism students and educators with a comprehensive understanding of Hispanics and Latino/a/x/s[1] communities and contribute with lessons to learn about how to better report on these heterogeneous groups. While there have been many attempts to educate journalists on how to cover diverse communities, to date there is no textbook that can be used as a guide to prepare journalists in covering the ever-evolving and heterogeneous groups that are becoming the majority minority of the country. This volume seeks to provide a comprehensive understanding of Latino/a/x/s and introduce a unique manuscript that can be used in the classroom to advance quality journalism. Yet, as years to come, what we propose here needs to be revisited, and we hope that in the next decade, when we learn about the new demographic of this country, we will be ready to keep advancing in our understanding of the transnational nature of Hispanics in America.

Latina/o/x communities have been part of the United States since, and even before, the annexation of Mexican and Puerto Rican territories, in 1848 and 1898, respectively. More recently, the 2020 U.S. Census showed how Latinxs have been key to the nation's growth. The Hispanic population was 62.1 million in 2020, almost 19 percent of the population, and it grew 23 percent. The population that was not of Hispanic or Latino origin grew 4.3 percent since 2010 (U.S. Census, 2021). By 2050, when the nation's racial and ethnic mix will look quite different than it does now, Hispanics are estimated to rise to around 30 percent of the U.S. population (Passel & Cohn, 2008). While Latinos of indigenous descent and Native Americans are the oldest groups to inhabit much

DOI: 10.4324/9781003212331-1

of what is today the United States, Hispanics in the United States could constitute the second largest country of bilingual peoples, only behind Mexico's 127 million. Latinxs have accounted for more than half of total U.S. population growth since 2010 and even though their growth is not as fast as previous years, they will still represent a very relevant group in the nation (Krogstad, 2020). Yet, for most of the contemporary decades, they have been marginalized or treated as foreigners in public discourse.

Why This Book?

Just 30 years after the Declaration of Independence of the United States, the very first Spanish-language newspaper was launched aiming at Spanish exiles who opposed Napoleon's conquest of Spain – *El Misisipí*, 1808. As Kanellos (2009) argues, because Hispanic intellectuals often went into exile in New Orleans, Philadelphia and New York, early Hispanic publications were founded in those cities. As the Southwest became part of the United States, so did their inhabitants and their cultural industries, which were incorporated in the American landscape (Retis, 2019). On the other coast, while Puerto Ricans became citizens, they were nonetheless still treated as foreigners (Gonzalez, 2011). Despite this situation, they have been contributing with their cultural production to the American public sphere but mostly in Spanish. Historical lenses help us understand how for more than two centuries, the American news media landscape has been composed of these binomial factors. On the one hand, English-language mainstream media reporting mainly for Anglo audiences, and on the other hand, Spanish-language media reporting mainly for Hispanic audiences. With the passage of the years and throughout more than two centuries, both components have contributed to what various authors have defined as in the middle of this multilevel media ecology, which is to understand the environment in which media is produced and used, and how they influence society or, in other words, understanding the relationship between media and individuals from an ecological perspective (McLuhan, 1964; Scolari 2012).

Today, many journalists, journalism educators and students are familiar with environmental issues. What we bring into the discussion is the understanding of demographic changes and the news media environment to find out what roles news media play and how media synergies intertwine in our post-digital world through the lenses of Latinxs communities. We found reporters, editors, producers and publishers trying to exercise the best practices they know about to cover the ever-changing communities at local, national and international levels. While professional preparation of journalists became the major contribution to this industry since 1908 when the first Journalism School was founded at the University of Missouri, there has always been a lack of comprehensive understanding of how to report on Latino/a/x/s communities. Latinos have been the fastest-growing ethnic group in the United States but remained almost invisible to the mainstream media. And when they become visible, they tend to be portrayed through stereotypes as criminals, law enforcers, cheap labors or hypersexualized beings (Retis & Badillo, 2015). In 2014, the National Association of Latino Independent Producers (NALIP) addressed what they called a "Latino media gap" (Negrón et al., 2014): as Latino consumer power grew, relative Latino media presence shrunk. Stories about Latinos constituted less than 1 percent of mainstream news media coverage, and the majority of these stories featured them as criminals. Furthermore, the NALIP survey of 19 primetime shows in 2013 revealed that there were no Latino anchors or executive producers in any of the nation's top news programs, and only 1.8 percent of news producers were Latinos. More recently, the latest diversity surveys conducted by the American Society of News Editors (ASNE) in 2019 and 2020 revealed that Hispanics comprised less than 7 percent of the workforce in newsrooms.

These studies confirmed the trend noted by previous reports produced by the National Association of Hispanic Journalists (NAHJ), *The Network Brownout Reports*. In 2005, they found that out of an estimated 12,600 stories aired by ABC, CBS and NBC, only 105, or 0.83 percent, were exclusively about Latinos or Latino-related issues, a slight increase from 2004 when Latino stories comprised 0.72 percent of coverage. Historically, as the National Council of La Raza (NCLR) argues, Latinxs have been out of the picture: they have been virtually absent as characters in the entertainment media and as correspondents and anchors in news media (NCLR, 2008: 21). Hispanics tend to be made invisible in the mainstream media discourse, and when they appear they are represented with a greater negative connotation than other ethnic minorities (National Council of La Raza, 1997). The analysis of the representation of Puerto Ricans in the *New York Times* and the *New York Post* found that three quarters of the news was centered on conflict (ibid). As Wilson and Gutiérrez (1985) stated, in the 1970s a major part of the news about Hispanics was around issues like youth in gangs, immigration or inter-racial violence. Historically, as Rodriguez argued, Latinas have been portrayed as either frilly *señoritas* or volcanic temptresses, with thick accents and aggressive sexual appetites (Rodriguez, 2008: 2). Furthermore, as Uriarte (2003) addresses, generalizations about Hispanic youth as gang members and drug dealers criminalize the Hispanic group in general.

Throughout the decades, bilingual and bicultural intellectuals, foreign-born journalists and contemporary diasporas moved around English-language and bilingual newsrooms in trying to do their best to cover the growth of Latina/o/x/s communities in their neighborhoods, cities, towns, states and the nation. The lack of professional preparation in the understanding of these complex socio-demographic changes became the main challenge for most of the newsrooms. The results brought lights and shadows, or *luces y sombras,* to the coverage of Latinxs communities in the United States. Two hundred years after the launch of the first Spanish-language publication, Latinxs are not a minority anymore but a relevant part of American society at 62 million and almost 19 percent of the U.S. population (Jones et al., 2021). Thus, journalists as well as journalism educators and students must be informed and advised on how to improve the quality of their reporting.

Contributors of this volume have all been journalists and became journalism educators at a certain moment of their professional career. All have faced the challenge of being sometimes the only Latinx in the newsroom or the only Latinx educator in their journalism school, while trying to improve the better coverage of our communities. Moving from the newsroom to the classroom implies bringing an in-depth understanding of news making to the professional preparation of younger journalists. All of us noticed the lack of a textbook that we could use in the classroom to better train journalism students in covering the Latinx communities. As we met in various academic conferences of professional gatherings, we all shared our needs as college educators. We needed a handbook that we could use to better prepare our students. Hence, we convened to write one. This is the result of a collective effort and our very first attempt to provide a handbook to reporting on Latino/a/x/s communities. All contributors are journalism educators, all work with students in English, Spanish or Spanglish. We are all part of the community we report about and have the cultural competency of sharing the dos and don'ts. We write this volume not only by and for our communities, but we are also seeking to contribute with a relevant document that can bring light to every newsroom and every journalism classroom. This is our main goal.

FIGURE 1.1 NAHJ chapter at CSULB

What Will You Find in the Following Chapters?

This book is meant to be a practical guide for aspiring journalists or early career journalists who want to understand how to cover the Latinx community in a more comprehensive way. Each chapter has an introduction, a case study, an interview with a Latinx journalist, tips, discussion questions and assignments. Each contributing chapter also examines a theme or a topic of coverage.

Portrayals of Latinos in the media are often negative in modern and historic times. It's important to examine some of this offensive coverage so we understand why fair and inclusive coverage is so important today. Chapter 2, by Melita M. Garza, Associate Professor of Journalism at Texas Christian University, examines some of the ways Latinos have been historically maligned in the media, especially with offensive terminology. She invites journalists to use history to give the coverage of Latinos greater context. The case study examines how *La Prensa,* the nation's most widely distributed Spanish-language newspaper in the 1930s, contributed to Mexican American identity formation by countering stereotypical images of Mexicans and immigrants in the English-language media and by advocating for healthcare, school desegregation and many other causes. This chapter also features an interview with Axios reporter Russell Contreras.

A beat is a subject area of news coverage. Latinos and immigration can be stand-alone beats. But the inclusion of Latinos in coverage should be included in all beats such as politics, sports or business. Latinos of all ages, professions, genders, races and classes should be included in beat coverage. There also are many respected Latino sources, from academics to community leaders and nonprofits to think tanks to be sourced. Chapter 3, by Professor Edna Negrón, Professor of Journalism at Ramapo College of New Jersey, examines how a reporter develops a beat. Latinos should be included in the coverage of any beat. This chapter offers guidance on how to develop Latinx sources, and the case study is about UnidosUS, a nonprofit, nonpartisan national organization with a network of nearly 300 community-based organizations that advocates for more equitable opportunities for Latinos, such as better healthcare, quality schools, increased voter participation and business growth. The chapter also features an interview with Monsy Alvarado, social justice writer for NJSpotlight.com, and *The Record,* a part of the USA Network.

Latinos can be of any race and Hispanics is an ethnicity, according to the U.S. Census. Almost 60 percent of U.S. Hispanic adults say they have experienced discrimination or been treated unfairly because of their race or ethnicity (Gonzalez-Barrera, 2019). There also is racism within the Latino community as historically, and in modern media, the whiter looking Latinos have been given more privilege. Chapter 4, by Claudia E. Cruz at the University of Reno, exposes colorism and race within the Latinx community. The case study examines the Washington Heights Riots of 1992 in the context of Black Lives Matter. It features an interview with Soledad O'Brien, formerly with CNN.

Latinas are 18 percent of the U.S. female population but expected to grow to 27 percent by 2060 (Catalyst, 2020). Based on full-time earnings in 2019, for every dollar white, non-Hispanic men earned, Latinas only earned 55 cents (Tucker, 2020). Hispanic women earned around 15 percent of Bachelor's degrees earned by U.S. citizen women and permanent residents in 2017–2018 (National Center for Education Statistics, 2019). These statistics alone show why reporting on issues, challenges and the success of Latina women is so important. Chapter 5 is written by Laura Castañeda, Professor of Professional Practice of Journalism at the Annenberg School for Communication and Journalism at the University of Southern California. This chapter explains the diversity of the Latina community and gender-based issues in reporting on Latinas. It features Jovita Idár finally earning an obituary in *The New York Times* thanks to the newspaper's effort to make up for its past decades-long neglect of many accomplished women. Idár, a writer, editor and feminist at *El Progreso* in Laredo, Texas, gained fame for blocking the Texas Rangers in 1914 when they showed up to try and shut down the newspaper.

The LGBTQ community is generally underrepresented in the news. There are even fewer stories of people who are LGBTQ and Latinx. The Association of LGBTQ Journalists (*NLGJA*), founded in 1989, is an organization of journalists, media professionals, educators and students working from within the news industry to foster fair and accurate coverage of LGBTQ issues. The organization published an *LGBTQ Stylebook*, has a mentorship program, a *rapid response task force* and a *Journalists Toolbox* with examples and best practices to cover the LGBTQ community in fair, balanced and accurate ways. In Chapter 6, Nathian Shae Rodriguez, Assistant Professor of Digital Media Studies at San Diego State University, explores the intersectional diversity of the Latinx LGBTQ community and how to cover it accurately and fairly. It also explores the meaning and history of the word Latinx. The case study is on news coverage of the Pulse nightclub shooting in June 2016. The chapter features an interview with Jorge Estevez, an anchor at WSB-TV Channel 2 Action News in Atlanta, Georgia, the first openly gay anchor and second Latinx on-air personality for the station.

The COVID-19 pandemic may be the biggest news story in our lifetimes. The impacts have been far reaching from the economy to education and health. Early in the pandemic, it became clear that not all communities were impacted equally. Latinos in particular had higher case and death rates than whites. Chapter 7, by Teresa Puente, Assistant Professor California State University, Long Beach, looks at how the pandemic impacted the Latinx community. It also features an interview with Los Angeles Times Reporter Brittny Mejia.

Immigration is the most commonly reported topic about Latinos in the media even though a majority of Latinos in the United States are not immigrants and are actually U.S. citizens. While much of the coverage surrounding immigration is negative, it's important to also report on the financial, cultural and historical contributions that Latinos have made in the current-day United States. Chapter 8, by Teresa Puente, Assistant Professor at California State University, Long Beach, offers context to reporting on immigration and how to look beyond stories of unauthorized immigration. This chapter features a case study on the Deferred Action for Childhood Arrivals (DACA) immigration policy as well as a timeline of immigration news stories. It features an interview with Dianne Solis of the Dallas Morning News.

Latinos are not a monolith, and this was clear in the last presidential election. While most Latinos voted Democrat, there still are significant numbers of Republicans. Nationwide, Latinos cast 16.6 million votes in 2020, an increase of 30.9 percent over the 2016 presidential election. In 12 states with largest Latino voters Biden won 2 to 1 but he lost to Trump 2 to 1 in Florida (UCLA Latino Politics & Policy Initiative, 2021). Chapter 9 is written by Journalism Professors Mercedes Vigón and Alejandro Alvarado Bremer, Associate Professor and Coordinator of the Spanish-Language Journalism Master's Program and Associate Director of the International Media Center and Associate Professor in the School of Communication and Journalism at Florida International University, respectively. This chapter examines how to report on Latinos and politics, the diversity of the electorate and the influence of the Latino voter. It features interviews with news leaders at Univision.

Latinos are an economic force in this country but this news is often underreported.

Latinos contribute $2.6 trillion to the nation's economic output, known as GDP, in 2018 (Hamilton et al., 2020). If Latinos were a separate nation, they would have the eighth largest GDP in the world, behind France and India (Hamilton et al., 2020). Chapter 10, by Melita M. Garza, Associate Professor of Journalism at Texas Christian University, delves into business coverage and the economic importance of the Latinx community in business coverage. She details how to use data to tell stories and features an interview with Nancy Rivera Brooks, Assistant Business Editor, at the Los Angeles Times.

International news comprises a small share of overall news content in the United States and an even smaller share of that news is from Latin America. Yet, Latinos in the United States overwhelmingly pay attention to international news in an effort to stay connected with their ancestral homelands. Through their informed reporting, foreign correspondents shape our understanding of the world by highlighting growing issues in specific countries, regions and the world at large. Chapter 11, by Jesús Ayala Rico, Professor of Broadcast Journalism and Multimedia at California State University, Fullerton, provides practical grooming tips for students who aspire to report abroad. As Ayala points out from personal experience, reporting overseas can be challenging, especially when reporting from authoritarian governments like Cuba or Venezuela, countries where journalists are often considered the enemy. The chapter includes multiple travel checklists, tips for trauma-informed journalism and an interview with National Public Radio's Mandalit Del Barco, a veteran correspondent who has covered breaking news across the world. Del Barco shares her insights after covering the unpresented 2021 Olympics in Tokyo amidst a global pandemic.

Univision and Telemundo are the two largest Spanish-language news outlets in the United States, although their audience has declined in recent years as more Latinos consume English-language news sources (83 percent). Still around 71 percent of Latinos said they still get some of their news in Spanish (Flores & Lopez, 2018). If you ask most students who their journalism role models are, they will likely mention veteran broadcasters like Jorge Ramos and Maria Elana Salinas. Yet, breaking into the competitive world of broadcast TV comes with its own set of barriers and challenges for Latinx journalists. Chapter 12, by Jesús Ayala Rico, Professor of Broadcast Journalism and Multimedia at California State University, Fullerton, explains how to put together a TV broadcast with a focus on the technical aspects and community reporting. The case study is an inside look at how a group of first-gen Latinx students from CSUF's bilingual newscast, Al Día, overcame imposter syndrome to Emmy-win their university's first student Emmy. It features an interview with John Quiñones, the beloved anchor of ABC News who speaks about his remarkable trajectory from a migrant farmworker to a pioneering broadcast Latino legend, and how he overcame rejection at a time when it wasn't acceptable to be a Latino in mainstream TV.

Public radio in the United States has long been a place to reach Latino audiences with networks like Radio Bilingüe and Latino USA. But the advent of podcasting has opened new opportunities and audiences for Latinx podcasters. Around 36 percent of Latinos have listened to a podcast in a month (Edison Research, 2021). Chapter 13, by Vanessa Vancour, bilingual strategist and podcaster, explores the growth of Spanish-language radio and bilingual podcasting and also explains how she launched an award-winning Spanish-language radio program.

Trends show more and more people in the United States are receiving their news from social media. Some 96 percent of Hispanic teens report having a smartphone (Anderson & Jiang, 2018). Three quarters of Latinos receive their news from internet sources (Flores & Lopez, 2018). Chapter 14 is written by Amara Aguilar, Professor of Professional Practice of Journalism at the Annenberg School for Communication and Journalism at the University of Southern California. This chapter analyzes the way Latinx millennials are consuming news and the growth of social media networks. This chapter features an interview with mitú Co-founder Beatriz Acevedo, who is a Latina entrepreneur and former Emmy Award winning journalist.

Whether you embark on a career in English-language or Spanish-language news, or both, it's important to master the elements of style and grammar. There are many guidebooks in English and Spanish. While the AP Stylebook is the primary book used in English-language news in the United States, there is not one primary stylebook used by Spanish-language journalists in the United States. However, some media outlets, mostly in Latin America, have published stylebooks that will be cited in this contributing chapter. Chapter 15, by Teresa Puente, Assistant Professor at California State University, Long Beach, provides guidance on how to report and write bilingually. It offers grammar and style tips for writing in Spanish and advice on how to translate quotes. It features an interview with bilingual journalist Patricia Guadalupe, who has freelanced for NBC News, Latino magazine and many other publications.

The rapid changing synergies of news production, distribution and consumption in the digital era have altered long-established journalism models. In the realm of these ever-changing scenarios, Latino media outlets have encountered new spaces to communicate with bicultural and bilingual audiences in the United States. Seeking to fill a gap, Jessica Retis, Professor and Director of the Master's in Bilingual Journalism at the University of Arizona, and Lourdes Cueva Chacón, Assistant Professor at San Diego State University, embarked on the task of identifying these news media projects to advance the study of contemporary professional practices. Their contribution in Chapter 16 explores the future of Latinx journalism and the growth in online news sites that focus on the Latinx community in English and in Spanish. It assesses the main trends in the Latinx community and the future of Latino media.

How to Use This Book?

This textbook is for journalism students and journalists who want to learn more about the nuances and complexity of reporting on the Latinx communities. This is a practical journalism textbook for reporting in multiple platforms on the diverse Latinx communities with cultural sensitivity. Some of the main themes of the book include reporting on immigration, race, age and gender. Also, the book covers how to report bilingually and in Spanish in different media platforms such as print, online, radio and television. This book gives context and advice about reporting on some of the most important issues impacting the Latinx community, including immigration, politics and business. It can benefit novice journalists as well as experienced journalists wanting to understand more about the Latinx community.

Each chapter also lists trade tools and tips for reporting on the Latinx community, assignments and also discussion questions. There are references at the end of each chapter. They are a guide for the reader to do more reading and research on each topic. They are not meant to be a conclusive list but to be a guidepost to additional reading and resources.

Lessons to Learn for the Post-digital Age

More than 62 million Latinx make almost 19 percent of the nation's total population. Projections predict this growth to reach about 106 million by 2050. The nation's Hispanic population has been one of its fastest growing in recent decades with 12 states having a population of 1 million or more Hispanic residents in 2019: Arizona, California, Colorado, Florida, Georgia, Illinois, New Jersey, New Mexico, New York, North Carolina, Pennsylvania and Texas (U.S. Census, 2020). Yet, understanding how to better cover these groups in daily news reporting remains challenging for newsrooms and journalism schools. With this manuscript, we hope to contribute to the advancement of these tasks.

One of the biggest challenges is the newsrooms' demography. Recent reports have demonstrated the failure in trying to match the percentage of racial and ethnic minorities in newsrooms to that of the population at large (American Society of News Editors, various years). "The structural forces that contribute to the problem are well known and largely reflect how race and privilege intersect. The main entry points into the profession —unpaid internships and journalism schools— tend to favor people who come from wealthy backgrounds. Many jobs are never posted; hires are made through existing networks, in which people tend to affiliate, and empathize, with those like themselves. When people of color do manage to get hired, they find a lack of formal mentorship and they are rarely promoted into management positions" (Arana, 2018). Newspapers, broadcast and digital networks, as well as social media enterprises are still failing in reaching what the National Association of Hispanic Journalists demanded through their Parity Project: "to increase the number of Hispanics in the newsrooms, because this can help make a difference in areas important to journalists: knowledge, connections, sources, staff and coverage" (Colón, 2006).

As the COVID-19 crisis showed flagrant racial health disparities in the United States, journalists from marginalized communities have increasingly demanded change. As Childers (2020) argues, one solution that has been exposed in corporate America over the years has been to emphasize the business case: greater diversity is better for business; but emphasizing the moral case is required for real and lasting change. Furthermore, many journalists of color have been talking about the racism and discrimination they've faced while working in newsrooms (Hazard, 2020). Several non-profit initiatives have been launched seeking to tackle this crucial scenario. In 2020, Report for America doubled the number of its partner newsrooms owned or operated by Black and Hispanic journalists and is increasing the number of beats covering communities of color in 2021 (Kille, 2020).

In addition to the efforts of professional organizations like NAHJ, Latinx journalists have launched various initiatives within their own newsrooms. In 2020, Gustavo Arellano wrote a piece about how Latinos and the Los Angeles

Times had a complicated past but a promising future. The paper was home to Ruben Salazar, whose columns explained the Chicano movement to the nation until he was killed by a tear gas projectile fired by a sheriff's deputy while covering a protest in East Los Angeles on August 29, 1970. In 1984, the paper ran a series titled "Latinos" which won the Pulitzer Prize for public service and taught news organizations to pay more attention to the changing demographics in their communities (Arellano, 2020).

In July 2020, Latinx journalists at the L.A. Times penned an open letter for better news representation: "For much of its history, the Los Angeles Times has covered the Latino community in dehumanizing ways, painting us as criminals or victims or simply ignoring us (...) For decades, we've asked management to hire more of us, promote us and make us editors. But those calls have largely gone unanswered. Today, only 13 percent of The Times newsroom is Latino. Of 109 editors and managers, only 11 percent of them are Latino. The Times has only ever had three Latino masthead editors." Inspired by Black journalists, Latinxs established the Latino Caucus at the Los Angeles Times in 2020 to call for a change. The collective mission claimed demands in various areas: (1) stand in solidarity with the Black Caucus; (2) stop treating Latinos as a minority group; (3) build a newsroom that reflects the demographics of L.A. County; (4) formally apologize for fomenting episodes of anti-Latino hysteria in California and the United States; (5) correct pay disparities for Latinos and other journalists of color and women whose salaries, post-Guild contract, remain glaringly low compared to white counterparts; (6) guarantee that at least two Latino Caucus members, in addition to Black journalists and other journalists of color, are kept informed about the creation of new jobs, the search for candidates and the vetting of finalists; (7) create a path for Latinos on staff to grow into influential roles – columnists, critics, editors and managers; (8) establish a robust pipeline for Latino talent, connect with and contribute to Latino journalism organizations such as the National Association of Hispanic Journalists and CCNMA: Latino Journalists of California; (9) guarantee that the paper will increase outreach and hiring from public university systems with large Latino student bodies; (10) provide *L.A. Times en Español* the resources it needs to succeed as a key L.A. Times brand representing Southern California's vast Spanish-speaking market; (11) institute employee reviews for management and hold managers accountable for their track records of recruiting and retaining Black, Latino and other journalists of color; (12) end the practice of relying on Spanish speakers and other multilingual journalists as translators without providing a byline or additional pay, hire Spanish-speaking translators or compensate Latino journalists for taking on additional labor translating for monolingual colleagues; (13) commit to adding more Latinos on The Times' business side, hire publicists, consultants, marketing specialists and salespeople who have an intimate sense of Los Angeles' diverse Latino market; (14) invest in having *The Times* brand present in Latino

Los Angeles, host food, music, sports and cultural events catering to Latino audiences, highlight Latino Times writers, invite them to create conversations and town halls across Southern California.

In August 2020, the Arizona Republic Guild's Diversity Committee launched a campaign "to promote diversity/equity/inclusion, address historic underrepresentation & strengthen our newsroom & journalism for years to come" (Arizona Republic Guild, 2020). The petition summarized various essential issues: (1) publicly post regularly updated diversity data for the newsroom; (2) release a pay-equity study of our newsroom; (3) prioritize coverage of diverse communities; (4) treat la voz equitably; (5) expand recruitment efforts for diverse journalists; (6) ensure diverse candidates are interviewed for every open position; (7) prioritize parity in promotions; (8) create diversity fellowships, editing and training programs to bolster retention and advancement of diverse journalists; (9) outline rules for social media policies and fairly enforce them; (10) ensure safety for journalists and interns during protest, pandemic coverage; (11) implement newsroom-wide diversity, cultural awareness training; (12) compensate the diversity committee for its work; (13) publicly restate our commitment to equity.

The efforts by journalists at the Los Angeles Times and The Arizona Republic are a call to action for newsrooms across the country to improve their coverage of Latinos and their treatments of Latinx journalists. This book also serves as a guide with the voices of Latinx journalists, analysis and assignments from journalism educators with history and context on covering some of the most important issues facing diversity within Latinx communities. The news media, working journalists and journalism students should see this as essential reading.

FIGURE 1.2 Latinx journalism students. Photo by Amara Aguilar

Note

1 In this collective project, we will use the terms Hispanic, Latino, Latino/a, Latino/a/x, Latinx interchangeably to describe a diverse group that makes up about 19 percent of the U.S. population. Pan-ethnic labels have been used for decades to describe a wide range of groups with ties in several Latin American countries. As journalism educators, we train journalism students to ask their sources how they identify themselves and use their preferred term when writing.

References

American Society of News Editors (various years). Newsroom Diversity Survey. Available at: https://members.newsleaders.org/newsroom_diversitysurvey

Anderson, M. and Jiang, J. (2018). Teens, Social Media and Technology, *Pew Research Center*, May 31, 2018. Available at: https://www.pewresearch.org/internet/2018/05/31/teens-social-media-technology-2018/

Arana, G. (2018). 17% of US Newsrooms Staff is Not White. Decades of Failure. *Columbia Journalism Review*, November 18, 2018.

Arellano, G. (2020). *For Latinos and the L.A. Times,* A Complicated Past — and A Promising Future, *Los Angeles Times*, September 27, 2020.

Arizona Republic Guild (2020). Twitter Campaign. Available at: https://twitter.com/azrepublicguild/status/1293322668679131136

Catalyst (2020). Women in the Workforce United States, Oct. 14, 2020. Available at: https://www.catalyst.org/research/women-in-the-workforce-united-states/

Childers, N. (2020). The Moral Argument for Diversity in Newsrooms is also a Business Argument-and You Need Both, *Niemanlab*. Available at: https://www.niemanlab.org/2020/11/the-moral-case-for-diversity-in-newsrooms-also-makes-good-business-sense/

Colón, A. (2006). The Parity Project: Making a Difference, One Newspaper at a Time, Poynter, February, 17, 2006.

Edison Research (2021). Latino Podcast Listener Report 2021. Available at: https://www.edisonresearch.com/the-latino-podcast-listener-report-2021/

Flores, A. & Lopez, M.H. (2018). Among U.S. Latinos, The Internet Now Rivals Television as a Source For News, *Pew Research Center*, January 11, 2018. Available at: https://www.pewresearch.org/fact-tank/2018/01/11/among-u-s-latinos-the-internet-now-rivals-television-as-a-source-for-news/

Gonzalez, J. (2011). *Harvest of Empire: A History of Latinos in America*, New York, NY: Penguin.

Gonzalez-Barrera, A. (2019). Hispanics With Darker Skin Are More Likely to Experience Discrimination Than Those With Lighter Skin, *Pew Research Center*, July 2, 2019. Available at: https://www.pewresearch.org/fact-tank/2019/07/02/hispanics-with-darker-skin-are-more-likely-to-experience-discrimination-than-those-with-lighter-skin/

Hamilton, D. et al. (2020). LDC U.S. Latino GDP Report. https://blogs.callutheran.edu/cerf/files/2020/09/2020_LDCLatinoGDP_CERF.pdf

Hazard, L. (2020). "I Continue to Have Nightmares That I Still Work There": Many, Many Journalists Speak Out About Racism in Newsrooms Across the Country, *NiemanLab*, June 11, 2020. Available at: https://www.niemanlab.org/2020/06/i-continue-to-have-nightmares-that-i-still-work-there-many-many-journalists-speak-out-about-racism-in-newsrooms-across-the-country/

Jones, N. et al. (2021). 2020 Census Illuminates Racial and Ethnic Composition of the Country. Available at: https://www.census.gov/library/stories/2021/08/improved-race-ethnicity-measures-reveal-united-states-population-much-more-multiracial.html

Kanellos, N. (2009). Pursuing Democracy: The First Hispanic Newspapers in the United States, Vol. 1, Issue 1. Available at: https://www.readex.com/readex-report/issues/volume-4-issue-1/pursuing-democracy-first-hispanic-newspapers-united-states

Kille, S. (2020). Report for America Boosts Diverse Newsrooms and Beats, Report for America, December 14, 2020.

Krogstad, J. (2020). Hispanics Have Accounted for More Than Half of Total U.S. Population Growth Since 2010. *Pew Research Center.* Available at: https://www.pewresearch.org/fact-tank/2020/07/10/hispanics-have-accounted-for-more-than-half-of-total-u-s-population-growth-since-2010/

McLuhan, M. (1964). *Understanding Media: The Extensions of Man.* New York, NY: Ginko Press.

National Center for Education Statistics (2019). Table 322.50: Bachelor's degrees conferred to females by postsecondary institutions, by race/ethnicity and field of study: 2016-17 and 2017-18 [Data set]. *2019 Digest of Education Statistics.* Available at: https://nces.ed.gov/programs/digest/d19/tables/dt19_322.20.asp

National Council of La Raza (1997). "Out of the Picture: Hispanics in the Media." In: Clara Rodríguez (Ed.), *Latin Looks. Images of Latinas and Latinos in the U.S. Media*, Boulder, CO: Westview Review, 21–35.

National Council of La Raza (NCLR) (2008). Out of the Picture: Hispanics in the Media. In: Clara Rodriguez (Ed.), *Latin Looks: Images of Latinas and Latinos in the U.S. Media*, New York, NY: Routledge, 21–35.

Negrón, F. et al. (2014). *The Latino Media Gap. A Report on the State of Latinos in the U.S. Media.* New York, NY: Columbia University-NALIP. Available at: https://www.nalip.org/latino_gap_study

Passel, J. & Cohn, D. (2008). U.S. Population Projections: 2005-2050. *Pew Research Center.* Available at: https://www.pewresearch.org/hispanic/2008/02/11/us-population-projections-2005-2050/

Retis, J. (2019). *Hispanic Media Today: Serving Bilingual and Bicultural Audiences in the Digital Age.* Washington, DC: Democracy Fund. Available at: https://www.democracyfund.org/publications/hispanic-media-today

Retis, J. & Badillo, A. (2015). *Los latinos y las industrias culturales en español en Estados Unidos.* (Latinos and Spanish-language Cultural Industries in the United States). Madrid: Real Instituto Elcano. Available at: http://www.realinstitutoelcano.org/wps/portal/rielcano_es/contenido?WCM_GLOBAL_CONTEXT=/elcano/elcano_es/zonas_es/lengua±y±cultura/dt01-2015-retis-badillo-latinos-industrias-culturales-en-espanol-en-eeuu

Rodriguez, C. (2008) Introduction. In: Clara Rodriguez (Ed.), *Latin Looks: Images of Latinas and Latinos in the U.S. Media*, New York, NY: Routledge, 2–12.

Scolari, C. (2012). Media Ecology: Exploring the Metaphor to Expand the Theory, *Communication Theory*, 22(2012), 204–225.

Tucker, J. (2020). 55 Cents on the Dollar Isn't Enough for Latinas, October, 2020. Available at: https://nwlc.org/wp-content/uploads/2019/11/Latina-EPD-2020.pdf

UCLA Latino Policy & Politics Initiative (2021). Vote Choice of Latino Voters in the 2020 Presidential Election. Available at: https://latino.ucla.edu/wp-content/uploads/2021/08/Election-2020-Report-1.19.pdf

U.S. Census (2020). Hispanic Heritage Month 2020, Available at: https://www.census.gov/content/dam/Census/newsroom/facts-for-features/2020/CB20-FF.07.pdf

U.S. Census (2021). 2020 Census Statistics Highlight Local Population Changes and Nation's Racial and Ethnic Diversity. August 12, 2021. Available at https://www.census.gov/newsroom/press-releases/2021/population-changes-nations-diversity.html

Uriarte, M. (2003). "A Problematic Press Latinos and the News." In: Fritz Cropp, Cynthia Frisby and Dean Mills (Eds.), *Journalism Across Cultures*. Iowa: Iowa State Press, 39–63.

Wilson, C. and Gutiérrez, F. (1985). *Minorities and Media*. Beverly Hills, CA: Sage.

2

Historical Representations of Latinos in the Media

Melita M. Garza

In 1954, when the U.S. Supreme Court heard the landmark Mexican American civil rights case, Hernandez v. Texas, one justice asked the San Antonio, Texas, lawyer Carlos Cadena to explain what a person of Mexican American descent was. Before Cadena could answer, yet another justice, Felix Frankfurter, interjected: "They call them greasers down there, don't they?" (The American Experience, 2009).

No one asked Frankfurter where he got that idea, or what he understood "greaser" to mean. Chances are good, however, that the justice picked up the epithet from popular media, a vehicle through which stereotypes, tropes and slurs become embedded in American culture over time. It is critical for journalists to know Latinx history, including the history of how Hispanics have been othered in the U.S. society through media representations. This chapter provides a brief conceptual understanding of the history of Latinx "othering" in the U.S. media, as well as theoretical tools that enable media practitioners to report, interpret and write about the nation's largest underrepresented group with credible journalistic authority. Understanding the Latinx stories of the past are essential to insightful coverage of the present and future of Latinos as a group, and the United States as a whole.

This conceptual understanding starts with the opening chapter anecdote about the "greaser" – a term that is a prime example of a stereotype. Conceptually, a stereotype is a heuristic – a mental shortcut – typically thought of in fixed, binary terms. Stereotyping, a form of bias, involves an unchanging positive or negative prejudgment about the nature, character and abilities of individuals based solely on their group membership. In other words, without even getting to know someone, your mind tells you that you already know what they are about.

DOI: 10.4324/9781003212331-2

FIGURE 2.1 U.S. Supreme Court

Although the history of "greaser" predates the twentieth century, it got a boost in 1918 when the Adams Newspaper Syndicate distributed a "Random Reels" column headlined "The Greaser" (Rann, 1918). Papers around the country, including the *Fort Worth Star-Telegram*, printed the piece, which the Adams Syndicate called a "Stickful Feature." The syndicate advertised that such features were "read by millions daily" and were meant to be memorable (Adams, 1916).

> 'Stickful Features' are short ... They have one big, vital idea—and they say it quick. They are habit-forming features. They are easy to read—and ARE READ. They create smiles. They make people think ....
>
> (Adams, 1916)

The "one big, vital idea" in "The Greaser" column? "The greaser is a full-blooded Mexican with the mild and human instincts of the masculine hyena." The column went on to describe greasers, as "alcoholized"; "ignorant"; and "a worse pest than the side-stepping mosquito" (Rann, 1918). Although the column may be considered a relic from the last century, the meaning of sentences like the following are clear: "It is hard to do business with a race of people who never went to school long enough to learn that crossing the Rio Grande with a machine gun is one of the most prompt forms of sudden death" (Rann, 1918). For Latinx people reading this, then or now, the column offered nothing to smile about.

Journalism doesn't bear the sole blame for the proliferation of racist media "othering." These ideas filter through society in songs, novels, films, television shows and via social media. It is important to recognize that stereotypical representations may be nuanced. For instance, ten years before the *Star-Telegram* published "The Greaser," American cinema pioneer D.W. Griffith released "The Greaser's Gauntlet," a film with a much-maligned Mexican as a main character. Scholar Juan Alonzo (2004) explained that this film shows the Mexican immigrant as both protagonist and villain. Griffith, best known for the racist film, "Birth of a Nation," which celebrated Ku Klux Klan violence against Blacks, produced a storyline in which the "the greaser" was framed for a crime. After being captured and strung-up by Anglo vigilantes, a white woman intervened, saving him from lynching. He descended into alcoholism, and years later heroically rescued the woman who had saved him earlier. In the end, he returned to Mexico having failed to achieve the American Dream of a better life.

Latinx tropes such as "the greaser" persist today, dating from the Hispanophobia that European colonizers brought with them as they settled the land that became the United States. Anglo Americans viewed their Spanish neighbors in the New World through this inherited, bigoted lens that Spanish historians have labeled the Black Legend (Weber, 1992). As the legend had it, Spaniards were lazy, greedy, corrupt and authoritarian, among other attributes that demonstrated their unworthy character. These epithets were transferred, in varying degrees to Mexicans, Puerto Ricans and others who traced their background to the Spanish conquest. These labels gained momentum in periods of economic strife, such as the Great Depression, and continued through the 1950s and 1960s through to the present day. For instance, the Latino Threat Narrative, a term anthropologist Leo R. Chavez (2013) popularized, is an update on the Black Legend. Chavez studied how media have stereotyped Mexican Americans as a threat by promoting various myths about them, including that they are unassimilable and unfit for citizenship.

Stereotyping is a form of symbolic annihilation, a concept that refers to the trivialization, condemnation, or erasure of an underrepresented group in the media (Tuchman, 2000). The lack of Latinx perspectives in many newsrooms is one factor contributing to the problem. According to the 2019 diversity survey of the American Society of News Editors, only 7.36 percent of all salaried reporters and editors in newspaper and digital newsrooms are Hispanic (American Society of News Editors, 2019). Representation in Hollywood is even more abysmal, with Latinos holding only 4.9 percent of all speaking parts in the top 100 movies in 2019 (USC Annenberg, 2020). These statistics are striking considering that Hispanics are the largest underrepresented group in the nation, accounting for roughly 18.5 percent of the population in 2019 (U.S. Census Bureau, 2019).

Consequently, many ideas about Latinx people circulating in the media, and therefore throughout society, are most often framed by white decision-makers, including reporters, as well as editors, producers and directors. Conceptually, framing refers to the way news stories, as well as other narratives, are constructed with bits and pieces of reality that the storyteller deems relevant and worthy of emphasis (Gitlin, 2003). News events and issues are framed and placed in a context that the journalist decides is significant, filtered through the reporter's ideas about society and what matters. The following historical case study illustrates how an important Mexican American media voice countered framing in English-language media.

A Closer Look: Framing Mexicans: *La Prensa,* the *San Antonio Express,* and the *San Antonio Light* and the Great Depression

On April 7, 1930, the year after the stock market crash kicked off the Great Depression, hundreds of jobless persons of Mexican descent marched in protest through the streets of San Antonio, Texas, in despair. Standing on the sidelines, a journalist for the English-language *San Antonio Light* newspaper reported on the reactions of the white crowd. "Send 'em back to Mexico if they want jobs" (*Light*, 1930), one onlooker said, framing the protestors as "other." The reporter captured even more explicit quotes. "Bet half of them are not American citizens," another observer commented as the protestors marched by. That assessment was too generous for at least one spectator who rebutted the idea: "Haven't seen one American yet" (*Light*, 1930). Given that journalists were not roaming the crowd asking to see citizenship papers, this coverage shows how Mexicans and Mexican Americans were framed as "other," simply based on their skin color, features and perhaps their language.

The Great Depression was not just a key period in the U.S. economic history but it was also a pivotal period in the nation's immigration history. For the first time it became a crime to enter the United States without proper permits. More than one half million Mexicans and Mexican Americans from across the country were repatriated to Mexico in immigration crackdowns. Meanwhile, those few who still tried to enter faced stricter enforcement of literacy, hygiene and financial tests.

In San Antonio, a city founded by Spanish-speaking immigrants in 1721, the politics, policy and reality of these immigration issues played out in three daily newspapers. One of these, the *Light*, was part of the eugenicist William Randolph Hearst's newspaper empire. It competed head-on with the other English-language daily in town, the *San Antonio Express*, an independent and locally owned newspaper that represented San Antonio's banking, ranching and railroad interests. The city's third daily newspaper, the Spanish-language *La Prensa,* was founded in 1913 by Mexican immigrant publisher Ignacio Lozano. In just a few years, Lozano had turned his paper into the most widely circulated Spanish-language newspaper in the country. Lozano expanded into Los Angeles, California, in 1926 with *La Opinión*, a paper still operating today. With networks of contributors throughout the United States, these papers, though San Antonio and Texas-based, offered an indelible national voice of identity and empowerment to persons of Mexican descent. This was most visible in *La Prensa's* publishing the names and localities of hundreds of Mexican Americans from around the country who made donations to various civil rights causes (Garza, 2018).

This case study shows how past media tropes proliferating in a city that was the centerpiece of the nation's Spanish-speaking immigrant myth and memory continue to resonate in today's news. By providing alternative frames through which Mexicans and immigrants might envision themselves, Lozano helped define what it meant to be Mexican and American. He contributed to Mexican American identity formation by countering stereotypical images of Mexicans and immigrants in the English-language media, and by advocating for healthcare, school desegregation and many other causes. Meanwhile, the English-language dailies dueled over the role, place and identity of Mexicans and immigrants in Texas and the country. Words were the tools the *Express* and the *Light* used as they faced off in their editorial pages.

For instance, while the *Light* offered insight into the anti-Mexican attitudes of San Antonians, as seen in the commentary of the crowd watching the jobless parade, it didn't seek out other sources to contradict those ideas. That position was left to *La Prensa*, a newspaper that showed Mexicans and Mexican Americans in a variety of roles, often as hard workers and patriots, sometimes as unfortunate victims, and other times as good citizens with agency who supported their community. Most importantly perhaps, *La Prensa* proposed a vision for Mexicans and Americans as people who belonged in the United States and would remain. Consider the words of columnist Rodolfo Uranga: "There will always be Mexicans in the United States, whether temporarily or permanently based. Even though some anti-Mexicanists and xenophobes shout furiously for the removal and the exclusion...they will not achieve it" (Uranga, 1929). Although Uranga's column was written about 100 years ago, it speaks today to those who question the presence of Mexicans and other immigrants in the United States.

The opinion pages of the two English-language dailies were just as forceful as *La Prensa* in expressing their ideas about immigrants. The war of ideas about Mexicans and immigrants these three newspapers waged in editorials was a contest to be the strongest "light of understanding" (Bush, 1932), as a then-prominent journalism textbook defined the goal of opinion writing.

One of the *Light's* more humanely written Depression-era editorials, published on October 12, 1933, called on Congress to support the American Legion's national defense platform, including urging the legislators "against any weakening by treaty or otherwise any safeguards … against any immigration from Asia and against any unrestricted immigration from any other parts of the world" (*Light*, 1933). In other editorials, the *Light* referred to immigrants as "undesirable human vermin" and "alien riff-raff" (*Light*, 1930). For the *Light*, immigrants were akin to animals, and this dehumanizing metaphor is a prime example of symbolic annihilation.

Meanwhile, the locally owned *San Antonio Express* argued that Mexicans played a vital, irreplaceable role in the economy. Mexicans were needed for their skill at "plowing, sowing, and reaping, chopping and picking cotton, transplanting onions and lettuce, digging potatoes, gathering and packaging spinach, tomatoes, oranges, and so on" (*Express*, 1930). This, argued the *Express*, was work that neither machinery nor Anglos would take on as these were tasks that "native white men generally will not do" (*Express*, 1930). Farming was not the only sector that relied on Mexicans. They were also "needed to lay pipes, dig ditches, put down pavement, grade rights-of-way, and build railroads," the editorial argued. While the *Express* characterized Mexicans as indispensable, or in today's language, "essential workers," the Express also racially marked Mexicans as "other," and specifically as people other than white.

In studying journalism history, whether from the 1930s or other eras, something called "the mediated Mexican" takes life form. Understanding how broadsheets and tabloids used themes, narratives, and rhetoric to construct the newspaper or "mediated" Latina/o (as opposed to those we meet in real life) gives us historical context to understand how Latinx people are portrayed in the media in our own time.

In Conversation with Russell Contreras, Axios

Russell Contreras is the Race and Justice Reporter for Axios, where, among other things, he co-writes the Axios Latino Newsletter with Mexico City-based Telemundo reporter Marina Franco. Prior to that, Contreras worked with the Associated Press in New York, New Jersey and Albuquerque, where he was a member of AP's race reporting team. He has also reported for the *Albuquerque Journal* and the *Boston Globe*. He graduated from the University of Houston in 1997 with a degree in history and English and earned an MFA in non-fiction writing from Columbia University in 2002. The following is an edited excerpt of an interview with Contreras. The complete interview is available in this chapter's web resources.

How did you use history when you were an AP reporter based in New Jersey?

Contreras: So, I went there doing everything: covering breaking news, doing broadcasts, coming up with stories. But it was in New Jersey that I found Mexican immigrants. I started fishing around, wanted to know "Why were you there? Why were you here, of all places?" and it was part of the great migration that was happening across the country. I wanted to know the history. So, I did what

FIGURE 2.2 Photo of Axios journalist Russell Contreras. (Photo by Russell Contreras)

I could. I went to Rutgers University, the library to find out what was going on. There was not a lot of material. So, that's when I realized that whatever I was writing would be the first draft of that history.

How did history play a role in moving from the Albuquerque Journal to the Boston Globe?

Contreras: I did a 40th anniversary of [the U.S. Supreme Court case] Brown versus Board of Ed [Education]. I also found out that George I. Sanchez, the well-known Mexican American scholar, education scholar, was from Albuquerque, and literally forgotten. Right? The building, University of Texas is named after him. He's got schools in Texas and California named after him. But his hometown of Albuquerque had forgotten. And it fascinated me because I'm like, "Why? Why is that? What's going on here?" And so, it got the ball rolling, where I started integrating my knowledge and history of stories, and I got positive reactions. And that's what got the attention of an editor by the name of David Beard at the *Boston Globe* who pulled me in to hire me and say, "We want you to come to Boston. We have a Latino community in Boston. And some of our towns that need coverage."

Why is knowing history and knowing how to do historical research more important for young reporters today than ever before?

Contreras: And I realized that all these places, when they laid off [journalists], they laid off their older staffers and kept the younger staffers because of cost. Well, then they lost her institutional knowledge. So, all of us that are at media outlets lack the institutional knowledge, and we could not explain things that were happening, and police violence was one of them. Why did this pop out of the blue? Well, it didn't pop out of the blue. So, I used my training as when I was a graduate student of history at the University of Houston to go back and try to find the story. And I did that constantly. So, when the race team was finally created, I was doing a couple of things pitching stories about race, Black Santa, for example, or John F. Kennedy's visit to Houston with LULAC [League of United Latin American Citizens] before his assassination, or LBJ's speech to Selma where he brings up his experience as a teacher in Mexican American schools. Those are things that I knew as a history that I knew nobody else did. And I would write these stories, and then we'd get positive feedback. So, when the [AP] race team formed, Sonya Ross, the editor, immediately said, "I want Russell on my team."

What would you say to journalism students today about why they should study history?

Contreras: I'd say history would really enhance your study of journalism because it's an investigation of the past. You're telling a story. You're going back in the past and trying to put together the pieces of the puzzle. You do that with journalism. A shooting happens, that's happened yesterday, or five hours [ago]. It's in the past. You're trying to put it together, even though it's contemporary, for today's audience. So, the shooting happened on Wednesday or in 1917. It's the same. You're trying to tell us the who, what, when and why and you're trying to put it in context, right? Why does it matter?

That's one of the axioms of Axios. It's the second line of all their stories, "Why it matters." So, in history, the Porvenir [Texas] Massacre, why it matters? Well, this shows the history of racial violence that Mexican Americans faced. Tulsa, why it matters? This shows the violence black people faced, and then the effort to prevent them from rebuilding tells a story about why things are today. So, I would advise to really consider history as a subject. Because if you really want to be strong in your field, if you really want to stand out as a reporter, you will have a leg up, no matter what market, if you have a basic historical foundation of that community. I would have been lost had I gone to Boston, had I not known the basic fundamentals of Lawrence or Boston. If I didn't know a thing about busing riots, if I didn't know anything about Lawrence's Bread Strike, I would have been lost. I went in there with some context, and it could help explain things that were happening at that moment. Not everything, but I would get a start.

So, when reporters flew in, or helicoptered in, they'd say: "Protests between demonstrators and police," I knew that this was a continuation of a longer story, that "some of those activists from 1974 were here." [But] when new people came in [they] didn't have that context. My stories were better. The photos were better. The context was better. And it was just a basic homework to look at history.

The other thing is that a lot of folks, I find a lot of reporters aren't reading their history or reading any books. We spend most of our time on social media. And we're not even clicking on stories. We're getting our education by headline and tweets. If one reads our history, it gives you a better foundation when you go in, and you immediately excel. So, political science: great minor. English is a great minor. I'm an English major too, as well. But history is really the one. It's really the discipline that has put me over and got me to where I am today. Because I'm able to put things in context and present previous historical events that people are fascinated by, right, that historians knew about, but the general public did not. And that has catapulted me to the top.

Trade Tools and Tips

1. Set aside a specific social media-free day and time to devote to expanding your historical knowledge, either through books, audio, or other formats.
2. Search for history-oriented podcasts that you might listen to while you're working out or cooking or driving to work.
3. Take current issues or controversies in your area – even those already in the news – and search for any overlooked historical angles to what is happening today in your community.
4. Contact your local, regional and/or state historical society and find out what those societies have in their collections.
5. Create a list of go-to sources, such as university historians, who might be able to provide historical insight on future stories.

Assignments

1. Based on information from this chapter, search your college library's historical newspaper databases to find the term "greaser" or other media tropes and memes of the past. You might use just one newspaper database, such as newspapers.com, NewsBank, or Proquest Historical Newspapers or comparing findings across more than one database. Use the bar chart found in your search results to create a historical and/or geographic timeline for the

word(s). If your library doesn't provide access to any historical newspaper databases, see exercise two below.

2. As a follow to the first exercise, use the Google Books Ngram Viewer to track the popularity of the words you identified in exercise #1 over time. What overlaps do you see between the popularity of these terms? How many terms appear to be no longer in use, according to the viewer? If you did the first assignment, explain any differences between the trends in the Ngram viewer and the newspaper database search.
3. To learn more about key figures in Latinx journalism who have paved the way for journalists of the present and future, research the life of a member of the NAHJ Hall of Fame and write a paper and/or develop a multimedia story, podcast, or column about their life and contributions. Alternatively, do the same for a longtime local Latinx journalist whose career has had an impact in your area.
4. Using your college's library database, retrieve Russell Contreras's scholarly article, "The X-factor: The struggle to get Latinos in US news stories amid a Latinx push and changing journalism landscape," *Cultural Dynamics* 2017, Vol. 29 (3), 177–175. After reading the article, write a 400- to 500-word reflection paper analyzing how Contreras shows the relevance of journalism history to understanding and reporting on Latinx people today. (If your library doesn't have access to this article, request it through inter-library loan.)
5. The induction of the early twentieth century Mexican American journalist Jovita Idár into the NAHJ Hall of Fame in 2021 put Latina journalists in the historical spotlight. Idár might have been more widely known or received recognition sooner had she written her autobiography. Fortunately, two contemporary U.S. bilingual journalists with a clear eye to their historical legacy, Ilia Calderón and Maria Hinojosa, natives of Columbia and Mexico respectively, have written memoirs that are available in English and Spanish. Read one or both books and write a 750-word book review that analyzes how the author(s) incorporate history in telling their life stories. To expand on this angle in your review, briefly explain why history and journalism history matter today. Tips on how to write and structure a book review, are available on the University of North Carolina at Chapel Hill's Writing Center website. See the entry on "Book Reviews" under "Tips & Tools" on the website.

   Books for this assignment:

   Ilia Calderón, *My Time to Speak: Reclaiming Ancestry and Confronting Race*, (New York: Atria Books, 2020)

   Maria Hinojosa, *Once I was You: A Memoir of Love and Hate in a Torn America*, (New York: Atria Books, 2020).

Discussion Questions

1. After reading this chapter and learning about the marketing of "Stickful Features," what insight have you gained about how the media has historically profited from memes and tropes of Latinos? What are some ways you see that playing out in media today, including social media?
2. What was the significance of San Antonio's *La Prensa* as a voice for Latinos, whether Spanish-speaking or not?
3. Why is being absent from news coverage often as damaging, or more so, than being ridiculed, trivialized, or attacked?
4. After reading the Q&A with Russell Contreras, discuss ways to find out about hidden Latinx historical events in your city, state and/or region.
5. Based on Russell Contreras's concerns that journalists spend too much time on social media and not enough time reading books, discuss specific ways you might learn more about history and Latinx history.

References

Adams Syndicate (1916, April). "The 'Stickful Feature Idea'" [advertisement]. *The Editor and Publisher*, 48(46): 1416.

Alonzo, J. (2004). From derision to desire: The 'Greaser' in Stephen Crane's Mexican stories and D.W. Griffith's early westerns. *Western American Literature*, 38(4): 374–401.

The American Experience (2009). "A class apart." *Documentary transcript*, p. 19. https://www-tc.pbs.org/wgbh/americanexperience/media/pdf/transcript/A_class_Apart_transcript.pdf

"American program endorsed by Legion." (1933, October 12). *San Antonio Light*.

American Society of News Editors (2019). "2019 ASNE Diversity Newsroom Survey," Table C. Whites and Minority Percentages of the Overall Workforce (including newsroom leaders and all others). Available at: https://static1.squarespace.com/static/5d2df6a6231a750001881b75/t/5d76c698c87c4c7550640ec2/1568065177406/Summary±Tables±2019_9.6.19.pdf

Bush, C.R. (1932). *Editorial Thinking and Writing: A Textbook with Exercises*. New York, NY: D. Appleton and Company.

Chavez, L. (2013). *The Latino Threat: Constructing Immigrants, Citizens, and the Nation*, 2nd Edition. Stanford, CA: Stanford University Press.

Garza, M. (2018). *They Came to Toil: Newspaper Representations of Mexicans and Immigrants in the Great Depression*. Austin, TX: University of Texas Press.

Gitlin, T. (2003). *The Whole World is Watching: Mass Media in the Making and Unmaking of the New Left*. Berkeley: University of California Press.

Rann, H. (1918, April 29). Random reels, "The Greaser." *Fort Worth Star-Telegram*.

Tuchman, G. (2000). "The symbolic annihilation of women by the mass media." In Lane, C. & Lockhart, C. (Eds.), *Culture and Politics: A Reader*. New York, NY: St. Martin's Press.

"Undesirable aliens heavy charge on Uncle Sam." (1930, August 4). *San Antonio Light*.

Uranga, R. (1929, Feb. 16) "Glosario del Día," *La Prensa*.

USC Annenberg Inclusion Initiative (2020). "Inequality in 1,300 films: Examining portrayals of gender, race/ethnicity, LGBTQ & disability from 2007 to 2019." https://assets.uscannenberg.org/docs/aii-inequality_1300_popular_films_09-08-2020.pdf

U.S. Census Bureau (2019). Quick facts. Retrieved from https://www.census.gov/quickfacts/fact/faq/US/RHI725219

Weber, D.J. (1992). *The Spanish Frontier in North America*. New Haven, CT: Yale University.

"Widespread opposition to the Box Bill." (1930, January 29). *San Antonio Express*.

3

Beat Reporting and Developing Sources in the Latinx Community

Edna Negrón

When New Jersey reporter, Monsy Alvarado, reported a story in April 2021 about the lag in COVID-19 vaccination rates among underserved communities (Alvarado, 2021), she knew where to get Latino perspectives on the vaccine.

"I knew of a park where a lot of older men tend to play dominoes. I spent an hour there talking to the different people there, men and a few women, too," Alvarado said. "I not only interviewed them, but also observed some of the dialogue that they were having about this particular subject."

Alvarado, a veteran reporter covering North Jersey's diverse communities, understands the importance of finding local Latino sources on her beat to tell relatable stories and localize national trends.

How to Cover Latinos on a Beat

A beat can be defined geographically as in a town or by a subject, such as sports, health or education. A reporter can cover Latinos on *any* beat. But what do you actually know about Latinos? What are facts from perceptions and how do you avoid stereotypes? How do you find the right sources?

The way a reporter approaches a beat shapes the types of stories she covers and how the public perceives Latinos. A beat reporter should aim to report stories that reflect the realities that Latinos live daily, their challenges, successes and views on general news stories.

Latinos are diverse. In the borough of Queens, New York City, for instance, Latinos make up more than 28 percent of the population, and hail from more than a dozen Latin American countries, including Colombia, Mexico and Ecuador. Each group has its own sociopolitical and cultural characteristics but

DOI: 10.4324/9781003212331-3

share a community identity. While *QueensLatino* covers the borough's diversity and nuances in its local Spanish-language publication, its mission is on its masthead: "*Por Nuestra Comunidad.*"

Investing time to research people and places in the Latino community is important to finding reliable local sources at the neighborhood school, civic and government levels to national groups that advocate for equity and social justice in education, law enforcement, politics, health, entertainment and immigration.

So, what should you know before you write a story about Latinos on your town beat?

Who are the Latinos on your beat and what do they care about?

Start by knowing which Latino groups are in your local community. Are they newer immigrants or have they been established in the community for generations? Knowing how Latinos identify (Gonzalez-Barrera, 2020) is a function of cultural competence (NAHJ, 2020) or awareness of who they are.

Latinos, for example, are largely a young demographic with a median age of 30, according to the 2020 U.S. Census. And they care about much more beyond immigration. An April 2021 survey of Latino voters commissioned by the national advocacy organization, UnidosUS, with Univision found that 45% of the respondents identified COVID-19 as their top concern followed by jobs at 41%, healthcare costs at 25% and immigration at 21%. (UnidosUS, 2020).

Locally, Latinos are taxpayers and also care about quality of life neighborhood issues, such as public safety, quality schools, voting rights and representations in the arts.

Latinos tend to keep close tabs on their native countries, where family members still reside. For example, Puerto Ricans in New York City and Orlando,

FIGURE 3.1 Photos of UnidosUS by Edna Negrón

Florida followed the developments and provided for the needs of those living without electricity on the island after Hurricane Maria's devastation in 2017. For example, U.S. mainland Puerto Ricans communicated through a Facebook group "Puerto Rico Maria Updates" to stay informed of the island's needs.

Understanding the local history of Latinos and their motivation for migrating to your town can provide important context. For instance, in the city of Paterson, New Jersey, historically an industrial town, Peruvians are a substantial Latino group along with Dominicans and Mexicans. Peruvians had come to Paterson (Chin, 2016) to work in textile in the 1950s. Many are now business owners in a section now called "Little Lima."

Where are the Latinos and who are the local sources? Observe. Meet. Listen.

Take a walk around your coverage area. Map the places where Latinos congregate. Is it a bodega, restaurant, soccer field, church steps, barbershop or block where day laborers gather? Attend a local town or school board meeting or cultural event. Is there a Latino business hub? Find and talk to the local Latino go-to leaders, such as parent advocates, coaches, activists, clergy, artists and restaurateurs. List sources by country of origin.

Finding sources and story ideas

Check the U.S. Census: Statistics are a good source of story ideas when you identify patterns and raise questions. https://data.census.gov/ provides detailed information about Latinos in your coverage area. What is the demographic profile, including specific Hispanic origin, age, median income?

Mine annual reports: For example, education is important to Latinos. School performance reports The National Assessment of Educational Progress (NAEP, https://www.nationsreportcard.gov/) usually required by the U.S. and state education departments show the schools with significant Latino enrollment. Achievement rates in key subjects, language learning and graduation rates are good indicators. You can search your state Education Department's database of school performance.

Check social media and verify sources: What are people discussing on social media? Who are the local Latino groups and personalities on TikTok, Twitter. Instagram or Facebook? Be sure to verify any potential sources and information (Urbani, 2019) that you find on social media. Check their digital footprint across other platforms and online searches. Use tools such as Tweetdeck to monitor multiple topics of interest to Latino communities; subscribe to specialized newsletters or coverage, such as nbcnews.com/latino.

Check past stories: What has been written about Latinos in your community? Check the archives or library databases. Who are the sources quoted in those stories? Who are the gadflies or catalysts raising concerns or complaints? Who are the experts, academics that explain research and trends?

National sources, local stories

The issue or specialized beat focuses on subjects including health, education, sports, business, criminal justice, immigration, politics and the arts. Advocacy and nonprofit organizations conduct studies and surveys that analyze Latino equity and access to affordable healthcare, quality education, voter registration, path to U.S. citizenship and entrepreneurship.

Localize the research to make the findings meaningful to your town beat. For example, a statistic about the rise in first-time Latino voters can be told locally through voter participation groups.

There are many national organizations that monitor and study Latino progress and problems. They include UnidosUS, Pew Research Center, the Mexican American Legal Defense and Educational Fund, Latino Justice PRLDEF, Hispanic Association of Colleges and Universities, The National Association of Latino Elected and Appointed Officials and League of United Latin American Citizens (LULAC), UCLA Latino Policy & Politics Initiative. The Journalist's Resource is a good source of more research.

A Closer Look at UnidosUS as a Latino Source

2020 was a year of unprecedented challenges for Latinos. The COVID-19 pandemic, protests that renewed calls for racial justice and a contentious presidential election tested the community's resolve. And the nation's largest civil rights organization for Latinos cast a critical spotlight on those issues through a number of studies and education campaigns (UnidosUS, 2021a).

UnidosUS is a nonprofit, nonpartisan national organization with a network of nearly 300 community-based organizations that advocates for more equitable opportunities for Latinos, such as better healthcare, quality schools, increased voter participation and business growth (UnidosUS, 2018).

Formerly the National Council of La Raza (NCLR), the organization changed its name to UnidosUS in 2017 to broaden its reach to the diverse Latino population growing in the United States.

Founded in 1968 in Arizona, NCLR is rooted in the civil rights movements of the 1960s when there was a need for an organization to rally Mexican Americans. Scholars and Chicano activists initially founded the Southwest Council of La Raza; the nonprofit organization that later became NCLR. The term *la raza* translates to race in Spanish, but activists applied the word to mean "community" or "our people," representing families who migrated from Latin America.

Conservatives targeted NCLR's use of the term "la raza" (Contreras, 2017) arguing that the organization was anti-white. But NCLR explained that the rebranding, in part, was a way to reach the younger Latino demographic. Beyond Mexican Americans, the word *raza* was not typically used by other Latino groups. The name change was initially met with mixed reaction at its 2017 conference in Phoenix; some saw the move as leaving Chicano history, rooted in the farmworkers movement, behind. But in the end, NCLR said it was building on that legacy as UnidosUS. *Unidos* means united in Spanish.

In its five decades of advocacy on behalf of all Hispanics, NCLR has been a primary source on Latinos by examining the disparities the community faces on a range of issues from the COVID pandemic to politics. 2020 was particularly tough and local news outlets reported UnidosUS' research findings to tell Latino stories.

The COVID-19 pandemic hit the Latino community hard. Though Latinos comprised 18.5 percent of the population in 2020 at the height of the pandemic, they represented more than a third of the COVID-19 cases. To arm the community with accurate information about COVID-19, UnidosUS developed, "*Esperanza Para Todos,*" a toolkit of facts they distributed to communities to make sure that Latinos received necessary and culturally relevant information.

Local papers reported on UnidosUS's efforts to educate and encourage Latinos to get vaccinated. In Texas, *El Paso Times* reported a story (Jackson, 2021) about two UnidosUS outreach workers who manned a table outside a local mall to distribute vaccine information to Latinos. The reporter localized an April Poll of Latino voters conducted by UnidosUS and Univision News that found that the COVID was their top concern (UnidosUS, 2021b). Latinos surveyed said they either were unsure about getting the vaccine or didn't know how to register to get it.

Many Latinos were essential workers in healthcare, construction and food service, and didn't have the luxury of quarantining or staying home during the apex of the pandemic in 2020. UnidosUS, collecting data, monitored COVID's impact by compiling key indicators, such as loss of employment, housing, food insecurity, remote education, included in "By the Numbers: Latinos in the Time of Coronavirus (UnidosUS, 2020)." The dashboard kept track of COVID's impact in six key states: Arizona, California, Florida, Nevada, Texas and Colorado. Unemployment during the height of the pandemic in 2020 triggered a ripple effect of social and economic problems, including homelessness and hunger.

In February 2021, *The Tampa Bay Times,* using the "By the Numbers" data (Faheid, 2021) published a story on the high levels of food insecurity among Latinos in Florida. The local angle focused on a Latina mom who had lost her housekeeping job would drive to a food line to wait with 700 cars to get a boxful of free fruits and vegetables, a scene repeated across the country where hard-hit Latino communities needed help.

Beyond the pandemic, UnidosUS studied the impact of systemic racism on Latinos following renewed calls for racial justice. The April 2021 paper, "Toward a More Perfect Union: Understanding Systemic Racism and Resulting Inequity in Latino Communities," (UnidosUS, 2021c) outlined how decades of inequities have affected Latinos in areas, including healthcare, employment, poverty, education, criminal justice and wealth.

The paper cited, for example, that some Latinos work in the lowest paying jobs with little or no health insurance, and children attend schools that are more segregated and have fewer resources.

Latinos contend with the criminality stigma associated with undocumented immigrants. *Al Día* published a story (Lopez, 2021) on the paper in both English and Spanish.

The report also found that the numbers of Latinos who die in police custody are disproportionately higher than whites and likely undercounted, a point mentioned in a *Washington Post* analysis (Foster-Frau, 2021).

On the political front, UnidosUs pushes for increased representation in government and immigration policies. As the presidential election approached in 2020, states like Arizona, where Latinos comprised 25 percent of eligible voters (Gonzalez, 2020), became key to turning from red to purple or swing state.

Angered by the 2010 racial profiling policy SB1070, requiring immigrants to show documents in Maricopa County, Latino voters in Arizona struck back at the polls in 2020. In recent years, UnidosUS, via its community affiliates and other grassroots groups, including Living United for Change in Arizona (LUCHA), helped to mobilize Latino voters for a significant win. UnidosUS' analysis found that 71 percent of Latino voters in the state supported Democrat Joe Biden and cited grassroots mobilization as a model for growing Latino voter influence (Murguia, 2020).

In Conversation with Monsy Alvarado, a Local Reporter, Who Uses Both Community and National Stories to Report Her Stories

Monsy Alvarado has reported on immigration and emerging communities in North Jersey for more than 20 years. At the time of this interview covered the beat for *The Record,* a part of the USA Network. Her journalism career spans coverage of the many Latino groups in North Jersey including Dominicans and Peruvians in Paterson, Mexicans and Puerto Ricans in Passaic, Guatemalans in Palisades Park and Colombians in Hackensack and Cubans in Union City.

Palisades Park is a community that is overwhelmingly Asian, but 20 percent of the population is Latino. This day in early June, Alvarado walks along Columbia and Broad avenues amid the din of truck traffic, and sits in a local

FIGURE 3.2 Photos of Monsy Alvarado by Edna Negrón

Latino restaurant where the menu includes local fare of *pupusas* (a thick stuffed corn tortilla) and *tamale.* In an interview, Alvarado talks about covering Latinos on this community beat and offers her advice to young reporters about localizing national stories and finding good sources. The transcript is edited for brevity.

Palisades Park is located about 20 minutes south of the George Washington Bridge. We're here in Palisades Park in a local restaurant called, "El Oliva." Can you describe this area?

Alvarado: Palisades Park is a community in Bergen County very close to New York City, so it's east just outside of Bergen County. There's a mix of different types of immigrants here, many Guatemalan day laborers live here, some also women day laborers who work in the local nail salons. They get picked up in the morning by the owners of the respective respected nail salons and are taken to wherever they work and they're brought back in the evening. [There are] a lot of Guatemalans here, Mexicans here as well and some Ecuadorians.

Latinos have been growing recently. You started seeing Guatemalans here. We could see that at the school district. There's a town here called Fairview, and a few years ago they had to start a new school program for the newly arrived children because they didn't know the language. That's another way to see how the immigrant population is growing.

The library started carrying more Latino offerings and more books in Spanish language so newly arrived people who just are not as comfortable reading in English can read things in Spanish.

So how do you approach a beat like a Palisades Park? When you're thinking about Latinos, how do you approach a beat?

Alvarado: When I would go to council meetings like any other municipal reporter, the Korean community tended to be a little bit more involved. It was easier to kind of get those Korean stories out of those meetings because they would ask for translation services because they wanted to understand what the council was saying.

With the Latino community, some of them weren't as involved. I had to really walk the beat, literally walk the streets, talk to restaurant owners, talk to the locals like a chamber of commerce to see what concerns were out there.

In the library, [there are] a lot of people who don't speak English. They go to the library to learn English; they have literacy programs there, so that's a way to meet people and just talk to them about their concerns. Here in Palisades Park, they actually started Spanish story time, and the mothers would take their children there, and that was the way of meeting some of the mothers. When you have an education question, you can reach out to that community because you had the mothers you had talked to about the story time program.

So, you were describing a story you did about someone who died a tragic death, and you were here a few times in Palisades Park.

Alvarado: There were a few tragic deaths, a couple of men who were found; they were homeless and they were found dead in a truck, also there are people who live under a bridge here. I would come here because when somebody passed away, whether through a car accident, if we wanted to find more about them, usually if you came around here, somebody would know about them. Sometimes, you would find donation bins in the restaurants with a picture of the person, and sometimes you would even get lucky enough to get a phone number. It was a way of reaching out to the family.

What about health issues involving Latinos in this area that have to do with COVID-19?

Alvarado: Since I've been covering the Latino community for a long time, I would, during the COVID pandemic, get calls from people asking, "Hey, I don't know where I can get this test." When you start receiving a lot of those calls, you think there has to be a story, right? Are they getting tested? And so, I think that's why it's so important to walk the beat because when a pandemic hits, you have those connections. That's how I was able to do stories about the racial disparities when it came to the vaccine.

Q: How do you find local sources?

Alvarado: So a variety of different ways. Some of the best places to get sources are churches. Latino people tend to go to church often and they have a good rapport with their priests, so a priest is always a really good person to talk to also the secretary of parishes. Then, also community liaisons. Even if you can't speak the language, there are people in the community who are bilingual who can connect you. You should always keep community liaisons handy, and also grow them if you find somebody that speaks both languages in the community. Take their number, make sure to keep in touch with them because they could connect you with people.

Q: What do you think is the most common misconception people have about Latinos?

Alvarado: I think a lot of people think Latinos are the same. Depending on where you're from, cultural traditions are different. Mexicans are different from Guatemalans, and we need to show that in some of our stories. Also, our political views are so different and diverse. We have Republican Latinos, Libertarian Latinos, Democratic Latinos. Always remember that you can't just assume because you're a Latina you're going to be voting a certain way or you're going to be thinking a certain way.

Q: What would you advise a young reporter covering a Latino beat?

Alvarado: I think one of the most important things that helped me is really grow your Latino source list. I have a document where I can constantly add people from certain parts of the world. If you were born in Colombia, I have a list of Colombian people; I have a list of people from Puerto Rico; I have a list of people from Central America, South America. We might want to write a reaction piece. I call them.

Usually, conversations are so important because if that person might not be able to help you they're well I know so and so who has a family member who's over there you know, and so that's really, really important. One piece of advice to especially new reporters is always keep a list handy and expand on and make sure to add ten new names from different backgrounds in that source list, because you'll need it one day and it's good to have them.

Q: Sometimes you have to write a story based on a national statistic or some kind of study that involves Latinos. How do you handle those kinds of stories?

Alvarado: We do a lot of stories on studies and so you read the study and then you start looking for people that might fit that, We might also have to pull information from national sources to support the study that you're trying to report on.

Q: What's one piece of advice you can give a reporter about filing a Latino story? What should they aim for?

Alvarado: Different voices. You can't just interview one Latino and just assume that he could speak for the greater Latino population. Always speak to more than one person because different people bring different perspectives to a story and they might actually change your mind on something that you're writing about because they bring something out.

Q: Is there anything else that you want to say to the young reporter who's covering the Latino community? Is there basic advice you could give?

Alvarado: Go out there and talk to people. It's so important. Texts are not the same, phone conversations are not the same. Sometimes when people see you, you can develop that rapport with them that's so important when you really need them when you're working on deadline. If you can, carve out some time to just really walk out there and just talk to the community not for a story, but just to develop those sources so -when you do need them you know where to go.

Trade Tips and Tools

Avoid the DON'Ts

- Don't patronize or assume a Latino does not speak English.
- Don't think all Latinos are immigrants. For example, Puerto Ricans are U.S. citizens.
- Don't exploit a vulnerable source, such as someone who has never talked to a reporter.
- Avoid stereotypes. For example, did you know that undocumented workers pay (Institute on Taxation and Economic Policy, 2017) more than $11 billion a year in taxes, according to a nonpartisan tax policy organization.

Practice the DOs

- Do become familiar with how Latinos identify in your coverage area.
- Find community sources who can introduce you to other sources or can translate for you, if needed.
- Do talk to people in the community even if you are not working on a story. Build rapport.
- Do compile a list of sources by country and keep adding to it.
- Do follow the SPJ code of ethics (https://www.spj.org/ethicscode.asp).

- Engage the community in idea development. What types of stories and solutions would they want to see in stories about their community?
- Do interview various Latino voices. No one Latino represents the community.

Discussion Questions

1. Search the archives for ten most recent stories about Latinos in the United States. Which Latino groups or Latin American countries are mentioned? What are the most common topics associated with Latinos in the news? What stories, sources are missing?
2. Find three stories about the Latino vote in the 2020 Presidential Elections. Consult research by national Latino organizations. What Latino leaders are most quoted in the stories, and whose voices are overlooked? Identify three significant findings. How would you localize one on your beat?
3. Then and now. Find a national trend story about Latinos on a specialized beat such as healthcare, sports, immigration, entertainment, politics. How are Latinos portrayed? Has coverage changed? If so, how? If not, what angles could better reflect Latinos today?
4. The 2020 Census count has been controversial. What is the impact of the latest numbers, and what issues do the numbers raise?
5. The COVID-19 pandemic had a devastating impact on Latinos, more than any other group. Essential workers had to go to work; students and teachers pivoted to remote learning, undocumented immigrants faced the worse consequences losing jobs and facing hunger and homelessness. What inequities did COVID lay bare about the Latino community? How did the media tell those stories in photos or multimedia?

Assignments

1. Find out which Latino groups are on your local beat. Look up Census data, what profile of the community emerges? Find a recent story for each group in your town. Identify five issues that Latinos care about. How are the different Latino groups portrayed?
2. Map your local town beat. Where are the Latinos? Their gathering places? Their businesses? The places of worship, schools, athletic fields. Be specific. Identify ten key sources. Include an activist, elected official, advocate; identify a civic group, a local artist.
3. Identify three national organizations that advocate for Latinos in areas such as education, health and politics. Find contact information and a study that they conducted. How can you localize the findings and make it relevant to your local Latino community? What sources would you talk to and why?

4. Search five stories about the young Latinx community. Identify three issues that they care about. Who are the sources? Why do these issues appeal to this demographic?
5. Search social media to see what Latinos are talking about. What groups do you see on platforms such as Facebook and Twitter? Identify five groups, five sources and five issues. Verify the sources. Which sources would you use? Identify one story idea.
6. **Reporting Assignment:** Identify local advocacy groups and meet members of the community and engage them in discussion about the types of stories that they would like to see. Identify an angle for one idea, what is the news value? What questions would you ask? What sources would you talk to? Write a story pitch. Why would this story idea matter to Latinos and what insights does it convey about Latinos to the general public?
7. **Reporting Assignment:** Identify a challenge or concern in the local Latino community. Report it. It can involve local schools, politics or be a quality of life in the neighborhood such as crime, public safety, the environment. Find a relevant study or statistic. Interview sources. Ask the community and experts for their ideas for solving it.
8. **Reporting Assignment:** Education is important to Latino families. Take a look at the local school report card for your school or district where Latinos comprise a significant population. What patterns do you observe? Is there a story idea there about gains, equity, access? Diversity? Identify a local education story angle and develop it using sources from your local district.
9. **Reporting Assignment:** Profile an ordinary person who does an extraordinary thing. There are many untold stories of Latinos who contribute to the community and society overall. Profile one person who is a local inspiration or hero.
10. **Research and Reporting Assignment**: Puerto Rico has been a colony of the United States since 1898. Puerto Ricans became U.S. citizens in 1917, but they cannot vote in the presidential election. They serve in the military. Currently, the future status of Puerto Rico has been again under review: Should the island become a state or remain an enhanced commonwealth. Should it seek independence? Find five stories and compare recent coverage about the future of Puerto Rico. What do you learn about the state of Puerto Rico? What do local Puerto Ricans say?

References

Alvarado, M. (2021, April 11). NJ Still Hasn't Bridged the Racial Gap in COVID Vaccination. Here's What's Going Wrong. The Record. https://www.northjersey.com/story/news/new-jersey/2021/04/05/nj-covid-vaccine-appointment-campaign-state-still-struggling-bridge-racial-gaps/4805037001/

Chin, M. (2016, May 18). Why Paterson, New Jersey, Is Famous in Lima, Peru. The Atlantic. https://www.theatlantic.com/business/archive/2016/05/peruvians-paterson/483288/

Contreras, R. (2017, January 12). AP Explains: Why Term 'La Raza' Has Complicated Roots in US. Associated Press. https://apnews.com/article/9572a239f3e441b6a0c33f18255b10e9

Faheid, D. (2021, February 23). Florida's Latino Population Hit Hard by Food Insecurity During the Pandemic. *Tampabay.com*. https://www.tampabay.com/news/health/2021/02/22/floridas-latino-population-hit-hard-by-food-insecurity-during-the-pandemic/

Foster-Frau, S. (2021, June 2). Latinos are Disproportionately Killed by Police But are Often Left Out of the Debate About Brutality, Advocates Say. Washington Post. https://www.washingtonpost.com/national/police-killings-latinos/2021/05/31/657bb7be-b4d4-11eb-a980-a60af976ed44_story.html

Gonzalez-Barrera, A. (2020, September 24). *The Ways Hispanics Describe Their Identity Vary Across Immigrant Generations*. Pew Research. https://www.pewresearch.org/fact-tank/2020/09/24/the-ways-hispanics-describe-their-identity-vary-across-immigrant-generations/

Gonzalez, D. (2020, October). Telemundo Poll: Biden Leads Trump Among Latino Votes in Battleground Arizona. *Azcentral.com*. https://www.azcentral.com/story/news/politics/immigration/2020/10/30/poll-biden-leads-trump-64-28-among-latino-voters-arizona/6069700002/

Jackson, A. (2021, April 23). Vaccine Hesitancy Concern for City and County; Latino Community Urged to Get Vaccinated. El Paso Times. https://www.elpasotimes.com/story/news/2021/04/23/el-paso-city-and-county-urge-latino-communities-get-covid-19-vaccines/7357725002/

Institute on Taxation and Economic Policy. (2017, March 2). Undocumented Immigrants' State and Local Tax Contributions. https://itep.org/immigration/. https://itep.sfo2.digitaloceanspaces.com/immigration2017.pdf

Lopez, O. (2021, April 27). Desde la inmigración hasta el COVID-19: Analizando las disparidades en las comunidades latinas. *Aldia.com*. https://aldianews.com/es/articles/leaders/non-profits/desde-la-inmigracion-hasta-el-covid-19-analizando-las-disparidades-en

Murguia, J. (2020, November 24). Opinion: Arizona is Now a Swing State Because of SB 1070 and the Latino Voters It Activated. https://www.azcentral.com/story/opinion/op-ed/2020/11/24/sb-1070-energized-latino-voters-why-arizona-now-swing-state/6286453002/

The National Assessment of Educational Progress (NAEP). Retrieved from https://www.nationsreportcard.gov/

National Association of Hispanic Journalists (NAHJ). (2020, August 18). Cultural Competence Handbook. https://nahj.org/wp-content/uploads/2020/08/NAHJ-Cultural-Competence-Handbook.pdfQueensLatino.com. Retrieved from https://queenslatino.com/media-kit/.

Society of Professional Journalists. SPJ Code of Ethics. Retrieved from https://www.spj.org/ethicscode.asp

UnidosUS. (2018) Fifty Years of An American Institution. https://www.unidosus.org/wp-content/uploads/2021/08/unidosus_history.pdf

UnidosUS. (2020, April). By the Numbers: Latinos in the Time of Coronavirus. https://www.unidosus.org/blog/2020/10/26/interactive-data-tool-latinos-in-the-time-of-coronavirus/

UnidosUS. (2021a, February 8). A Year of Resistance and Resilience, 2020 Annual Report. https://www.unidosus.org/wp-content/uploads/2021/08/unidosus_2020 annualreport_digital.pdf

UnidosUS. (2021b, April 6). COVID remains Latinos' Top Concern in New Poll by Univision News and UnidosUS. https://www.unidosus.org/press-releases/040621-unidosus-univision-release-latino-covid-poll/

UnidosUS. (2021c, April 8). Toward a More Perfect Union: Understanding Systemic Racism and Resulting Inequity in Latino Communities. http://publications.unidosus.org/bitstream/handle/123456789/2128/unidosus_systemicracism_executivesummary.pdf?sequence=5&isAllowed=y

Urbani, S. (2019). Verifying Online Information. First Draft. https://firstdraftnews.org/wp-content/uploads/2019/10/Verifying_Online_Information_Digital_AW.pdf

U.S. Census Bureau. Search engine for more detailed information about a population's characteristics in a location. https://data.census.gov/cedsci/

4

Race, Colorism and Policing in Latinx Communities

Getting the Real Story

Claudia E. Cruz

When CNN Reporter Omar Jimenez began to cover the unrest in Minneapolis after the killing of George Floyd, he never thought the assignment would land him in jail.

A few months after Minnesota State troopers detained him and his news team, he told the Chicago Tribune, "I never would have considered we would have ended a live report in handcuffs" (Ryan, 2020).

Though authorities released him, his detention triggered questions about the treatment of the media by police (CNN, 2020) and whether the officers targeted him for being Black (Macaya et al., 2020).

Jimenez, an Afro-Latino whose father is Colombian and mother African-American, told the Chicago Tribune how worried his mom had been. In a text sent to him during the ordeal, his mother lamented, "I didn't want to be another mother whose beautiful Black son died in police custody" (Ryan, 2020).

The behavior of police toward members of the African-American and Latino communities in the United States has come under increased societal scrutiny in the past several years. This, despite how some journalists have sought attention to the unequal treatment of Black and Brown bodies by police. Even as early as 1892 the investigative reporting of Ida B. Wells, a Black journalist, documented the lynching of Black men by white mobs (Walker, 2020).

The coverage has been unbalanced for many reasons including the lack of diversity in newsrooms, the dearth in the understanding of policing in minority communities and for the purposes of this textbook, the limited knowledge of the Spanish-language by reporters.

Hispanics or Latinos make up 18.7% of the U.S. population, according to the U.S. Census 2020 figures. That's nearly 62.1 million people of various racial

DOI: 10.4324/9781003212331-4

categorizations since "Hispanics may be of any race" reads the footnote. But what exactly does this mean?

It's not uncommon for a journalist to hear that the classification of people by race is solely or mostly a phenomenon of the United States where the legal rights and privileges of citizens have been limited or expanded upon over time due to whether they are "white" or "Black" (Haney Lopez, 2006, p. 7). This is only part of the truth.

A Latinx journalist, especially if they can speak Spanish and communicate with newer immigrants, should also understand the role race has played in the creation of "colorism" in Latin America. Colorism is a caste or categorization system based on someone's phenotype – in this case, skin color – inherited by a population from its ruling class (Chavez-Dueñas et al., 2014, p. 8).

A recent study (Figure 4.1) by the Pew Research Center on Hispanics, immigration and demographics found that "Latinos with darker skin are more likely than those with lighter skin to report a specific incident of discrimination" (Gonzalez-Barrera, 2019). What does this mean and how does it manifest within the Latinx community and their interactions with the police?

School lessons about Latin America in the United States usually begin and end with mentions of the Spanish settlers, the indigenous populations that lived in the region upon the arrival of the Europeans in 1492 and the beginnings of the slave trade from Western Africa to the Western Hemisphere.

Seldom taught is the hierarchical racial framework developed through a caste system inherited by Latin Americans from its colonial class (Figure 4.2). This colorism-based structure gave rise to the various labels used for the mixed-race offspring of the colonizers, indigenous and enslaved Africans (Chavez-Dueñas et al., 2014, p. 7). As this population migrated north during the 20th Century, it found itself further embroiled in the complicated issues of the racialized and systemic discrimination already prevalent in the United States.

Discussions about race and colorism in the Latinx community have taken place mostly in academic circles for years. However, questions of representation have gained national attention recently.

One example arose after the June 2021 movie theater release of "In the Heights," an adaptation of the 2008 Tony Award-winning musical of the same name created by Lin-Manuel Miranda and written by Quiara Alegria Hudes, both light-skinned Latinos of Puerto Rican ancestry.

The vibrant and joyfully scripted and choreographed scenes depict the struggles of the multigenerational, mostly Dominican immigrant neighborhood of Washington Heights near the Northern tip of Manhattan. Yet, immediately after its screening, the conversation became: Why were most of the principal actors light-skinned Latinos instead of being a true representation of the dark-skinned Afro-Dominican population it's supposed to reflect? (León, 2021).

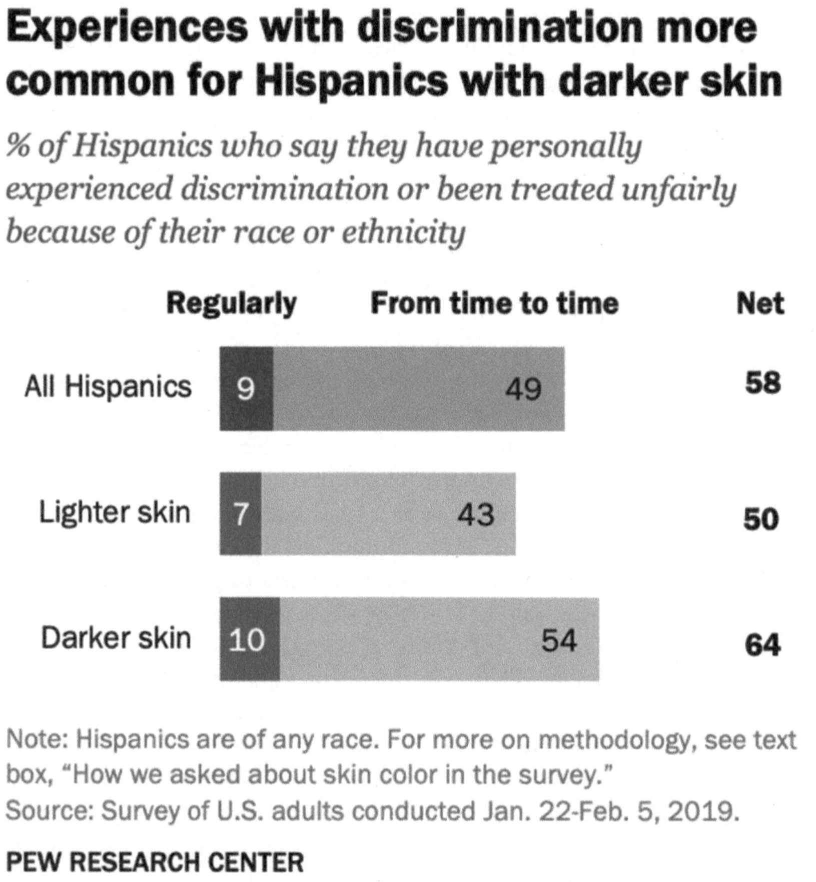

Experiences with discrimination more common for Hispanics with darker skin

% of Hispanics who say they have personally experienced discrimination or been treated unfairly because of their race or ethnicity

	Regularly	From time to time	Net
All Hispanics	9	49	58
Lighter skin	7	43	50
Darker skin	10	54	64

Note: Hispanics are of any race. For more on methodology, see text box, "How we asked about skin color in the survey."
Source: Survey of U.S. adults conducted Jan. 22-Feb. 5, 2019.

PEW RESEARCH CENTER

FIGURE 4.1 Pew Research Center chart showing that darker-skinned Hispanics claim to experience more discrimination compared to their lighter-skinned counterparts (Gonzalez-Barrera, 2019)

On Twitter Miranda publicly apologized for the shortcoming and acknowledged that he could "hear the hurt and the frustration over colorism" (Miranda, 2021).

If an individual who lives and works in Washington Heights – like Miranda – "fell short" and misrepresented the predominantly Afro-Dominican neighborhood that he grew up in, then how would a Latinx journalist, perhaps bilingual, come to quickly understand the racial makeup of a community that is not their own? What roles do race, colorism and language play in news gathering? What should you consider, especially or specifically, when the police are involved?

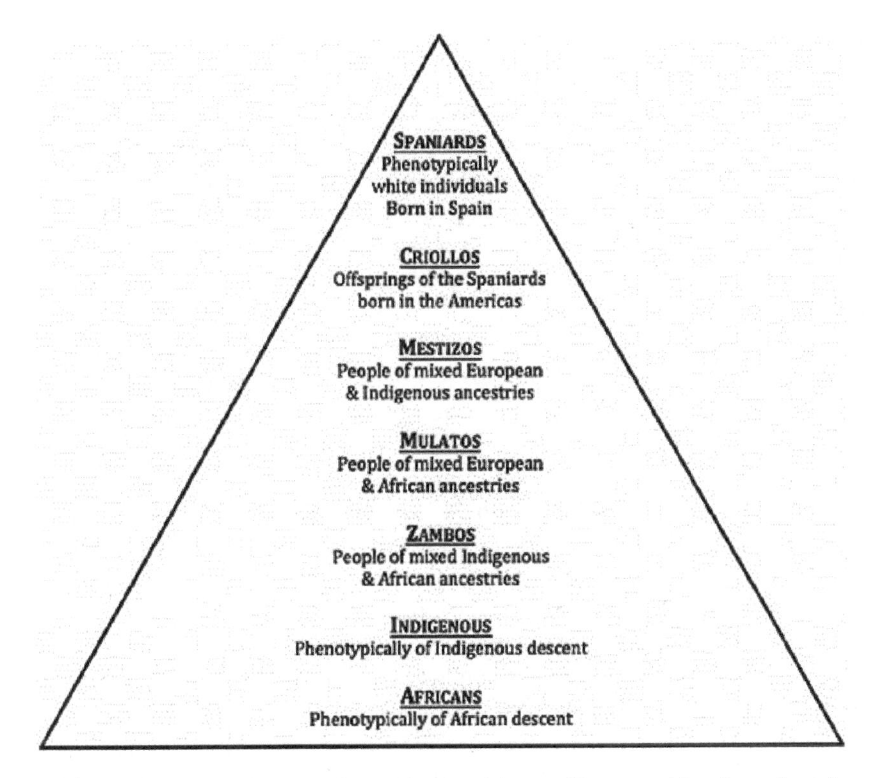

FIGURE 4.2 Triangular image shows the racial hierarchy created by the colonizing Spanish settlers of Latin America (Chavez-Dueñas et al., 2014, p. 7)

The implications of race and colorism among Latinos is extremely nuanced. It may be influenced by where in the United States the Latinx community is located, how many generations their family has been in the country, their personal experience with discrimination, their age and gender and their immigration status. But how does the lack of enough bilingual media coverage impact our understanding of these communities?

The next section of this chapter will present a case study to explore the historical news coverage of police brutality in Washington Heights and also investigate the current day conversation about race and colorism in the Afro-Latino neighborhood.

A Closer Look: Race as an Identifier in an Afro-Dominican Community

As the world learns about Washington Heights – albeit through the lens of a glossy Hollywood production – the predominantly Afro-Caribbean neighborhood also made national headlines during an uprising against the New York

Police Department (NYPD) nearly 30 years earlier (HabichuelaConDulce, 2020).

For a period of six days starting on July 3, 1992, Dominicans protested the murder of 23-year-old island-born Jose "Kiko" Garcia. Witnesses claimed he was brutally beaten and shot by New York City Police officer Michael O'Keefe, while on patrol in a street identified by the NYPD as a "known drug location" (Sullivan, 1992). O'Keefe said it was Garcia who first drew a .38-caliber pistol on him. A grand jury cleared him of charges that September, ruling the death a justifiable homicide.

The disturbance spanned nearly 70 city blocks (H M, 2015) and took place a little over two months after the Los Angeles riots that also found four police officers not guilty in the beating of Rodney King.

Those intense days began to shape the "local claims to racial justice" of the burgeoning Dominican community, according to race, class and immigration Professor Pedro Regalado (Regalado, 2019, p. 963; Simon, 2018).

"It was a disaster. People were in the streets burning cars and businesses. It was like Rodney King, but Dominican. It was a disaster," Belkis Tamayo, a local resident, told Regalado in an interview (Regalado, 2019, p. 967).

Regalado suggested that despite the community's almost three-decade attempt since their mass arrival in the late 1960s to become part of the larger fabric of New York City, other factors, including the negative portrayal of Dominicans in the English-language media as "criminally inclined" and the additional "threat of force and containment that local police harassment embodied" demonstrated there was still a lot of work to be done (Regalado, 2019, p. 969).

All this while also being challenged that year by the "demonization" and "racial antagonism" of mayoral candidate Rudolph Giuliani who vied for the top job in city leadership against the incumbent, New York City's first Black mayor, David Dinkins (Regalado, 2019, p. 962).

Giuliani went on to win the 1993 mayoral election and afterward heightened law enforcement in Northern Manhattan with his appointment of William Bratton as Police Commissioner who implemented the Broken Windows theory of policing (Allman, 2021).

It can be difficult for a journalist, Latino or not, to have an understanding, even if a modest one, of a community when they arrive to cover a protest after police violence. However, every journalist, especially Spanish-speaking ones, should find out who the mavens are in the area (PrestonLopezShow, 2014). Veteran race and policing journalist Soledad O'Brien said that once a reporter starts to ask, they'll notice that "the same five names start coming up."

After the death of George Floyd in May 2020 and the nationwide Black Lives Matter protests, the families of Latinos killed by police began to join the BLM movement to bring attention to the violence against their own community by law enforcement officials (Associated Press, 2020). The data supports

FIGURE 4.3 Poster for an exhibit about the history of Dominicans in New York from 2008 (Courtesy Dominican Studies Institute)

their discontent as several databases that track police killings, including Mapping Police Violence and the Police Shooting Database from The Washington Post, show that "Latinos are killed by police at nearly double the rate of white Americans" (Foster-Frau, 2021). The numbers could be higher depending on whether the Latinos were classified racially as "white" or "Black."

Few cases do make national headlines. Unfortunately, the ones that do often occur when the Latino killed by the police officer is a child, as in the cases of 13-year-olds Andy Lopez in Santa Rosa, CA in 2013 (Matthews, 2014) and Adam Toledo in March 2021 in Chicago, IL (Howe and Boyle, 2021). Jesse

Romero, a 14-year-old, died in 2016 after being shot by an officer in the Los Angeles neighborhood of Boyle Heights (Mather, 2018). None of the officers have faced charges.

Experts like, now-retired Mexican American Studies professor and scholar on police violence, Roberto Rodriguez thinks "society has this notion that [police violence] is a Black and White issue, and not for Latinos. It's kind of like, That's not your issue. Your issue is immigration" (Foster-Frau, 2021). Rodriguez has kept a list of Latino deaths at the hands of police (Rodriguez, 2020), which he told the Washington Post is "off the charts."

Sometimes when Latino communities do try to bring attention to issues of police violence, it's not always understood why. Marisol Márquez, a community activist in Los Angeles, told the Los Angeles Times in August 2020 that when her organization convened a group of Latinos to speak at a Black Lives Matter protest, the participants drew some backlash.

"We got an angry message that said we really needed to have had way more speakers who were not Latino or Chicanos ... I was so angry. Who they were referring to were people who had family members who had died at the hands of LAPD ... Chicanos," Márquez said (Associated Press, 2020).

If Latinos have faced significant police violence, and even protested against it like in the unrest of Washington Heights in 1992, what's been the barrier or challenge to tell more of these stories? How do race and color play into this narrative? Do darker-skinned Latinos, including those of indigenous descent, get ignored? Do light-skinned Latinos, including reporters, overlook the violence against their darker-hued counterparts? How can we overcome our own bias and prejudices to tell the stories of police violence throughout the Latinx community?

Several days after the death of George Floyd, another notable event took place in Washington Heights. On June 1, some businesses in the Bronx were vandalized and unverified social media videos claimed that something similar would happen on Dyckman Street, a heavily Dominican thoroughfare immediately north of Washington Heights (Dyckman's Diary, 2020a). Community leaders called upon the police for protection. Many young men from the neighborhood also volunteered to help the police watch the storefronts (Dyckman's Diary, 2020a).

No vandals ever appeared, but several young African-American men were chased off Dyckman Street. The video of those young Black men being run out by Dominican-Americans infuriated many on social media and the Dominicans were accused of "racism" for working alongside the 34 Precinct to protect businesses that day (Segura, 2020).

Those young Black men came back later for an apology (Dyckman's Diary, 2020b) and that weekend – close to 30 years after Kiko Garcia's death – a new generation of community members doubled-down on their commitment to Black Lives Matter (Dyckman's Diary, 2020b).

Hispanic experiences with discrimination can differ depending on skin color

% of each group saying each of the following has happened to them because of their race or ethnicity

	Hispanic, lighter skin	All Hispanics	Hispanic, darker skin
People acted as if they were not smart	36%	48%	55%
Been subject to slurs or jokes	34	46	53
People acted as if they were suspicious of them	27	37	43
Feared for their personal safety	23	30	35
Been treated unfairly in hiring, pay or promotion	19	26	30
People assumed they were racist or prejudiced	18	21	23
Been unfairly stopped by police	11	19	24

Note: Hispanics are of any race. For more on methodology, see text box, "How we asked about skin color in the survey."
Source: Survey of U.S. adults conducted Jan. 22-Feb. 5, 2019.

PEW RESEARCH CENTER

FIGURE 4.4 Pew Research Center infographic depicting how Hispanics experience discrimination differently because of colorism (Gonzalez-Barrera, 2019)

But it was a very different optic than that of 1992 because the new young Dominican demonstrators grew up with a different understanding of the colorism dynamics within their own community (Figure 4.4). "Don't confuse the passion for our community with racism. We all are victims of the [sic] authority and we must unite even more!" said the Dyckman's Diary's Instagram post.

The next section of this chapter will present an interview with award-winning journalist Soledad O'Brien who over the course of her career has reported on the intersection of race and policing. She shared how her experiences with racism and colorism propelled her to tell stories often overlooked by the mainstream media.

In Conversation with Soledad O'Brien

Soledad O'Brien (pictured in Figure 4.5) is an award-winning documentarian, journalist, speaker, author, philanthropist and entrepreneur dedicated to telling stories on a broad range of social issues, including race and policing. The daughter of an Afro-Cuban mother and White-Australian father, O'Brien leans on her cultural background to give space for others to share their experiences.

The busy mother of four spoke to me over Zoom in June 2021 from her home in New York City. We conversed about how to report on race, colorism and policing, and

FIGURE 4.5 Photo of Journalist Soledad O'Brien (Courtesy of SO'B Productions)

particularly discussed how one of the many benefits of speaking the Spanish-language is telling more diverse stories.

Tell me about your experience with the Spanish language as a child and as a reporter and why a second language is useful in the type of work that we do?

O'Brien: A second language is essential, and yet I really struggle with it, which is ironic because my [Black and Cuban] mom was a Spanish and French teacher ... I think that was a tremendous loss. My kids actually speak Spanish far better than I ever did. I started taking it in high school.

As a local reporter, on KRON TV in San Francisco, CA, you needed the language much more in your daily interactions. As I moved away from doing local news, into more national news, I needed it far less and so I just didn't really practice. So, my Spanish has really mostly been Spanglish.

What other tools, skills and talents should young reporters have to help them in their coverage? Is it important to be well-rounded?

O'Brien: For me, it's always about being able to have conversations and have the people you're interviewing feel like you get them. You don't have to be on their side. You don't necessarily have to be their friend. But it has to be, "I understand where you're coming from."

I have found lots of domestic coverage being comfortable with poor people; being comfortable with people who don't necessarily speak English perfectly. And if English could be their first language, being comfortable in places that might seem a little bit unsafe because you don't know them well. Sitting down to eat food you haven't eaten before … I'm not sure everybody would describe that as well-rounded, but that to me is well-rounded.

How do you approach reporting on stories about race and colorism? What advice would you give a young reporter assigned this type of story?

O'Brien: We've done a lot of reporting on race and colorism, including a documentary as part of our "Black In America" coverage that looks specifically for an hour at colorism. Issues like this that are very informed by people's personal experience, but then can be undergirded by a lot of data. I try to approach them that way.

It's why all these conversations [are] about what is "objectivity," right? If you actually have had experiences that make you an expert in the conversation or make you at least someone who has something to add to the conversation.

I would say be quiet and ask a lot of questions. Constantly think, "I'm trying to understand your point of view." It's not about me and what I'm doing there. It's about that person – until I'm pushing back or doing follow-ups and then it is about me … Where you can use your own lived experience is to push back and form questions and ask intelligent follow-ups.

The data shows young men are more likely to be involuntarily stopped by the police. What kind of experience did your Afro Latino brothers have?

O'Brien: I have three sisters and two brothers. I think about my younger brother, Orestes. He's a big guy, probably 6 feet 2 inches tall, 200-something pounds. When he was … at Harvard Medical School, he was attending a party in Brooklyn when they were stopped by police.

I think this is a typical story, change the details. I just don't know very many young men of color who don't have a story like this.

He said, "All of a sudden the cops pulled up and they stopped them." Someone had knocked over … a subway toll taker. He'd been knocked over by three guys … kind of as close as they got. What he described … really did affect how I covered policing, police violence and police brutality – and how I just thought of it as a person.

We know from the data, certainly in New York City, about stop and frisk. When you see the large number of times that young men of color were stopped by the police for pretty much no reason at all – nothing came out of the stop. Just how humiliating! How that wears on your psyche!

How can a young journalist develop stronger questioning and interviewing techniques to best cover police violence in communities of color? How have those techniques changed after the Summer of 2020?

O'Brien: 2020 has been an interesting dividing line. So, in 1993 [when I was a local reporter] we assumed the police and the police statement was … the word of God. Now we know that those statements are frequently made up, that they're often inaccurate, that sometimes they're just wrong, but not intentional. Sometimes it is intentional.

But you need to come back to [what's] the information that I need to get out of this interview: "What happened? Do you recognize who it was? Can you tell me what's going on?" Stick to the reporting.

Also remember there's not always video. Sometimes there's video, but often it's subjective. And just like the police version, it's a subjective take on what happened. Sometimes it's intentionally misleading. Anybody who's involved, anybody who has a stake in it – sometimes they're misleading you. You have to make sure that you're really trying to piece together the best you can of the story that unfolded.

If you're bilingual, do you have a better opportunity to connect with the community about the stories that are affecting them when it comes to police violence?

O'Brien: One hundred percent, there's no question. Listen, first of all, often in these communities, people don't want to talk, right? Sometimes the stories are a little bit murky and a little complicated.

I speak Spanglish, but my producer is fluent and the number of times we've had great access because she has pulled up on someone on the street and said, "I want to talk to someone about this." They say, "oh, let me introduce you to my cousin. They don't speak any English at all." All of a sudden you find yourself in this whole new world of all new people, none of whom have been interviewed in any way, shape or form, because the bulk of reporters didn't speak the language. Because they didn't speak the language, it was almost as if their story had no merit.

They, for the intents and purposes of the journalism, didn't exist. Maybe the Spanish language press would interview them, but maybe not. But let me promise you, a reporter who came in and who didn't speak the language was never going to interview this large group of people who had something to say.

Any time there's a group of people whose voices have essentially been ignored by the mainstream media, I think it's a goldmine for a reporter to get in there. Just because they don't speak English doesn't mean that they don't have a valuable message, that they're not great interviews.

How can journalists who might be lighter-skinned understand or check themselves for this prejudice?

O'Brien: It's a great question … To a large degree, if you're a reporter, you just have to understand bias and do research and really read into bias and understand your own bias. Everybody has bias.

Having a great friend, a great producer who you can just say, "Are we doing this the right way?" … I think finding that is really important to recognizing your own bias …

Also, tracking your numbers, literally keeping a spreadsheet. Who am I talking to? What's the data telling you about your own reporting? Do you look and say, "oh, my God, I'm quoting old guys." … Tracking will do you a world of good in terms of really keeping yourself where you were you want to be.

You have parachuted into chaotic and still unfolding news scenarios, what advice do you have to quickly get up to speed?

O'Brien: You land on the ground, you start reporting about what you're seeing and who you're talking to. But then you sit down in restaurants and you say, "I'm looking for a really interesting, blah, blah, blah." Ask your waiter and ask the guy who's, you know, I don't know, sitting next to you.

Never start extrapolating from things in communities that you don't know. You have to have a lot of humility about places that you don't know. Talk to the people who do know. That's kind of the strategy, I would say.

How can a young journalist bring their most authentic self to reporting?

O'Brien: I think being authentic and an honest person in your dealings with people and telling stories in communities is really essential. I don't know that I always did that with my bosses … I think they need to know that you're a good worker, you're a hard worker, that you have interesting stories to pitch. But I think the people you're interviewing need to understand, like, here's what I'm here to do and I would like to tell your story.

Trade Tools and Tips

Your assignment editor tells you to promptly head to the site of a police-involved shooting in a predominantly Latinx neighborhood. You have an hour until you arrive at the site of the incident. How do you prepare on the drive (or subway ride) there? The following are some practical tips to consider.

Research Methods

- What do you know about the neighborhood? (Check city government website)
    - No two Latino communities in the United States are the same. Therefore, a journalist arriving on the scene to cover an anti-police violence protest in a Hispanic community should quickly ask questions to understand the makeup of the Latinx population in the area.
        - Queries should cover: What's the ethnic makeup of the community, average and median age, main economic industry and prior involuntary policing issues.
        - Don't misrepresent the community because you could lose their trust and the goal is the opposite
    - Ask questions of:
        - Neighborhood-based organizations
        - The public. Talk to a lot of people.
        - Public officials
- What's the local news of the day/week/month? (Do Google Searches)
    - What are the headlines, especially related to police, in the Spanish-language press?
        - Don't duplicate, that is, aggregate information from other media sources that you have not verified yourself
    - What's the dynamic between the community and the police department?
- Sourcing
    - Can you find strong community-based organizations you can speak to (ideally on the scene) for context? (Can you get a quote or soundbite in Spanish?)
    - Finding trustworthy sources quickly can help you gain context, and the best way to do so is to show up. Journalism is not a game of telephone. It's about observation.

Production Tools

- Shoot photos, and if possible, video as soon as you arrive. Don't focus on details yet.
    - Don't worry about processing images until the moment you find a temporary-permanent location to set-up.

    - If asked to move by law enforcement, politely comply.

- Ask witnesses what they saw as soon as you can. Jot down some details (use paper and pen, or online memo software).
    - Try to get the facts behind these details by talking to as many people as you can.
        - Get their full name, telephone number and email if necessary. Ask them where they live in the neighborhood. You may need to contact them again.
    - Don't add information that you did not observe or cannot attribute to a reliable source.
- Keep an updated list of facts and important contact handy.

Discussion Questions

- How can a bilingual journalist – whether new to the field or with years of experience – provide the best, most accurate coverage of race and cultural identity in a community?
- What prior knowledge and tools can help them quickly evaluate and encapsulate a tense police event in a Latino neighborhood and be ready for the live camera hit, breaking news article, audio report or social media post?
- What is the impact of the use of race-based identifiers in media coverage of police violence?
- What terms do your newsroom colleagues use and how might that contribute to inaccurate and biased reporting about Latino communities? (Kelly, 2021)
- If you ran a newsroom, how would you cover unrest about police violence in a Latinx community now?

Assignments

1. Watch the PBS documentary "Zoot Suit Riots," which aired on February 2002 and read this accompanying article about the Murder at Sleepy Lagoon (Figure 4.6) to get additional background on the issues between the Mexican American community and the police and white serviceman in Los Angeles.

   Documentary: https://www.pbs.org/wgbh/americanexperience/films/zoot/

   Article: https://www.pbs.org/wgbh/americanexperience/features/zoot-rise-riots/

   What socioeconomic similarities do you find between the Mexican American/Chicano community in Los Angeles in the early 1940s and that of Dominicans in Washington Heights 50 years later? What are some differences?

FIGURE 4.6 Group portrait of eight Mexican American males taken in for questioning in the 1942 Sleepy Lagoon murder investigation, Los Angeles, Calif. (Los Angeles Daily News, Public domain, via Wikimedia Commons)

How did the depiction of Chicanos by the English-language media influence the attempts to seek justice for the murder of José Gallardo Díaz at Sleep Lagoon? (Find articles in the Los Angeles Times to assist with this assignment.) (Gerson, 2021).

Bonus question: What is the connection between the term Zoot Suits and the Mexican American community? How did the police racialize this article of clothing to legitimize their treatment of the youths in the area?

2. Listen to this podcast segment between two Mexican American Latina journalists, Maria Garcia and Maria Hinojosa.

   www.npr.org/2021/06/21/1008735322/what-does-it-mean-to-be-latino-the-light-skinned-privilege-edition?

   What did you learn about Hinojosa's view on Latinx light-skin privilege and how she feels in her own skin? What about her colleague Garcia? Where do the two agree?

   Bonus question: What steps can a Latinx journalist take to understand if a privilege they have affects how they conduct their reporting?

References

Allman, Rupert. "*Bill Bratton on Fixing Broken Windows and American Policing,*" The 1A, June 10, 2021. Audio segment accessible via https://the1a.org/segments/bill-bratton-on-fixing-broken-windows-and-american-policing

Chavez-Dueñas, Nayeli, Adames, Hector and Organista, Kurt. "Skin-Color Prejudice and Within-Group Racial Discrimination: Historical and Current Impact on Latino/a Populations." *Hispanic Journal of Behavioral Sciences.* Vol. 36, p. 3–26 (2014). Article accessible via https://www.utep.edu/liberalarts/george-floyd/Skin-Color-Prejudice.pdf

Contreras, Russell. "*Activists: Police killings of Latinos lack attention,*" Associated Press, Aug. 17, 2020. Article accessible via https://apnews.com/article/shootings-race-and-ethnicity-ca-state-wire-mexico-tx-state-wire-059f64f61b8d348611af6c6a00a71e4e

"*CNN Photojournalist, Crew Arrested On-Air While Documenting Minneapolis Protests,*" U.S. Press Freedom Tracker, May 29, 2020. Blog post available via https://pressfreedomtracker.us/all-incidents/cnn-photojournalist-crew-arrested-air-while-documenting-minneapolis-protests/

@DyckmanDiary, "Dyckman Street apology," Instagram uploaded June 3, 2020a. Post accessible via https://www.instagram.com/p/CA-3ln7jTWC/

@DyckmanDiary, "They tried to divide us," Instagram uploaded June 3, 2020b. Post accessible via https://www.instagram.com/tv/CA_qxPbgwiH/

Foster-Frau, Silvia. "Latinos are Disproportionately Killed by Police But Often Left Out of the Debate About Brutality, Some Advocates Say," *Washington Post*, June 2, 2021. Article accessible via https://www.washingtonpost.com/national/police-killings-latinos/2021/05/31/657bb7be-b4d4-11eb-a980-a60af976ed44_story.html?

Gerson, Daniela. "Latinos and the LA Times," Twitter screenshot uploaded June 4, 2021. Tweet accessible via https://twitter.com/dhgerson/status/1400908222437879808/photo/1

Gonzalez-Barrera, Ana. *"Experiences With Discrimination More Common for Hispanics With Darker Skin,"* Pew Research Center, July 2, 2019. Article and tables accessible via https://www.pewresearch.org/fact-tank/2019/07/02/hispanics-with-darker-skin-are-more-likely-to-experience-discrimination-than-those-with-lighter-skin

HabichuelaConDulce, "*1992 Washington Heights riots,*" Reddit, uploaded Sept. 15, 2019. Video accessible via https://www.reddit.com/r/nyc/comments/d4ux19/1992_washington_heights_riots/

Haney Lopez, Ian. *"White By Law,"* New York University Press, 2006.

H.M. "*Washington Heights Riots,*" YouTube, uploaded Nov 26, 2015. Video accessible via https://youtu.be/6I6ukojlLhI

Howe, Jesse and Boyle, Andy. "*A Detailed Timeline of the Adam Toledo Shooting,*" Chicago Sun-Times, Apr 26, 2021. Article accessible via https://chicago.suntimes.com/news/2021/4/26/22386140/adam-toledo-shooting-timeline-video-police-cpd-little-village

Kelly, Mary Louise. *"How Newsroom Leaders Wrestled with Covering a Tumultuous Year"* NPR All Things Considered, June 9, 2021. Audio segment accessible via https://www.npr.org/2021/06/03/1003020225/we-hold-these-truths-how-newsroom-leaders-wrestled-with-covering-a-tumultuous-ye

León, Felice. "*Let's Talk About in the Heights and the Erasure of Dark-Skinned Afro-Latinx Folks,*" The Root, June 9, 2021. Article accessible via https://www.theroot.com/lets-talk-about-in-the-heights-and-the-erasure-of-dark-1847064126

Macaya, Melissa, Hayes, Mike, Alfonso III, Fernando, Diaz, Daniella, Yeung, Jessie, George, Steve, Kottasová, Ivana and Thompson, Nick, "*A Black Latino CNN Reporter was Arrested. A White CNN Reporter was Not,*" CNN, May 29, 2020. Video accessible via https://www.cnn.com/us/live-news/george-floyd-protest-updates-05-28-20/h_9023ffd063def0b1af22cb3ecdc72a06

Mather, Kate. "*No Charges for LAPD Officer who Fatally Shot 14-year-old in Boyle Heights,*" Los Angeles Times, Mar. 5, 2018. Article accessible via https://www.latimes.com/local/lanow/la-me-ln-jesse-romero-lapd-shooting-20180305-story.html

Matthews, Mark. "*No Charges in Shooting of 13-Year-Old Andy Lopez By Sonoma County Sheriff's Deputy,*" NBC Bay Area News, July 8, 2014. Article and video accessible via https://www.nbcbayarea.com/news/local/no-charges-expected-in-shooting-of-13-year-old-andy-lopez-by-sonoma-county-sheriffs-deputy/1973364/

"*Minnesota Police Arrest CNN Team on Live Television,*" CNN, May 29, 2020. Video accessible via https://www.cnn.com/videos/us/2020/05/29/minneapolis-protests-omar-jimenez-arrested-newday-vpx.cnn

Miranda, Lin-Manuel. "Apology," Twitter post uploaded June 14, 2021. Tweet accessible via https://twitter.com/Lin_Manuel/status/1404565413116141570/photo/1

PrestonLopezShow. "Washington Heights Riots News (1992)," *YouTube*, uploaded July 4, 2014. Video accessible via https://youtu.be/UyzH54pmIQU

Regalado, Pedro A. "The Washington Heights Uprising of 1992: Dominican Belonging and Urban Policing in New York City," *Journal of Urban History*, Vol 45(5), 2019. Doi: 10.1177/0096144218788304

Rodriguez, Roberto. "Is there Room for Red-Black-Brown Voices in National Conversation about Race,?" August 28, 2020. Blogpost accessible via http://drcintli.blogspot.com/2020/08/is-there-room-for-red-black-brown.html

Ryan, Shannon. "*Omar Jimenez, a Former Northwestern Basketball Walk-On and Journalism Student, has a 'Front-Row Seat' to History as a CNN Correspondent,*" Chicago Tribune, Nov. 15, 2020. Article accessible via https://www.chicagotribune.com/sports/college/ct-omar-jimenez-cnn-northwestern-journalism-20201115-uui4ykrcp5h5ro-vacrnh2ozh24-story.html

Segura, Olga. "Remembering the NYPD Shooting of Dominican Immigrant Kiko García and What if Means during Today's #BlackLivesMatterMovement," *Latino USA*, June 8, 2020. Article available via https://www.latinousa.org/2020/06/08/kikogarcia/

Simon, Scott. "*Crime is Down in American Cities, and 'Uneasy Peace' Explains Why,*" NPR Weekend Edition Saturdays," January 20, 2018. Audio segment accessible via https://www.npr.org/2018/01/20/579116484/crime-is-down-in-american-cities-and-uneasy-peace-explains-why

Sullivan, Ronald. "New York Officer Said to be Cleared in Fatal Shooting," *New York Times*, Sept. 10, 1992. Article available via https://www.nytimes.com/1992/09/10/nyregion/new-york-officer-said-to-be-cleared-in-fatal-shooting.html

U.S. Census Bureau, Quick Facts, 2021. https://www.census.gov/quickfacts/fact/table/US/PST045219

Walker, Malea. "*Ida B. Wells and the Activism of Investigative Journalism,*" Library of Congress Blog, February 12, 2020. Article accessible via https://blogs.loc.gov/headlinesandheroes/2020/02/ida-b-wells-and-the-activism-of-investigative-journalism

5

Reporting on Latinas

"She" Se Puede!

Laura Castañeda

Here's a quick quiz before we begin studying Latinas and journalism:

1. Name a Latina journalist from the late 1900s.
2. Name a Latina journalist working today.
3. What are some of the key issues currently facing Latinas?
4. What percentage of the U.S. population is Latina/o/x, and how many are women?
5. What are the largest Latino/a/x groups by country of origin in the United States?

Don't be surprised if you can't answer most of these questions. Latinos/as/x in general across the United States suffer from what scholars, journalists and think tanks have for years described as "erasure" or "invisibility," even though Latinos, at almost 19% of the total U.S. population, represent nearly one in five Americans today and are projected to account for nearly one in three Americans by 2060 (U.S. Census, 2015). "Locked into one-dimensional narratives about immigration or neglected in our primary black and white narrative of America — Latinos, like Native Americans and Asians, rarely see themselves represented at all (let alone accurately) in the American story" (Aspen Institute, 2019).

The erasure problem is even worse for Latinas (in this chapter, the terms "Latina/o" and "Latinx" will be used interchangeably). First, men of any race or gender are far more likely to be seen than women in the media. For example, around the world, women appeared as subjects of stories in a quarter of television, radio and print news, comprised just 19% of experts featured in news stories and accounted for 37% of reporters telling those stories (Global

DOI: 10.4324/9781003212331-5

Media Monitoring Project, 2015). Second, "this gender-imbalanced picture of society can reinforce and perpetuate harmful gender stereotypes" (Rattan et al., 2019).

What are these stereotypes? The Latino/a/x community in *national* news media are portrayed negatively as violent, criminal, undocumented, comic or overly sexualized, and in *local* news Latinos are overly represented in immigration and crime stories with negative-only racial stereotypes (Sui & Paul, 2017). Latina-specific images in *news* media are similar, but other common and damaging misconceptions stem from *entertainment* media, which has long portrayed Latinas as everything from sexy, sensual, exotic, spicy and fiery to subservient, family-oriented and self-sacrificing (Rodriguez, 1997).

Past research has shown that there are many reasons why news media coverage of Latinas does not necessarily improve as more Latinas get hired and rise through the ranks within newsrooms. Journalists of color often have limited influence on news content, they may find it difficult to challenge news norms and routines favoring the dominant white perspective, they are eager to be perceived as professionals and are therefore less likely to challenge well-established newsgathering practices, they are likely to remain neutral rather than advocate for their group, they are likely to choose official sources that are often white sources, they occupy lower-ranked positions in the newsroom, are assigned to less prestigious beats, and have less editorial power in determining the selection, content and placement of stories (Johnston & Flamiano, 2007; Pritchard & Stonbely, 2007; Nishikawa et al., 2009).

Recent news events, however, are changing this narrative. Following the Black Lives Matter uprisings, an increasing number of Black, Latino and other journalists of color began strongly advocating for better coverage of their communities – and an increased emphasis on hiring, retention and promotion in newsrooms. At the Los Angeles Times, a new Latino Caucus was formed and one of its outspoken early leaders was a woman – journalist Esmeralda Bermudez (see Figure 5.1). In an open letter, the caucus denounced the newspaper's past racist coverage of Latinos and pointed out that Latinos comprise 13% of the newsroom in a city that's more than half Latinx (Thiel & LaRue, 2021).

TABLE 5.1 Latina/o/x Employees/Leaders in English-Language U.S. Newsrooms

Radio	5.6%
Radio News Directors	3%
TV	12.2%
TV News Directors	10.3%
*Print + Online	7.24% (Latinas@3.34%)
Print + Online Leaders	17.61%

Sources: Radio & Television News Directors Association, 2021; *News Leaders Association, 2019

FIGURE 5.1 Members of the Los Angeles Times' Guild/Latino Caucus

The Times and its former owner, Tribune Publishing, settled a pay disparity lawsuit for $3 million that gave 240 current and former Black and Latino reports back pay. However, LA Times Latina food critic Patricia Escárcega said her salary was two-thirds that of another food critic, and eventually left the publication when editors refused to boost her pay, which she described in a series of tweets (Chan, 2021). Three Latina journalists whose contracts were not renewed at KUSA 9News in Denver, Colorado, spoke out about the various challenges they faced there (Folkenflik, 2021). The National Association of Hispanic Journalists (NAHJ) set a record, signing up 4,325 members as of July 2021 (Y. Bonaparte, personal communication, July 27, 2021). Journalist Andrea González Ramírez in 2020 launched the Latinas in Journalism Mentorship Program to connect "women and non-binary femmes" working in the news industry (see Figure 5.2).

FIGURE 5.2 The Latinas in Journalism Mentorship Program

Covering Latinas and Latina Issues

When it comes to covering Latinas and the issues that affect them, it's important to remember that although Latinas are large in number, they are not one homogeneous group. Women make up about half of the more than 60 million Latinos/Hispanics in the country (Pew, 2019). While the largest Latino/Hispanic origin group by far is Mexican at almost 37 million people, the next largest in descending order are Puerto Rican at 5.6 million, followed by Salvadoran, Cuban, Dominican, Guatemalan, Colombian, Honduran, Spanish, Ecuadorian, Peruvian, Nicaraguan, Venezuelan, Argentinian and Panamanian (Pew, 2019). Note: The term "Latino" refers to any person of Latin American descent living in the United States while "Hispanic" refers to people who share Spanish as a common language (Garcia-Navarro, 2015). So technically, Spaniards or those with Spanish heritage living in the United States are Hispanic, but not Latino. At the same time, Portuguese-speaking Brazilians or those of Brazilian heritage living in the United States are Latino, but not Hispanic.

It may seem obvious, but not all Latinas are alike. Spaniards, Brazilians, Cubans and Mexicans and their descendents living in the United States can be worlds apart socially, culturally, politically, racially, economically and linguistically. The immigrant experience is starkly different from that of U.S.-born Latinx women. Increasingly, the concept of Latinidad, or having a common Latino identity, has been under fire by a growing number of young, Black and indigenous critics who say it favors "white and Mestizo elites and the American political class" (Salazar, 2019). Here in the United States, even the terms "Latino," "Hispanic" and "Latinx" spark controversy. Preza (2021) writes that the term "Hispanic" came to define people of "Latin America during the 1970 census" and is resisted by those who reject its association with Spain and colonialism; "Latino" became popular in the 1990s and is a shortened way of saying Latinoamericano, or "Latin-American;" and Latinx is "a gender-neutral and non-binary version of Latina/o." LGBTQ communities abroad are using an even newer term – Latine (Del Real, 2020). Of course, most people use and prefer far more specific ethnic identifiers, such a Salvadoran or Salvadoran-American.

When researching Latinas for a story, ask yourself: Are you writing a national story about Latinas? If so, it is important to disaggregate the data by sub-group such as country of origin and/or geographic area, immigrant vs. non-immigrant, income levels, educational attainment, etc. The Maynard Institute for Journalism Education [MIJE], a nonprofit dedicated to making newsrooms reflect the diversity of our country, developed a program called "Fault Lines" aimed at addressing personal bias that also can be used to tell more accurate and inclusive stories and build diverse source lists (SPJ Toolkit). Maynard's "Fault Lines" are race, gender, sexual orientation, generation, geography and socio-economics. For instance, if you are assigned a story about the college completion rate for Latinas, you could use the Fault Lines to remind you to obtain data about the race, age and economics of Latinas earning college degrees. This could lead to a more interesting story with richer details, and how those factors affect who earns degrees and why. Similarly, a story about racism and white privilege and how both are viewed by younger Latinas vs. older generations of women is a way to add generational nuances to a story. Fault Lines also can be used to build a database of Latina news sources. In addition to adding experts on race, gender, sexual orientation, etc., you can add voices from the medical/health fields, public safety, the economy and education and the community, to name a few. The key is to make sure there are an equal number of female sources as male sources. You also should schedule informational interviews with as many of these sources as possible to learn about the community's biggest challenges, successes, movers and shakers.

One of the biggest stories about Latinas is the pay. Salary differentials between men and women are already stark, but it's even more extreme for Latinas, who earn 45% of what white men do, or 55 cents for every dollar earned by a white non-Hispanic man (Fundamedios, 2021). This affects Latinas in newsrooms small and large. A pay study by the Washington Post Newspaper Guild (2019) found that Latinas earned an average annual salary of $80,250, lower than Black women ($87,808), Asian women ($94,875) and white women ($99,931).

Most important, learn about the history of Latinos in your area and how your local news outlets have or haven't covered their stories. Many national publications also report on Latinos. The Los Angeles Times in 2021 launched a newsletter called "The Latinx Files" and a vertical on its website called "Latino Life" featuring stories about Latinos. Axios also has a Latino newsletter. Latino USA airs stories about Latinos on public radio stations across the country. Univision and Telemundo have national television shows and local affiliate stations that produce Spanish-language news shows. Online-only publications such as Palabra, Latino Rebels, NBCLatino, Remezcla and CNN en Español focus on Latinos. Many local publications such as L.A. TACO in Los Angeles are innovating coverage about food and culture and breaking local stories focusing on social justice. For Latino-focused content, there's *Latina* and *Latina Style* magazines, and Latinamoms.com and HipLatina.com online.

A Closer Look at: From Jovita Idár to the White House Press Corp

Perhaps the most recognized early journalist is Jovita Idár, who finally earned an obituary in The New York Times thanks to the newspaper's effort to make up for its past decades-long neglect of many accomplished women. Idár, a writer, editor and feminist at El Progreso in Laredo, Texas, gained fame for blocking the Texas Rangers in 1914 when they showed up to try and shut down the newspaper (Medina, 2020). She first began working for her father's newspaper, La Crónica.

Since then, Latinas have made their marks in newspapers, magazines, radio, television and now digital media. Washington Post Reporter Alma Guillermoprieto (1982) was one of two journalists who broke the story of the El Mozote massacre in El Salvador in which hundreds of people were killed by Salvadoran armed forces. Broadcast journalist and Afro-Latina Soledad O'Brien began her broadcast career in the early 1990s and now heads her own production company, Starfish Media Group. Maria Elena Salinas began her career in Spanish-language news at Univision affiliate KMEX-TV in Los Angeles, and today is a contributor to CBS News (Steinberg, 2019). Maria Hinojosa is the anchor and executive producer of Latino USA on National Public Radio, which she launched in 1992, and is president and CEO of Futuro Media Group, which produces the show (Davis, 2020).

In recent years, more Latinas are producing groundbreaking work than ever including Lulu Garcia-Navarro at National Public Radio, Esmeralda Bermudez, Brittny Mejia, Carolina Miranda, Mariel Garza and many others at the Los Angeles Times, Jennifer Medina at the New York Times, and several Latinas covering the Joe Biden White House including Cecila Vega (ABC News), Monica Alba (NBC News), Arlette Saenz (CNN),

In Conversation with Rebecca Aguilar

Award-winning TV Broadcaster, Fights for All Journalists, But Especially Latinas

Rebecca Aguilar comes by her passion for helping others honestly (see Figure 5.3). She grew up in Ohio watching her Mexican immigrant parents – her father was a union organizer for United Auto Workers and her mother was a migrant rights advocate – fighting daily to improve the lives of others.

During her 40-year career, Aguilar has been recognized with 50 journalism awards or nominations for her journalism work at TV stations in Ohio, Texas, Arizona and California. Her leadership and mentorship are equally extraordinary. In 2020, she became the first Latina and woman of color elected president of the Society of Professional Journalists. Previously, she served for four years as vice president of the National Association of Hispanic Journalists.

Aguilar's commitment to Latinas also is evident through two Facebook groups she launched: Wise Latinas Linked, with more than 9,000 members, and Latinas in Journalism, with almost 2,600 members (see Figure 5.4). Wise Latinas

FIGURE 5.3 Rebecca Aguilar

FIGURE 5.4 The Latinas in Journalism Facebook Group

was launched in honor of Supreme Court Justice Sonia Sotomayor. Latinas in Journalism shares job and internship postings, news stories, advice and encouragement for Latinas who work in news. This interview has been edited for space and clarity.

Did you have a mentor or support system as a young reporter?

Aguilar: When I started in June of 1980, there wasn't any [support system]. There wasn't even a big group of women of color in the business. It was run by a lot of white men. So I pieced together what I call my "posse" of strength.

Did you ever find it tough to stand up for yourself in the newsroom?

Aguilar: I saw people who wanted to build walls and stop me. You know there's this cliché about "pick and choose your battles." For people of color the battles choose you. They've always chosen me. Whether you like it or not, you just have to decide, will you be a leader or a follower? And if you're a follower, don't complain. Leaders are the ones that are opening doors for you and I think a lot of people would say that I have led in this world of journalism, not only for Latinas, not only for people of color but all journalists.

Would you say there's enough news media coverage of Latinas and Latina issues?

Aguilar: It's getting better. We can't depend on the Wall Street Journal, the Washington Post, the New York Times, ABC News, NBC News, NPR. We can't expect them to do all the stories. But what's beautiful today is that we have community papers and non-profits, websites, newsletters, podcasts and social media. People are not waiting for someone to cover a story. I'm going to do it and I'm going to get it out.

Latinx reporters sometimes complain about being assigned Latinx-only stories or being prohibited from covering Latinx issues due to charges of potential bias. Can you speak to these concerns?

Aguilar: If I hear that from anyone I'm like, "Get out of my face, okay." I've worked at seven TV stations. In certain areas, I wanted to cover the Latino community. I hear people say, "I don't want to be on the taco beat." First of all, that's derogatory, so don't be saying that. Second, you should embrace it. Because, let me tell you, when I negotiated my contract with the Fox station [in Dallas], which was a CBS station when they hired me, I got $15,000 more because I said

I'm bicultural-bilingual. I want to cover my community – who better to tell the stories of Latinos? I speak the language.

What can Latinx reporters do to make newsrooms more equitable?

Aguilar: We need to be a louder voice. I mean, I know so many Latinas who are frustrated right now but don't feel free to speak out because they don't want to jeopardize their jobs. If you're good at what you do they're not going to get rid of you.

What should journalism students do while in college to better inform themselves about Latinx issues?

Aguilar: All student journalists should read about our community. We're not just one group. We're a variety of groups – Cubans, Puerto Ricans, Nicaraguans, etc. We have layers to us. We have different histories. A Mexican is different from a Cuban. You must get to know the immigrant communities within the larger Latino community.

What do you say to journalists who want to cover the Latinx community, but are nervous to try because they are neither a part of nor an expert on the community?

Aguilar: Please stop using that excuse. I've never said, "oh my God I can't cover that – that's all white people." All right, you're probably saying, "I don't speak Spanish." Well, there's a lot of Latinos who don't speak Spanish and they're still in there, covering the community. Drive into Latino communities. Go to restaurants. Take a Spanish class. Get to know people. A good reporter can cover anything. I've covered everything from golf with Tiger Woods to basketball playoffs. Do I know anything about golf? Hell no. I never even played it. But I covered it.

Any final words of advice for college students?

Aguilar: Remember, you're going to meet other student journalists. And just because you may go to a private elite school and the person next to you goes to a community college, you're not any better. And for you people going to a community college, don't ever think you're less than a person going to Harvard or Northwestern. The bottom line: In a newsroom you're all the same. If you don't know how to gather news you're not going to last. Embrace your differences. Also, think about becoming a leader in a journalism organization. You will expand your network, and you can do it as a student and as a professional.

FIGURE 5.5 Sonia Gutierrez

A Closer Look at

Three Latina Broadcasters Ousted from Denver TV Station Help Make Change

In early 2020, Lori Lizarraga, Kristen Aguirre and Sonia Gutierrez were happily ensconced at KUSA 9News, the market leader in Denver, Colorado (see Figures 5.5, 5.6 and 5.7). By March 2021, all three Latina journalists were gone, and charges of discrimination were making national headlines.

Since their departure from the station, however, they have been lauded, won awards for their bravery and held up as cautionary tales of what Latinx and other journalists of color – women in particular – often face in mainstream newsrooms. Their experiences at the station also led to positive changes there.

Technically, they weren't fired; their contracts were allowed to lapse without renewal, a common method stations and reporters part ways in the news business. But the story at KUSA, which is owned by Tegna, Inc., and is an NBC affiliate, is far more complicated (Folkenflik, 2021, Lizarraga, 2021). Here's what happened:

Lizarraga was two weeks into her job at KUSA when she was told to say in a story that a source was "here illegally" or "illegally in this country" instead of "undocumented" (Lizarraga, 2021). She tried to explain to her producers

FIGURE 5.6 Kristen Aguirre

FIGURE 5.7 Lori Lizarraga

that this language was problematic but they wouldn't budge, and her story did not run. She said this pattern continued for two years until she left the station. During her tenure there, she said she also was told not to wear her hair in a bun with a middle part – a style she has worn as a Mexican and Ecuadorian woman all her life – because it was not a good look (Folkenflik, 2021). In addition, after George Floyd's murder and subsequent Black Live Matter protests, she said supervisors resented her after she demanded that African American colleagues be consulted on coverage (Folkenflik). She moved back to her hometown of Dallas, Texas, after leaving Denver.

Aguirre in 2019 suffered a traumatic brain injury after a stroke that paralyzed her on her left side (Lizarraga, 2021). When she returned to KUSA, she was given studio time for practice hosting and with help carrying equipment on assignments (Folkenflik, 2021). About six months later, both arrangements dropped off, then disappeared, she said. Aguirre has filed a formal amended complaint with the U.S. Equal Employment Opportunity Commission, which is in mediation (Folkenflik, 2021). She moved to WLOS-13 in Asheville, North Carolina.

Gutierrez was told that she had to disclose her own status whenever she reported on immigration (Lizarraga, 2021). She had been a DREAMer, and as such was protected from deportation through the Obama-era policy called Deferred Action for Childhood Arrivals, or DACA but became a legal permanent resident through marriage (Folkenflik, 2021). Gutierrez said she never got a clear response when she asked for an explanation or for examples of her work that showed bias (Lizarraga, 2021). She remained in Denver to work for Rocky Mountain PBS.

A group of elected local officials in Denver and the National Association of Hispanic Journalists met with KUSA and Tegna officials, calling for the dismissal of three top station executives, which did not take place (Folkenflik, 2021). Tegna has faced allegations of racial bias in the past. However, since the Black Lives Matter protests and the complaints from Lizarraga, Aguirre and Gutierrez came to light, the company announced a diversity, equity and inclusion initiative, new corporate training programs, promoted diversity in hiring and coverage at its 64 stations and hired its first chief diversity officer (Folkenflik, 2021).

Tegna and KUSA declined to comment on what happened to the Latina journalists, saying those are personnel matters. However, Tegna did enact new standards of immigration coverage, eliminating the use of "illegal" to describe undocumented immigrants (Folkenflik, 2021).

For their efforts to improve immigration coverage at KUSA, Lizarraga, Aguirre and Gutierrez won the NAHJ's 2021 Dale Award, which said in a tweet, "Because of their bravery, a bar was raised for standards of fair & accurate representation within an institution that holds a lot of weight in our industry & communities" (Tweet NAHJ). The ACLU Colorado also announced plans to honor the women at its 2021 Bill of Rights Event "for fighting discrimination in the newsroom" (ACLU tweet).

Assignments

1. Choose a local, state or national news source and examine coverage (including photos, videos and social media) of a major story that focuses on women or women's issues. Analyze whether Latinas included in the story as subjects or sources.
2. Examine social media activity, such as Twitter, around an issue involving women or women's issues. Analyze whether Latina voices are amplified as part of the original post(s), as responses to the original post(s), or separately by Latina commentators.
3. Research the demographics of your community to find out which Latinx communities are represented, how large they are, and what their most pressing issues might be. How many of these stories focus on women's issues? Develop a list of potential story ideas.
4. Develop a database of news sources that includes a range of Latina voices from your diverse Latinx community.
5. Research the Latinx-focused media outlets in your community, and conduct interviews with the editor or a reporter from that outlet to learn how many reporters and editors are women, and about how it engages with its readers/viewers/listeners, especially women.
6. Research, pitch and produce a story about Latinas in your community. Think about the Maynard Institute's Fault Lines approach and the possible intersection of race/ethnicity, age, socio-economics, sexual orientation and geography when developing a story about Latinas.
7. Choose a U.S. Latina journalist pre-1980 and produce a report about her.
8. Conduct role playing exercises where you as a journalist attempt to a) pitch a story about a Latino issue that an editor/producer is skeptical about, b) ask for a raise and get turned down and/or c) asks for a promotion and is gaslighted. Discuss possible next steps.
9. Create a professional networking group for Latinas at your school or local area.
10. Join an existing local or national professional group for Latinas/os in journalism, such as Latinas in Journalism, the National Association of Hispanic Journalists or CCNMA: Latino Journalists of California.

Discussion Questions

1. Why should journalist students learn more about the historic contributions of Latina journalists?
2. What are some of the challenges Latina journalists have faced in newsrooms, and what are some strategies for overcoming them?
3. Why have the numbers of Latina journalists in newsrooms remained low despite decades of efforts to diversify?
4. What can be done to increase the numbers of Latinas in newsrooms as well as those in top leadership positions?
5. What are some of the top issues facing Latinas locally, regionally, nationally and internationally? How can you, as students, develop these issues into stories?

Journalism Resources

Society of Professional Journalists, How to Cross your FaultLines: https://www.spj.org/dtb2.asp
Women's Media Center: https://womensmediacenter.com/
The Journalism & Women's Symposium: https://jaws.org/
Latinas in Journalism (on Facebook)
Wise Latinas Linked (on Facebook)
The National Association of Hispanic Journalists: https://nahj.org/
CCNMA: Latino Journalists of California: https://www.ccnma.org/
Latinas in Journalism Mentorship Program: https://www.latinajournalists.com/

The Journalist's Resource Guide: How the news media portray Latinos in stories and images: 5 studies to know: https://journalistsresource.org/race-and-gender/news-media-portray-latinos/

References

ACLU Colorado (2021). *Bill of Rights Event.* Retrieved Aug. 1, 2021 from https://aclu-co.org/bill-of-rights-event-2021/

Chan, J.C. (2021, April 1). LA Times Restaurant Critic Patricia Escárcega Exits After Pay Dispute. *The Wrap.* Retrieved July 30, 2021 from https://www.thewrap.com/la-times-restaurant-critic-patricia-escarcega-exits-after-pay-dispute/

Davis, A. (2020, Sept. 15). Maria Hinojosa: 'I was the First Latina in Every Newsroom I Ever Worked In.' *Oprah Daily.* Retrieved Aug. 1, 2020 from https://www.oprahdaily.com/entertainment/books/a34015265/maria-hinojosa-once-i-was-you-latina-memoir-interview/

Del Real, J.A. (2020, Dec. 18). 'Latinx' Hasn't Even Caught On Among Latinos. It Never Will. The Washington Post. Retrieved July 30, 2021 from https://www.

washingtonpost.com/outlook/latinx-latinos-unpopular-gender-term/2020/12/18/bf177c5c-3b41-11eb-9276-ae0ca72729be_story.html

Folkenflik, D. (2021, July 18). Latina Journalists' Ouster From Denver TV Powerhouse Spark Outrage. *NPR*. Retrieved July 30, 2021 from https://www.npr.org/2021/07/18/1002474866/latina-journalists-ousters-from-denver-tv-powerhouse-spark-outrage

Fundamedios. (2021). *Pay Gap Training Toolkit*. https://www.fundamedios.org/pay-gap-toolkit/

Garcia-Navarro, L. (2015, Aug. 27). Hispanic Or Latino? A Guide For The U.S. Presidential Campaign. *NPR*. Retrieved Aug. 1, 2021 from https://www.npr.org/sections/parallels/2015/08/27/434584260/hispanic-or-latino-a-guide-for-the-u-s-presidential-campaign

Global Media Monitoring Project. *Who Makes the News?* (2015, November). http://www.media-diversity.org/additional-files/Who_Makes_the_News_-_Global_Media_Monitoring_Project.pdf

Golden-Vasquez, A. (2019). *The Invisible Latino In America*. The Aspen Institute. https://www.aspeninstitute.org/blog-posts/the-invisible-latino-in-america/

Guillermoprieto, A. (1982, Jan. 27). Salvadoran Peasants Describe Mass Killing, *The Washington Post*. Retrieved July 30, 2021 from https://www.washingtonpost.com/archive/politics/1982/01/27/salvadoran-peasants-describe-mass-killing/bc5bb029-b5e6-4282-bd24-35739ea5b38c/

Johnston, A. & Flamiano, D. (2007). Diversity in mainstream newspapers from the standpoint of journalists of color. *The Howard Journal of Communications*, *18*, 111–131.

Krogstad, J.M. & Noe-Bustamante, L. (2020, Sept. 10). *Pew Research Center*. Key Facts About U.S. Latinos for National Hispanic Heritage Month. *Pew Research Center*. https://www.pewresearch.org/fact-tank/2020/09/10/key-facts-about-u-s-latinosfor-national-hispanic-heritage-month/

Lehrman, S. (2021). SPJ Toolkit Society of Professional Journalists. Diversity Toolbox. *How to Cross your 'Faultlines.'* Retrieved Aug. 1, 2021 from https://www.spj.org/dtb2.asp

Lizarraga, L. (2021, March 28). *LatinXed: 9News Got Rid of Three Latina Reporters This Past Year, Including Me*. Westword. Retrieved Aug. 1, 2021 from https://www.westword.com/news/9news-latina-reporter-kusa-media-discrimination-diversity-11925702

Medina, J. (2020, Aug. 7). *Overlooked No More: Jovita Idár, Who Promoted Rights of Mexican Americans and Women*. The New York Times. Retrieved July 30, 2021 from https://www.nytimes.com/2020/08/07/obituaries/jovita-idar-overlooked.html.

News Leaders Association 2019 Diversity Survey (2019). https://www.newsleaders.org/2019-diversity-survey-results

Nishikawa, K.A., Towner, T.L., Clawson, R.A., & Waltenburg, E.N. (2009). Interviewing the Interviewers: Journalistic Norms and Racial Diversity in the Newsroom. *The Howard Journal of Communications*, *20*, 242–259.

Preza, C. (2021, Dec. 2). Latino, Hispanic, and Latinx: What the Terms Mean and How to Use Them. *Reader's Digest*. Retrieved Feb. 18, 2022 from https://www.rd.com/article/latino-hispanic-and-latinx/

Pritchard, D. & Stonbely, S. (2007). Racial Profiling in the Newsroom. *Journalism & Mass Communication Quarterly*, *84*, 231–248.

Radio & Television News Directors Association/Newhouse School at Syracuse University Newsroom Survey 2021. (2021). https://www.rtdna.org/article/research_local_news_diversity_reaches_records_but_representation_gap_shrinks_slowly

Rattan, A., Chilazi, S., Georgeac, O., & Bohnet, I. (2019, June 6). *Tackling the Underrepresentation of Women. Harvard Business Review.* Retrieved July 30, 2021 from https://hbr.org/2019/06/tackling-the-underrepresentation-of-women-in-media

Rodriguez, C. (1997). *Latin Looks: Images of Latinas and Latinos in the U.S. Media.* Routledge.

Salazar, M. (2019, Sept. 16). *The Problem with Latinidad.* The Nation. Retrieved July 30, 2021 from https://www.thenation.com/article/archive/hispanic-heritage-month-latinidad/

Steinberg, B. (2019, July 22). *CBS News Names Maria Elena Salinas Contributor.* Variety. Retrieved Aug. 1, 2021 from https://variety.com/2019/tv/news/cbs-news-maria-elena-salinas-1203275594/

Sui, M. & Paul, N. (2017). Latino Portrayals in Local News Media: Underrepresentation, Negative Stereotypes, and Institutional Predictors of Coverage. *Journal of Intercultural Communication Research*, *46*(3), 273–294.

The Washington Post Newspaper Guild (2019). *A Study of Pay at The Washington Post.* Retrieved Aug. 1, 2021 from https://postguild.org/2019-pay-study/

Thiel, D. & LaRue, F. (2021, Jan. 16). Vol. 2. Dissed. *Palabra.* Retrieved July 30, 2021 from https://www.palabranahj.org/archive/dissed

U.S. Census Bureau. (2015). *Projections of the Size and Composition of the U.S. Population: 2014–2060.* https://www.census.gov/content/dam/Census/library/publications/2015/demo/p25-1143.pdf

6

Intersectional Latinx/a/o

Journalism Coverage and the LGBTQ Community

Nathian Shae Rodriguez

The Pulse nightclub shooting is the deadliest mass shooting incident in the history of violence against LGBTQ people in the United States (Goldman, 2016). On June 12, 2016, Omar Mateen entered Pulse, a gay nightclub in Orlando Florida, and shot and killed 49 people and wounded 53 others. Pulse was hosting "Latin Night" on the night of the mass shooting and a majority of the victims, over 90%, were Latinx, particularly of Puerto Rican, Cuban, Dominican, Columbian and Mexican ancestry (Alvarez & Madigan, 2016; Thrasher 2016). The national mainstream news coverage that followed Americanized the event and rendered the victims and their loved ones culturally invisible by failing to include mention of their intersectional identities (Flores, 2016). The coverage tended to focus more on the LGBTQ community at large as a tool to talk about United States/Middle Eastern relations and other political power dynamics given that the shooter was a U.S.-born Muslim American and a son of Afghan immigrants (Kalish Blair, 2016; Schwartz et al., 2016).

The victims of the mass shooting identified intersectionally as both Latinx and LGBTQ, among other identities. Therefore, the coverage of the event should have also been intersectional. Intersectionality works to illuminate multiple systemic oppressions and discriminations an individual experiences as their marginalized identities overlap and intersect (Collins, 2015; Crenshaw, 1990). Oppression "cannot be reduced to one fundamental type, oppressions work together in producing injustice" (Collins, 2000, p. 18); it is crafted and recrafted by both micro (intersectional) and macro (interlocking) processes. Kimberlé Crenshaw's articles "Demarginalizing the Intersection of Race and Sex" (1989) and "Mapping the Margins: Intersectionality, Identity Politics, and Violence Against Women of Color" (1990) are credited as the introduction of

DOI: 10.4324/9781003212331-6

intersectionality into the academic lexicon (Collins, 2015). Crenshaw conceptualized the term using race/ethnicity and gender to evidence the two identity categories were not mutually exclusive, but rather intersect to create multiple discriminations in Black women, specifically in the workforce and with domestic abuse. Crenshaw highlighted Black women often have less access to economic, social, and political gains and are disproportionately subjugated to violence, making their lived experiences subordinated to other identity groups. These issues were the direct result of power and oppressive institutions. Crenshaw argued the intersectional experiences of Black women evidence that multiple legal, political, and social structures are weighted against individuals with multiple marginalized identities.

In addition to Crenshaw, other scholars have noted that intersectionality also operates on the notion of difference, particularly how some identity categories are excluded, whereas others are inherently included because of their privilege in society (Nash, 2008). Identity categories are socially constructed to emphasize differences between and among identity groups, differences that are then perpetuated and reinforced by social systems of power (Gillborn, 2015). Some identity categories are seen as more desired than others, forming a hierarchy, whereas some identities are excluded at the expense of others (Nash, 2008). Latinx/a/o and LGBTQ identities are examples of such excluded identities. Intersectionality is an analytical tool that helps to "investigate how intersecting powers relations influence social relations across diverse societies as well as individual experiences in everyday life" to illuminate how categories of race, ethnicity, gender, sexuality, class and ability, among others, are interconnected and mutually shape one another (Collins & Bilge, 2020, p. 2). Thus, intersectionality can be employed as an analytic tool by journalists and journalism instructors to address issues of inequity and social issues when reporting on the Latinx community.

The term Latinx is a gender-neutral ethnic identity marker that transcends beyond traditional binary identifiers of masculine and feminine. Latinx includes those of "Latin American descent whose gender identities fluctuate along different points of the spectrum, from agender or nonbinary to gender non-conforming, genderqueer, and genderfluid" (Reichard, 2015, p. 1). The term first emerged online in the early 2000s within LGBTQ of color communities. The use of the identity marker rose to popularity around the mid-2010s and was used in physical spaces, particularly U.S. universities and colleges. By 2015, Latinx was incorporated into the names of student organizations and academic programming in Pomona College, Columbia University, and the University of Maryland, among others. The term was also popularized in news media during the 2016 U.S. Presidential Election. It became a term of contention amongst ethnic minorities who have traditionally identified as Hispanic, Chicana/o, and Latina/o. Latinx has now come to represent identities beyond LGBTQ and is used by many as inclusive term that encompasses identities of ability and disability, migration, age, ethnicities, American latinidad and issues of citizenship status.

This chapter focuses on "what intersectionality does rather than what intersectionality is" (Cho et al., 2013, p. 795). The chapter offers a brief history and context on Latinx news coverage to situate the case study on the Pulse Nightclub Massacre. The case exemplifies how intersecting power relations in media socially exclude, underrepresent, and misrepresent traditionally marginalized populations at the intersection of sexuality and race. The chapter concludes with an interview with a Latinx journalist who covered the Pulse Nightclub Massacre and ways in which journalists and journalism instructors can use intersectionality in their reporting to better represent the Latinx community.

Media's Impact on Latinx/a/o Identities

Research has shown LGBTQ identities and issues in the media to be underrepresented, heteronormative, and reliant on stereotypes (Bond, 2014; Darde & Morigi, 2012). Journalism, in particular, can contribute to the social exclusion of LGBTQ individuals though homophobia within the news media, journalists' lack of awareness and/or understanding of the social concerns of LGBTQ individuals, public pressure, and the lack of communication between journalists and the LGBTQ community (Şahin, 2021).

In a similar vein, Latinx/a/o identities, regardless of sexuality, have predominantly been portrayed negatively and framed using stereotypes (Bleich et al., 2021. These stereotypes include criminals, *illegal* immigrants, economic threats, burdens, hyper-reproductive, immoral, uneducated, domestic workers, and less articulate and less likely to have a high status occupation compared to their white counterparts (Barreto et al., 2012; Gutiérrez, 2008; Monk-Turner et al., 2010; Padín, 2005). Even when voting citizens of the United States, Latinx/a/o identities are still depicted in the news media as foreign to the nation (Soto-Vásquez, 2020). Distorted depictions and stereotypes can negatively influence self-esteem and ethnic-racial identity in Latinx/a/o emerging adults (Rivadeneyra et al., 2007; Shafer & Rivadeneyra, 2020).

There are, however, instances where the news media does have more positive representations. For example, Bleich et al. (2021) examined 17 U.S. newspapers between 1996 and 2016 to better understand Latinx/a/o depictions. The researchers found the papers presented themes of criminality and illegal immigration with more negative affect, however with more neutral tone, and themes of achievement and culture with more positive affect and tone. Overall, Latinx/a/o coverage in newspapers, in particular, has been relatively neutral rather than predominately negative. Important to note is that negative news depictions carry greater weight than positive depictions (Padín, 2005).

Media not only recount events and disseminate information daily but also affect how others recollect and interpret the news (see Kligler-Vilenchik et al., 2014). In other words, media not only tell the stories of today, but also archive and shape the public memories of yesterday. According to Houdek and Phillips (2017), public memory is a concept that denotes the "circulation of recollections among members of a given community" (par 1). The recollections of the given community members are not perfect historical accounts, but rather are a combination of the aspects individuals remember, forget, and ways in which the events or subjects are framed. Indeed, there is a difference between public memory and history. The difference between the two is that "memory is subjective and immediate, history is objective and mediate" (Collingwood, 2005, p. 366). At its most basic, public memory is personal and informal, whereas history is formal and official (Houdek & Phillips, 2017).

In the case of the Pulse Nightclub Mass shooting, the role of news media was to report on the violent event and tell the stories of the victims and survivors. Negative valence in the coverage and misrepresentation of the bodies affected can have adverse consequences for the Latinx community and its members. Negative media coverage seemingly supports acts of targeted violence and may also help amplify cultural overtones of homophobia and/or xenophobia. Although media can have negative effects on traditionally marginalized identities, they can also be agents of positive cultural change through social visibility and the challenging of inequalities (Bond, 2014; Darde & Morigi, 2012). Positive valence and nuanced representation of the bodies affected can have more constructive consequences. Journalism, in particular, through its communicative processes of deliberation and visualizations, can afford traditionally marginalized identities, such as the Latinx community, a form of "mediatized recognition and possible political advance" (Cottle, 2007, p. 36).

A Closer Look: Pulse and the Media

This chapter uses the Pulse Nightclub mass shooting as a case study to help orient readers on how journalistic coverage of a national tragedy, centering on intersectional Latinx identities, should be covered in the media. I will use intersectionality as an analytic tool to examine the Pulse mass shooting and the role of journalism. Particularly, I will use the intersectional domains of power – structural, cultural, disciplinary, and interpersonal – as a heuristic to scaffold the analysis and better exemplify the complexity of the concept of intersectionality. The Pulse nightclub shooting, the deadliest mass shooting in U.S. history against the LGBTQ community (Goldman, 2016), occurred on June 12, 2016, when Omar Mateen shot and killed 49 people and wounded 53 others at Pulse, a gay nightclub in Orlando Florida. The shooting took place on "Latin Night," a weekly event where musical genres of reggaeton, bachata, merengue, salsa, and cumbia were played by Latinx DJs and performers. The event attracted a predominately Latinx crowd, both gay and straight. Consequently, most of the victims, over 90%, were Latinx, particularly of Puerto Rican, Cuban, Dominican, Columbian, and Mexican ethnicity (Thrasher 2016). Of the 49 killed, 23 of them were of Puerto Rican ethnicity (Alvarez & Madigan, 2016).

In the wake of the mass shooting, the U.S. national mainstream media excluded intersectional identities of the Pulse mass shooting victims and tended to present the event, and the LGBTQ community, as a monolithic group to highlight national and international power dynamics (Flores, 2016, Kalish Blair, 2016; Schwartz et al., 2016). The media in and of itself is an example of the structural domain of power, "the fundamental structures of social institutions" (Collins & Bilge, 2020, p. 7). In the United States, the vast majority of media outlets are English-language only and are controlled by only six companies – often referred to as media concentration, media consolidation and/or media convergence. This means media is dominated by only a small number of elite groups, reflecting their interests, and catering editorial content towards the preference of owners (Bailard, 2016). Media organizations are also viewed as seemingly complicit with powerful interests and are often used extensively by politicians and other "power-brokers" to sway public opinion, policy, and political participation (Cottle, 2007). These mediated structures foster racial, classist, gendered, and heteronormative advantages and disadvantages that trickle down to not only to mediated content, but identities in the newsroom. In regard to Latinx news media, there are only a little more than 100 outlets, most of which are fairly small operations, are privately funded, offer primarily Spanish content, and are concentrated in a few states (Retis & Chacón, 2021).

In the case of the Pulse mass shooting, this meant that national mainstream news coverage presented an "Americanized" monolithic framing of the victims (Flores, 2016); a presentation that differed from the visuals found at the local memorial sites in Orlando, FL (see Figures 6.1 and 6.2). Such framing is a sanitized news story for public consumption that erases the intersectional complexity of the violent event. The media disseminated condolences "to bodies and loved ones extracted from any mention of queerness, brownness, or nationality" (Cram, 2016, p. 147). Mainstream news narratives of Pulse rendered the Latinx bodies who were Brown and Black culturally invisible (Flores, 2016). The Pulse mass shooting was specifically "a continuation of violence that has been enacted upon LGBTQ communities of color," adding to decades of federal- and state-sanctioned violence (Flores, 2016, para. 8).

Non-mainstream Latinx/a/o journalism and media sites and collectives such as *Remezcla, Pero Like on Buzzfeed, Latino Rebels, HuffPost's Latino Voices, Al Día,* and *Latina.com* often depicted the Pulse mass shooting and the victims and families using more racial and ethnic lenses. These digital media outlets tend to have more Latinx writers and creatives, with almost all having LGBTQ identities on staff. Most of the content used the label "LGBTQ Latinx" in their headlines and copy, as well as provided cultural nuance regarding the nightclub, the patrons,

FIGURE 6.1 Photo of Pulse nightclub by Nathian Rodriguez

FIGURE 6.2 A memorial to honor the victims of the shooting. Photo by Nathian Rodriguez

and the city of Orlando, Florida. These types of digital media sites and collectives have sometimes been dubbed as "alternative media"; however, as of 2020, Latinx/a/o individuals account for over half of the U.S. population growth, reaching 62.1 million (Gamboa & Acevedo, 2021; Krogstad & Noe-Bustamante, 2021). As Remezcla writes on its About Us page, "to us, what we were covering was our new mainstream." Previous research highlights digital-native Latinx news media as fostering heightened interconnectivity and intermediality practices that transcend beyond geographical boundaries, language barriers, and audience fragmentation (Retis & Chacón, 2021).

The shooter, Omar Mateen, was also a central foci of U.S. mainstream news coverage. National news outlets characterized Pulse as a "typical nightclub, while regenerating national fear of racialized terrorism" based on minimal knowledge of Mateen's motivations (Cram, 2016, p. 147). Mateen, a U.S.-born Muslim American and son of Afghan immigrants, pledged allegiance to ISIS and claimed the mass shooting as vengeance of the Islamic State (Schwartz et al., 2016; Thrasher, 2016). News coverage labeled Mateen a "homegrown terrorist" and treated the mass shooting as both an act of terror and a hate crime (Schwartz et al. 2016). Such declarations, claims Kalish Blair (2016), overlooked the complexity involving race, ethnicity, sexuality, ideology, and nationality.

Kalish Blair (2016) states that the Pulse massacre was a "dramatic act of violence begat by long-standing structural violence, fused at the nexus of militarism, U.S. imperialism, and neoliberal multiculturalism" (p. 111). Systemic power relations between the United States and continuous warfare in the Middle East, neoliberal policies that influence Puerto Rico and migration, "neoliberal multiculturalism" in gay spaces, and LGBTQ consumption patterns are instrumental in the explanation of the disproportionate murder of Latinx people, particularly Puerto Rican LGBTQ people (p. 112). He argues these connections illuminate the lack of diversity and inclusion mechanisms and their direct linkage to biopolitics of life and death. Cram (2016), in their critique on the aftermath of the Pulse mass shooting, highlighted clickbait headlines such as "Orlando shooting: 49 killed, shooter pledged ISIS allegiance," "49 killed in shooting at Florida nightclub in possible act of Islamic terror," and "Islamic State linked to worst mass shooting in U.S. history" from *CNN, Fox News*, and *USA Today*. National news outlets also broadcasted messages from U.S. leaders that framed Mateen as radical, jihadist, and promised to protect the LGBTQ community from ISIS. "Whitewashed queer bodies mattered when weaponized as regenerative instruments of national violence" (Cram, 2016, p. 147).

Both Kalish Blair and Cram's critique highlight the necessity for cultural context in journalism. The cultural domain of power "emphasizes the increasing significance of ideas and culture in the organization of power relations" (Collins & Bilge, 2020, p. 9). The Pulse nightclub mass shooting exemplifies the media's power of representation, misrepresentation, and erasure, which normalizes cultural attitudes about social inequalities, particularly in intersectionally marginalized communities. Furthermore, it highlights Crenshaw's (1990) conceptualization of political intersectionality where social justice activism for a marginalized group can often overlook other facets of identity in the group members. In this case, mainstream news coverage focused on the LGBTQ aspect of the Pulse victims, but neglected their ethnicity and other cultural contexts.

Why does this matter? What is the role of media in these power relations and intersectional identities? For one, news media have both watchdog and civic-oriented functionalities that increase accountability (Hellmueller et al., 2016). The disciplinary domain of power emphasizes "how rules and regulations are fairly or unfairly applied to people based on race, sexuality, class, gender, age, ability, and nation, and similar categories" (Collins & Bilge, 2020, p. 12). News media reflect disciplinary power that produce and reproduce significantly different cultural experiences for privileged and marginalized identities. As mentioned previously, over 90% of the Pulse mass shooting victims were Latinx (Thrasher, 2016). Non-intersectional journalism practices reinforce normative disciplined practices of marginalization. Puar (2007) has argued there exists patterns of inclusion and exclusion by which nonwhite migrants and LGBTQ individuals have been promised a sense of Americanized belonging through consumption, both mediated and not, and U.S. capital imperialism. Such patterns reify "binary normative frameworks" and normalize violence (Kalish Blair, 2016, p. 111). Furthermore, news media not only influence the present but also the past. The interpretation of public memory and how it is manifested is open to interpretations that lead to diverse, and often conflicting, recollections about the past that exist in the present (Browne, 1995; Zelizer, 1995).

The interpersonal domain of power "refers to how individuals experience the convergence of structural, cultural, and disciplinary power" (Collins & Bilge, 2020, p. 15). In other words, it evidences how a person experiences interlocking and intersecting systems of oppression at not only the individual level, but also the systemic and cultural level. Intersectionality highlights how an individual's simultaneous membership to a multitude of identity groups can affect how they experience compounded oppressions. Journalism can help make visible those intersectional experiences through mass media. Thus, journalism has the power and the responsibility to properly represent those intersectional identities to the viewing audience. To exemplify how localized media operated within the interpersonal domain in the aftermath of the Pulse mass shooting, this chapter includes an interview with an openly gay journalist who covered the event. In the next section, Jorge Estevez recounts his experiences and provides guidance on covering the Latinx community.

Estevez' intersectional identity provided him with an insider perspective to report from and identify with informational needs of the various community members impacted. He was able to speak from a place of understanding and contextualize the news coverage and those involved. Estevez' position in the overlapping communities made him privy to information on the victims' lives, locations and times of makeshift vigils, and the impact of the tragic event on the victims' families and communities. He was also asked to cohost a memorial because and read the names of the victims because he could speak Spanish and roll his r's. Estevez was both speaking to them and representing them, his identity provided him certain amount of credibility through his connection with the communities. Estevez' intersectional identities, including that of being a journalist, exemplify the interpersonal domain of power and how the stories of the Latinx LGBTQ victims and families were covered in the aftermath of the shooting.

A Conversation with Jorge Estevez, Anchor at WSB-TV Channel 2 Action News

Jorge Estevez (pictured in Figure 6.3) is an anchor at *WSB-TV Channel 2 Action News* in Atlanta, Georgia. He is the first openly gay anchor and second Latinx on-air personality for the station. Estevez was born in West New York, New Jersey to Cuban immigrant parents. He attended Rutgers University and graduated with a dual degree in journalism and communication. Estevez started his journalism career at *News 12 The Bronx* in New York and has worked at WFTV in Orlando, Florida and at WFOR-TV in Miami, Florida. Estevez was working in Orlando when the Pulse nightclub mass shooting occurred in 2016. The following is a portion of our interview that centers on his experience covering

FIGURE 6.3 Photo of television journalist Jorge Estevez

the Pulse mass shooting, as well as the importance of representation in news coverage.

Estevez: The night of the shooting, when I heard about it, I was at a weekend getaway in Cocoa Beach, an hour away from Orlando, and I just heard the news when I woke up. So I got up and I went to work. I was there all day gathering information and doing breaking reports. Then the victims' names started coming down, and I was like, I knew them. I knew people who knew the victims. And then people started calling me and messaging. As you can imagine, as an anchor in Orlando, a smaller city, a lot of people knew me. Everyone knew each other. So I got text messages, phone calls, like, "hey, that's, you know who, or that's my friend or, you know, I was there for a birthday party or something. So all these stories because of my connection to the community. And the Hispanic community and the gay community, the LGBTQ+ community, everything just kind of morphed. So it just became covering the story that became intensely personal.

In regards to it being personal to you, how were you able to of balance that, you know, personal connection? Did it help? Did it hinder? Was it something that was always there during your coverage?

Estevez: It was awfully sad, from a from a personal note, to know that people would attack both sides of my communities, right? Both the Latin community and you know, the Hispanic community and the LGBTQ+ community. So it's devastatingly personal for me. Pulse happened on Sunday morning at 2:02 a.m. And then a week later, the following Sunday was a vigil at Lake Eola, which is the center of town. I was then contacted and asked, "can you read the names?" They got the mayor to speak, the police chief to speak, and then I got roped in, too. And before I knew it, it was 50,000 people. And the organizer called me to read the names in Spanish. I was on stage with thousands of people staring at me in the amphitheater and tens of thousands behind the amphitheater all around the lake. And that's when it dawned on me how huge this was, the impact! It was a moment of healing, sadness, coming together, family appreciation, anger, resentment, frustrated, it was a moment of so much! So that's when it really hit me. I mean, I don't know how I didn't cry. My eyes were watering the entire time.

Yes, and, you know, when you speak about representation, it's also the people who were there at the nightclub, the people who knew people, the family members looking at you and your co-host there. But also seeing some of themselves in you, delivering the memorial in Spanish and English, being able to speak to them and represent them. How was that for you?

Estevez: Looking back on that, there was a certain level of credibility that I had in doing that. Not that you needed that to get your point, not that you needed to be a member of either community, you just needed to be human to feel. But for me, I had an extra connection and that led to credibility. When I said I'm sad, they understood. When I said I'm sad for our communities, they understood what that meant. And there was a level of sincerity there that everyone had. Again, I want to stress that you didn't have to be LGBTQ+ or Hispanic to be sad and angry at the same time. But it does add another layer of credibility. And I did it. And then, subsequently, you know, parents would reach out to me on Facebook or Instagram or other social media or come up to me in the streets or email me and say: "thank you, thank you for representing. My son came out to me today. Thank you for being part of the community, I now feel connected." Or "I use you as an example for my son. Look, you could do that one day." You know, because he's Hispanic or the gay part, you know, or LGBTQ-identifying kid who's not Hispanic. And the emails I got, and the messages and the DMs! I was like, wow, like this is, this is deep that I can even help you know, a smidge. That I can even help these parents a smidge, to teach their kids a lesson or encourage them somehow was just overwhelming for me.

I bet. I remember watching the memorials and they were bilingual. It was in Spanish and in English, which I think is important for the people who usually watch one language or the other in terms of news.

Estevez: It was very important to be able to do that, to be able to say the names in Spanish, to say the sentences in English and Spanish. And to say it in their language, it was just so special to them.

So, in terms of being part of the LGBTQ community, do you feel that you were able to deliver a more complex, or more holistic picture, of what happened? Using terms and lingo that people who are not part of the community may not know?

Estevez: Sure. I went to the club. I broke down what the club looked like, the difficulty, the ins and outs, the exit. Sure, there were some mechanical things that I was aware of because I had been in there. It was a very straight-friendly club. And obviously being gay, you know. When we would do stories on parents not wanting to claim the bodies of their children because they didn't want to accept that they were gay, like, I get it. Because to this day my father doesn't speak to me after I came out 14 years ago. So when you say that, people are like, "how's that possible? That can't be true?" And I'm like, yeah, it could be true. And it is true. Because I live it every single day, with my father, not wanting to claim me as his son, or recognize me as his offspring, or acknowledge my existence after I came out and told him I was gay. So I totally get it. And that's a perspective that a lot of cultures have, let's not say it's only the Hispanic culture, but also a lot of cultures don't. So I can understand that people don't get, but I can remind them very efficiently, that it's true.

What a way to be able to put things in perspective and humanize the story to people who are watching. You mentioned being out and the relationship you have with your father. Now you're in Atlanta and you're the first openly gay on-air anchor and only the second Latinx person at the station. What does that feel like for you? Is there a responsibility representing both of those different demographics?

Estevez: So Hispanic population here is like 10, 11% in the metro. This is a legacy station, the number one station, WSBTV, in the market. We've been around for 70 something years and the fact that I'm the second Hispanic to be on air here and then to be the first openly gay presenter/anchor behind the anchor desk at the station is insane to me. Like when you wrap your head around 2020, you're like, Oh, wow. I had no idea. You think Atlanta, big metropolitan area, we're market number seven now, huge LGBTQ+ community, and embracing. And you're like, oh, I guess they just haven't gotten around to it or maybe they weren't looking for someone? To be first of anything is great period. It comes with responsibilities, which I accept and embrace, and I'm looking forward to accomplishing it. But hopefully, at one point, it won't matter who's gay or who's not. Who's Hispanic or who's not. It'll matter who cares about the community, who's good at his or her job. Who's effective, who's positive, who's a pleasure to be around? Who can communicate a message, who can share a story? Those are the things that I'd like to think will be what the criteria will always be. And if they happen to be gay, Hispanic, Black, white, Asian, female, male, six feet to five foot eight. Great, that's fine, too!

I think that's awesome. And something that we as a society should strive for. We haven't achieved it yet, but maybe slowly going that that same direction.

Estevez: Yeah, people have come up to me and said, "Thank you for being here. Thank you for representing us. Thank you for being a member of the community." And then people who don't identify as LGBTQ+ have sent me emails saying: "Hey, you're a breath of fresh air." People who don't identify as Hispanic or LGBTQ+ have also welcomed me and it's been great.

How Can Journalists Do Better?

News media can contribute to the social exclusion and othering of LGBTQ individuals through underrepresentation and misrepresentation; however, media can also contribute to social inclusion by challenging stereotypes and giving voice and visibility to traditionally marginalized populations (Şahin, 2021). As Estevez stated, journalists need to be informed and recognize their own subjectivity on an issue. There are also a few resources, many of them free, that journalists can use to help establish best practices and guidelines for reporting on the Latinx community.

The Gay & Lesbian Alliance Against Defamation (GLAAD) is an organization founded in 1985 dedicated to shaping the media narrative around LGBTQ identities to promote cultural change and LGBTQ acceptance. The organization produces annual reports that analyze the state of media in regards to LGBTQ inclusion, such as the *Where We Are on TV* report, the *Studio Responsibility Index*, and the GLAAD *Media Reference Guide*. The guide is free and offers tools journalists can use to tell LGBTQ individual's stories fairly and accurately such as a glossary of terms/language and foci on covering the transgender community, HIV/AIDs, conversion therapy, marriage, parenting, religion, and sports, among others. There is also a directory of community resources and media contacts included in the guide.

The Association of LGBTQ Journalists (*NLGJA*), founded in 1989, is an organization of journalists, media professionals, educators, and students working from within the news industry to foster fair and accurate coverage of LGBTQ issues. The organization offers a variety of resources such as an *LGBTQ Stylebook*, a mentorship program, a *rapid response task force*, and a *journalists toolbox* to name a few. The NLGJA *Journalists Toolbox* provides examples and best practices to cover the LGBTQ community in fair, balanced, and accurate ways. Practicing journalists, as well as students, can be members of the organization.

This chapter and its case study on the Pulse mass shooting argued that journalism should include intersectionality of identities and experiences that reflect power relations across structural, cultural, disciplinary, and interpersonal

TABLE 6.1 Trade Tools & Tips: Jorge Estevez' Tips for Covering Latinx/a/o communities.

Gather facts, and gather more facts.
Talk to one side, talk to the other side, then talk to both sides again.
Make sure you recognize where people are coming from; everyone has their own stories. But sometimes their stories are marred with their own opinions and their own experiences and you have to be careful and mindful of that.
When covering a Latinx issue, know that there are deep-seated emotional responses to certain topics regarding the Latinx community, from both sides. You have to filter that out and get to the facts.
When talking about LGBTQ identities, you have decades of history that people are coming from and speaking from. Some good and some evil. You have to recognize that.
When you're dealing with hot topic issues, such as politics, religion, education, among others, you have to dig through the surface and then dig some more and more to find people's interpretation of the truth – which is not the same as the actual truth. The challenge is digging through the layers of people's own biases to get to what they really want to tell you.

Note: From personal communication with Jorge Estevez, August 6, 2021.

domains of power. The media is taxed with the responsibility to reflect this intersectionality through their social interaction with the identities they report on, as well as through the public images they broadcast to audiences. "Context is a condition of struggle" (Cram, 2016, p. 147). Media can better serve Latinx communities by imparting on journalists the necessity to understand the informational needs of Latinx audiences, as well as craft transnational spaces that those audiences demand (Retis & Chacón, 2021). Media and Communication courses need to integrate pedagogical processes and resources that help future journalists provide contextual, accurate, and intersectional coverage of Latinx populations, among other traditionally marginalized identities.

Discussion Questions

1. Which identifiers should journalists use and which should they avoid when reporting on the Latinx community? Why is this important to both your sources and the audience?
2. How can journalists avoid deadnaming transgender, non-binary, and gender nonconforming Latinx individuals? What other important guidelines should journalists employ?
3. How do you properly cite intersectional LGBTQ identities in conjunction with race, ethnicity, disability, socioeconomic class, and other identity markers? Why is intersectionality important?
4. What is the role of editors in fair, accurate, and inclusive news media coverage of Latinx communities? What about the roles of other newsroom staff? Is more intersectional diversity needed in the newsroom? Why or why not?
5. What resources are available for reporting in regard to the Latinx community and how can you employ them? How can you fact check these resources?

Assignments

1. Introduce the concept of intersectionality in your course. Choose two to three local news sources and two to three national news sources. Conduct a search for their respective coverage of the Pulse Nightclub Massacre. Have students compare and contrast their coverage. Is it intersectional and inclusive?
2. Develop a list of Latinx celebrities, politicians, and other public figures who might garner mediated attention. Have students conduct Internet and social media searches for journalistic coverage of the individuals on the list. Identify examples of poor and good coverage of intersectional Latinx LGBTQ individuals. Utilizing the *NLGJA Journalists Toolbox*, outline ways in which the reporters/organizations could have done better.

3. Select a recent Latinx-specific event. Have students practice writing a "filler" of 300–500 words for a fictitious online magazine (the magazine can be hard news, entertainment, sports, politics, or any other niche that is related to your particular course or topic). Have students trade fillers and then play "editor." Students can use the *NLGJA Journalists Toolbox* and/or the *GLAAD Media Reference Guide* to analyze the filler and suggest edits.
4. Place students into small groups and assign them a transgender, gender non-binary, and/or gender nonconforming Latinx trailblazer (such as Bamby Salcedo, MJ Rodriguez, Indya Moore, Sylvia Rivera, Jennicet Gutiérrez, Leiomy Maldonado, Diane Marie Rodríguez Zambrano, among others). Have students practice using pronouns and inclusive language by writing and recording a short featurette on their subject. This can be in the form of an audio story for radio or a short video for online news sites/social media. Students can use the *GLAAD Media Reference Guide – In Focus: Covering the Transgender Community* as a guideline.
5. Place students into small groups and have them examine social media activity surrounding Latinx celebrities, politicians, and activists. Have students select photos from their findings and practice writing intersectional and inclusive captions for the photos. Students can also practice writing headlines and social media blurbs for the pictures.

References

Alvarez, L., & Madigan, N. (2016, June 14). *In the Dead in Orlando, Puerto Ricans Hear a Roll Call of Their Kin*. New York Times. http://www.nytimes.com/2016/06/15/us/in-orlando-victims-puerto-ricans-hear-a-roll-callof-their-kin, accessed July 30, 2016.

Bailard, C. S. (2016). Corporate ownership and news bias revisited: Newspaper coverage of the supreme court's citizens united ruling. *Political Communication 33*(4), 583–604.

Barreto, M. A., Manzano, S., & Segura, G. (2012). *The Impact of Media Stereotypes on Opinions and Attitudes Towards Latinos*. Pasadena, CA: National Hispanic Media Coalition and Latino Decisions.

Bleich, E., Callison, J. P., Edwards, G. G., Fichman, M., Hoynes, E., Jabari, R., & van der Veen, A. M. (2021). The good, the bad, and the ugly: A corpus linguistics analysis of US newspaper coverage of Latinx, 1996–2016. *Journalism, 22*(6), 1522–1539.

Bond, B. J. (2014). Sex and sexuality in entertainment media popular with lesbian, gay, and bisexual adolescents. *Mass Communication and Society, 17*(1): 98–120.

Browne, S. H. (1995). Reading, rhetoric, and the texture of public memory. *Quarterly Journal of Speech, 81*, 237–250.

Cho, S., Crenshaw, K. W., & McCall, L. (2013). Toward a field of intersectionality studies: Theory, *applications, and praxis. Signs: Journal of women in culture and society, 38*(4), 785–810.

Collingwood, R. G. (2005). *The idea of history* (rev. ed.). Oxford: Oxford University Press.

Collins, P. H. (2000). *Black feminist thought: Knowledge, consciousness, and the politics of empowerment* (2nd ed.). New York, NY: Routledge.
Collins, P. H. (2015). Intersectionality's definitional dilemmas. *Annual Review of Sociology, 41*(1), 1–20. Doi:10.1146/annurev-soc-073014-112142
Collins, P. H., & Bilge, S. (2020). *Intersectionality.* Medford, MA: Polity.
Cottle, S. (2007) Mediatised recognition and the 'other.' *Media International Australia Incorporating Culture and Policy, 123*(1), 34–48.
Cram, E. (2016). Pulse: The matter of movement. *QED: A Journal in GLBTQ Worldmaking, 3*(3), 147–150.
Crenshaw, K. (1990). Mapping the margins: Intersectionality, identity politics, and violence against women of color. *Stanford Law Review, 43*(6), 1241–1299.
Darde, V., & Morigi, V. (2012). Sexual diversity in Brazilian journalism: A study of the representations of LGBT people in the newspapers Folha de S. Paulo and o Estado de S. Paulo. *Brazilian Journalism Research, 8*(1), 144–159.
Flores, V. B. (2016, June 13). The Pulse nightclub shooting robbed the queer Latinx community of a sanctuary. *Remezcla.*
Gamboa, S., & Acevedo, N. (2021, September 15). The new Latino landscape: The swift growth of U.S. Latinos is reshaping big states and small towns. NBCnews.com.
Goldman, D. (2016, June 13). Putting 'deadlist mass shooting in U.S. history' into some historical context: The two-way. *National Public Radio.* http://www.npr.org/sections/thetwo-way/2016/06/13/481884291/putting-deadliest-mass-shooting-in-u-s-history-into-some-historical-context, accessed June 24, 2016.
Gillborn, D. (2015). Intersectionality, critical race theory, and the primacy of racism: Race, class, gender, and disability in education. *Qualitative Inquiry, 21*(3), 277–287.
Gutiérrez, E. 2008. *Fertile matters: The politics of Mexican-origin women's reproduction.* Austin: University of Texas Press.
Hellmueller, L., Mellado, C., Blumell, L., & Huemmer, J. (2016). The contextualization of the watchdog and civic journalistic roles: Reevaluating journalistic role performance in US newspapers. *Palabra Clave, 19*(4), 1072–1100.
Houdek, M., & Phillips, K. R. (2017). *Public memory.* Oxford Research Encyclopedias. Doi: 10.1093/acrefore/9780190228613.181
Kalish Blair, Z. S. (2016). The pulse nightclub shooting: Connecting militarism, neoliberalism, and multiculturalism to understand violence. *North American Dialogue, 19*(2), 102–116.
Kligler-Vilenchik, N., Tsfati, Y., & Meyers, O. (2014). Setting the collective memory agenda: Examining mainstream media influence on individuals' perceptions of the past. *Memory Studies,* 7(4), 484–499.
Krogstad, J. M., & Noe-Bustamante, L. (2021, September 9). Key fact about U.S. Latinos for National Hispanic Heritage Month. Pew Research Center.
Monk-Turner, E., Heiserman, M., Johnson, C., Cotton, V., & Jackson, M. (2010). The portrayal of racial minorities on prime time television: A replication of the Mastro and Greenberg study a decade later. *Studies in Popular Culture, 32*(2), 101–114.
Nash, J. C. (2008). Re-thinking intersectionality. *Feminist Review, 89*(1), 1–15.
Padín, J. A. (2005). The normative mulattoes: The press, Latinos, and the racial climate on the moving immigration frontier. *Sociological Perspectives, 48*(1), 49–75.
Puar, J. K. 2007. *Terrorist assemblages: Homonationalism in queer times.* Durham, NC: Duke University Press.

Reichard, R. (2015, August 29). *Why We Say Latinx: Trans Gender Non-Conforming People Explain. Latina.Com.* http://www.latina.com/lifestyle/our-issues/why-we-say-latinx-trans-gender-non-conforming-people-explain

Retis, J., & Chacón, L. M. C. (2021). Mapping digital-native US Latinx news: Beyond geographical boundaries, language barriers, and hyper-fragmentation of audiences. *International Symposium on Online Journalism, 11*(1), 35–64.

Rivadeneyra, R., Ward, L. M., & Gordon, M. (2007). Distorted reflections: Media exposure and Latino adolescents' conceptions of self. *Media Psychology, 9*(2), 261–290. Doi: 10.1080/15213260701285926

Şahin, S. (2021). Coming out: The role of journalism in social exclusion of LGB people. *Journalism, 22*(1), 215–230. Doi: 10.1177/1464884918769462.

Schwartz, F., Campo-Flores, A., & Al Omran, A. (2016, June 13). *Obama says Orlando shooter was a 'homegrown' terrorist.* The Wall Street Journal. http://www.wsj.com/articles/officials-hunt-for-details-from-orlando-shooting-1465823030.

Shafer, J., & Rivadeneyra, R. (2020). The impact of televised stereotypes on the state self-esteem of Latino/a emerging adults: The moderating role of ethnic–racial identity. *Emerging Adulthood.* https://doi.org/10.1177%2F2167696820921308

Soto-Vásquez, A. D. (2020). *Mobilizing the U.S. Latinx vote: Media, identity, and politics.* New York, NY: Routledge.

Thrasher, S. W. (2016, June 14). Latino community mourns Pulse shooting victims: '90% were Hispanic'. *The Guardian.* Retrieved from https://www.theguardian.com/us-news/2016/jun/14/latino-hispanic-orlando-shooting-victims

Zelizer, B. (1995). Reading the past against the grain: The shape of memory studies. *Critical Studies in Mass Communication, 12*(2), 214–239.

7

COVID-19 and the Impact on the Latino Community

Teresa Puente

The entire world experienced the impact of the COVID-19 pandemic as it began in spring 2020 as travel was restricted, schools closed down for a year and Zoom became a part of our vocabulary with online meetings and classes. Essential workers from those in the medical profession to service workers and farm workers, among others, risked their health for the country.

A short time into the pandemic it became clear that not all people were impacted equally. The pandemic revealed divides in this country in terms of wealth and power. Many of those people with greater economic privilege were able to work from home and have groceries delivered.

Others went to work on the front lines to keep the country moving and safe. Within the first few months of the pandemic, it became clear that the Latino community in the United States was disproportionately impacted in terms of cases and deaths.

Early in the pandemic racial disparities were documented. The New York Times reported in April 2020 that the coronavirus was killing Black and Latino people at twice the rate of white people (Mays & Newman, 2020). In New York City, the preliminary death rate for or Hispanic people was about 22 people per 100,000; the rate for black people 20 per 100,000; the rate for white people 10 per 100,000; and the rate for Asian people 8 per 100,000.

Mayor Bill de Blasio told the Times it was due to economic inequality and lack of access to healthcare. Those and other inequities in housing and transportation all were factors that contributed to the disparities.

In May 2020 Chicago Public Radio WBEZ reported that COVID-19 testing lagged in Latino neighborhoods which had the highest and fastest-growing rates of COVID-19 in Cook County (Zamudio, 2020). The five ZIP codes that

DOI: 10.4324/9781003212331-7

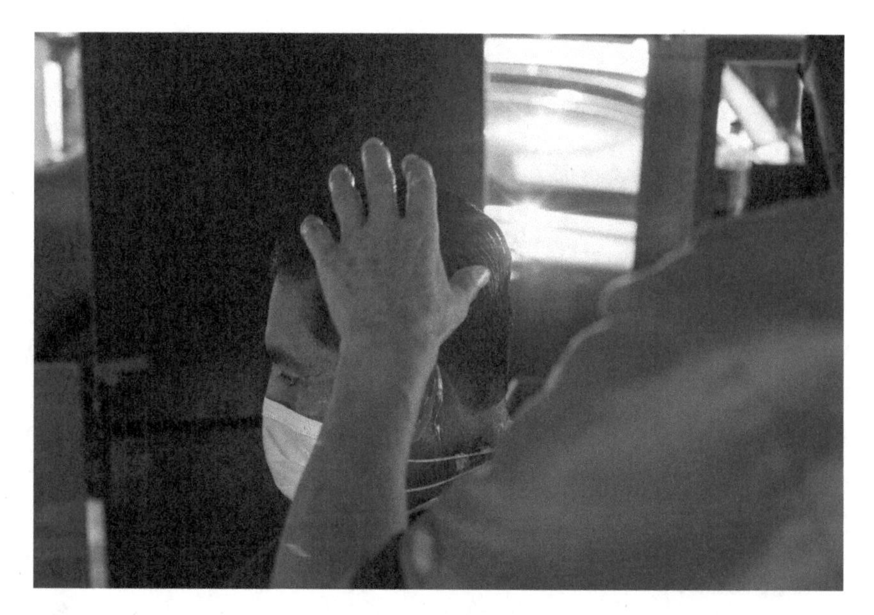

FIGURE 7.1 Photo of Latino barber in Long Beach, California by Pablo Unzueta

ranked among the county's top ten for both the rate of confirmed cases per 1,000 residents and the percentage of confirmed cases among the total tested were all in Latino areas of Chicago.

The Los Angeles Times reported in May 2020 that Latino essential workers were disproportionately impacted by COVID-19 (Branson-Potts, et al., 2020). In May 2020, Latinos comprised about 40% of California's population but 53% of positive cases (California Department of Public Health, 2020). Also, around 42% of Latinos polled said they could work from home, compared with 53% of blacks, 59% of Asians and 61% of whites (Mora & Schicker, 2020).

Spanish-language media also adjusted its coverage to offer expanded coverage. In March 2020, Estrella TV launched a one-hour newscast *Noticiero EstrellaTV: Reportaje Especial, Coronavirus la Pandemia* (Villafañe, 2020).

Also in March, Univision preempted the 3 p.m. broadcast to air a network-wide special, *Diario del Coronavirus*. This included Public Service Announcements featuring Dr. Juan Rivera, Univision's chief medical correspondent. He informed the Hispanic community about the coronavirus and how to stay safe during this period of time (Jacobson, 2020).

Telemundo also launched a late-night newscast *Noticias Telemundo Presenta – Coronavirus: Un País en Alerta*. It focused on the latest developments regarding the coronavirus and its impact on the Latino community (Jacobson, 2020).

Also student journalists with Al Día at California State University, Fullerton under the guidance of Professor Jesús Ayala Rico produced a 40-minute

FIGURE 7.2 Photo of Latino business owner in Long Beach, California by Pablo Unzueta

Spanish-language newscast *Coronavirus: Pandemia Mundial.* It won several national student media awards.

Beyond health reporting on the pandemic crossed into other issues such as the economy, housing and education.

Also, who has access to the vaccine, fears over getting a vaccine and how to vaccinate more people became an important part of the coverage.

The Guardian reported out of Georgia a story about community groups reaching out to Latino communities to increase vaccination rates (Pratt, 2019). As of September 2021, around 73% of all Hispanic adults in the United States had received at least one dose of the vaccine. Vaccination rates for Hispanics initially lagged but they increased in the summer of 2021 (Brodie, 2021).

A Closer Look: The Pandemic, Race and Ethnicity Data

At the start of the pandemic in spring 2020, data by race was not readily available. The CDC, the John Hopkins and the New York Times were not reporting their initial data by race and ethnicity (Kendi, 2020).

The Atlantic magazine created The COVID Tracking Project and also with Boston University's Center for Antiracist Research they started The COVID Racial Data Tracker. They asked each state to report data by race and ethnicity. They created guides as to how to use the data as well as a training video on how to use the data.

The Atlantic reported that the COVID Tracking Project was among the first to identify virus surges in the Sun Belt and how nursing homes were driving the

COVID death. Also their data was used by *The New York Times*, Johns Hopkins University and two presidential administrations. However, as of March 2021, the Atlantic stopped collecting new data as the government made some progress in tracking data (Meyer & Madrigal, 2021).

The Centers for Disease Control Has a COVID Data Tracker

With cases, death totals and vaccination rates. It even breaks the data down by county and age, race, ethnicity and sex. The CDC also has a page en español (CDC, 2021).

KFF is an endowed, nonprofit organization that provides independent information on national health issues. It has a vaccine monitor dashboard, a tracker for cases and deaths and Vaccine FAQ videos, including links to interviews with medical experts in Spanish supported by (UnidosUS, 2021).

Bloomberg also created a Vaccine Tracker that details which states are making the most week-by-week progress in closing their racial vaccination gaps.

It's important for journalists to look at the data to determine a range of factors from death and infection rates to vaccination rates and more. There are many sources of reliable data from the U.S. government as well as from news organizations that are gathering data.

But The Atlantic also warned that data has limitations: "Data are just a bunch of qualitative conclusions arranged in a countable way. Data-driven thinking isn't necessarily more accurate than other forms of reasoning, and if you do not understand how data are made, their seams and scars, they might even be *more* likely to mislead you" (Meyer & Madrigal, 2021).

In Conversation with Brittny Mejia

Brittny Mejia is a metro reporter at The Los Angeles Times. She also has worked at The Arizona Republic, the Arizona Daily Star, the Oakland Tribune and the Phoenix Bureau of The New York Times. She was a Pulitzer Prize finalist with her colleague Jack Dolan at the Los Angeles Times for exposing failures in Los Angeles County's safety-net healthcare system that resulted in months-long wait times for patients, including some who died before getting appointments with specialists. Mejia also has reported in depth on the pandemic and the impact on the Latino community in Los Angeles County.

What got you started in journalism?

Mejia: I was in elementary school. I thought I wanted to be a spy. I had a tape recorder and a notebook. I would lift people's fingerprints and put them in a notebook. And then one of my sisters said you should become a journalist. I didn't know anything about it. I looked it up and it sounded like a really cool

FIGURE 7.3 Photo of Brittny Mejia of The Los Angeles Times

profession. No one in my family is a journalist and it was an unusual path to take. I was the second in my family to go to college. My parents' mindset was like if you're going to spend money on an education you should be a lawyer or a doctor. It took landing at the Los Angeles Times for my parents to understand it was a real profession for me.

My mother immigrated from Mexico at 14 and grew up in L.A.

How did you become interested in reporting on health?

Mejia: I've always been interested in health-based reporting. This last year it really became more of a focus especially with the pandemic. This last year is actually when I started to spend the time and see who is impacted the most by COVID, which communities were hit the hardest and obviously the Latino community was way up there. That became more of a focus. This last year my family went through and I saw the impact in Mexico on my family and my uncle here. Actually, when I reported in an ICU for Christmas, my uncle was in a different ICU. I definitely saw it first-hand within my own family and it became a motivation for me to focus on those stories and try and tell those stories. This last year changed everything for me.

When did it become clear to journalists there was a disproportionate impact of COVID-19 on communities of color?

Mejia: Going into it for me, I thought who is going to be more at risk here? If we look at essential workers, if we look at who takes public transportation, in my mind this is who I cover mostly already. I already know those are the more vulnerable populations. When I reported on housekeepers (Mejia, 2020), they took the bus to the west side. Many of them don't have cars. We should have known who was going to be vulnerable at the very beginning. Then a little bit later we actually saw the data.

Tell me more about some of the stories you reported on during the pandemic and the Latino community?

Mejia: I went to the intensive care unit and I had spent a shift there in the ICU (Mejia, 2020b). A lot of the patients were Latino. One of them had been intubated for quite a while, a month. I ended up speaking with his wife and he was an essential worker. She talked about the risk and about how quickly it can spread. That's what really stuck out to me. In these situations, it can be difficult, people are going through a hard time. Obviously I'm not trying to retraumatize them or cause them more pain. It takes a lot for people to open up. You have to give them that space and not push. She was FaceTiming with her husband and then we did a call with her. We had many more conversations.

The big thing I learned especially over this last year is how important it is to build trust and build these relationships up in these communities. I think often there is a lack of trust as to whether we will be able to tell these stories accurately and fairly.

Another story I did was about a family who lived in a one-bedroom apartment (Mejia, 2021). It was five people in the one bedroom and a lot of them were essential workers. They worked in grocery stores. The dad was a mechanic. It wasn't like any of them could stay home and shelter in place. They didn't have the luxury of that. Once all the kids got sick, the dad was the only one who tested negative. He ended up getting it, going to the ICU and passing away.

Stories like that really stick with me. One of the first things I tried to do when I met them was say, Tell me about him. Tell him about who he was. I want to memorialize this person. A lot of times (reporters say) I can't imagine what you're going through. Some of us can imagine it. At that point my uncle was in the ICU. We were sharing and they opened up and shared about mental health and we ended up talking about that and things that weren't going into the story. We should have an open conversation and an open dialogue to build trust.

How did you report differently and also safely during the pandemic?

Mejia: Initially, I was doing a lot of my interviews over the phone or from home. That required more work, asking them to send me photos, asking them to send me videos, asking them to give me something so I can recreate the scene. I mostly do narrative writing. It's very hard if I can't visualize the space. When I'm out reporting, I take pictures and video for myself so I can remember. Having that taken away was stressful at first.

My biggest concern was going to a place and getting someone else sick. I was very, very careful. Once I started going out in the field I wore a fit-tested N95 mask, I had hand sanitizer looped on my jeans, I started using my phone to take notes so I could disinfect it after. I shifted some of the aspects of what I was doing out in the field to stay safe. I wanted to make sure they felt comfortable or they felt safe.

What are some of the issues or stories journalists should still cover about pandemic?

Mejia: What the pandemic did was lay bare a lot of inequities that have existed for a long time and that maybe we didn't think about at the level that we should have.

Looking at the story about overcrowded housing and that family in the one bedroom. That's a story that we're looking at and will continue to look at because the areas that were the most overcrowded were the hardest hit by COVID.

Just because we're starting to pull out of this (pandemic) that doesn't change the housing for a lot of people that doesn't change the risks there.

One of the other things that is important is how much Latinos were impacted economically.

I do want to report on the mental health impacts. If you look at families who lost jobs and just felt so disillusioned through this whole pandemic. They had all of this stress. I'm hearing from immigrants who were like I was told by my primary care doctor I should see a therapist. There was a little bit of resistance but this woman ended up doing it and felt better.

I wonder about mental health and how that's going to look over the next year especially if you look at Latinos and how they were disproportionately impacted. They are the ones who lost family members. They lost friends. That trauma carries with you and it needs to be addressed because if not it builds over time.

Some people aren't privileged enough to be able to sit and grieve that loss. That is something we have to think about.

You investigated delays in the Los Angeles County health system. What was the impact of that project?

Mejia: You had so many Latinos waiting so long for specialty care. Patients who waited months on end to see a specialist and who died waiting. The majority were Spanish-speaking or immigrants. It's not knowing how to navigate the system or not knowing that they should be seen sooner for specialty care.

It was months of trying to get all the records and really building trust with families. And having experts look at the records to see if what we were seeing lined up.

It was a finalist for the Pulitzer (2021), which was great. I'm amazed by that. These stories are so important and some families would not have known what happened to loved ones had it not been the investigation.

It launched internal reviews through the department and an investigation from the state. It did actually change the waiting times. It was so sad and terrible to see how underserved communities were treated this way.

There was one woman who was the lede of our story. She had kidney issues. They gave her a three-to-six-month time frame. She died waiting for an appointment with a nephrologist. We had experts saying she shouldn't have waited that long.

Before this investigation, this wasn't my lived experience with healthcare. That was a big shock to me seeing how long these waits were. These stories are important because things do need to change for the better. Communities that are underserved deserve these stories to be told.

Besides the pandemic, we have an infodemic with so much misinformation out there. What can journalists do about it?

Mejia: Disinformation, especially in Latinos communities, it's bad. It started really kicking up ahead of the election. There was so much disinformation, and it persisted now with the vaccine.

I see that when I'm doing interviews. I have people tell me that my niece or granddaughter saw on TikTok that the vaccine causes infertility.

I also have those conversations with my family. I'm very open with them. I say, let's talk through this. Tell me your misgivings and we will work through it.

I did a story at a vaccine clinic with Latinos who were finally getting it but waited months. I talked to people who said I already got COVID so I don't need to get vaccinated. That became a big part of my story.

Some of our stories on L.A. Times en Español have gotten a lot of clicks and views from people. Those explainers can really change things. It is important to have it in English and Spanish and have it readily available to communities.

Note: This is an edited transcript of the interview.

Trade Tools and Tips

While there is a health pandemic, it also has brought with it a pandemic of misinformation. Conspiracy theories have run rampant about the cause of the pandemic as well as fake news about the vaccine. The World Health Organization (WHO, 2021) has classified the fake news about the virus as an infodemic. They describe it as such: An infodemic is too much information including false or misleading information in digital and physical environments during a disease outbreak. It causes confusion and risk-taking behaviors that can harm health. It also leads to mistrust in health authorities and undermines the public health response. The WHO also is documenting some of the biggest myths about the virus and the vaccine with links to report misinformation that often spreads first on social media.

It is the responsibility of journalists to report accurately and also dispel some of the myths about the virus and the vaccine.

Here are some suggestions adapted from (First Draft, 2021), a nonprofit coalition that offers practical and ethical guidance in how to find, verify and publish content sourced from the social web.

1. Avoid sensationalist language that causes fear
2. Not every rumor deserves coverage
3. Talk to more than one expert
4. Use data, maps and graphs to help your audience
5. Guide your audience to official and verified sources of information

A #CoronavirusFactsAlliance was launched by the Poynter Institute (Poynter, 2021), International Fact-Checking Network (IFCN) and others to bring together more than 100 fact-checkers from around the world to combat the misinformation spreading about the new coronavirus.

The Poynter Institute also offered recommendations (Tompkins, 2020). They include:

1. Limit the use of subjective adjective like "catastrophic" and "deadly"
2. Statistical stories are less frightening than anecdotal ones
3. Frame stories with context
4. Explain what readers can do with recommendations

Discussion Questions

1. Which media outlets did some of the best coverage of the impact of the pandemic on the Latino community? Why?
2. What are some of the story angles that still merit additional coverage in your community? Identify subject areas of coverage.
3. How has COVID impacted the lives of people in your family and community? Does your personal experience contribute to the story or possibly hinder a story?
4. What are some of the limitations of data about COVID?
5. What can journalists do to address the infodemic?

Assignments

1. Using one of the data sets, identify whether COVID cases and deaths are up or down over the last month for the Latino population in your county. Use this data as a starting point for a news story.

2. Using one of the data sets, identify whether vaccination rates are up or down over the last month for the Latino population in your county. Use this data as a starting point for a news story.
3. Interview Latinx health professionals about the impact of COVID on the community.
4. Interview local Latinx business owners about the impact of COVID on the community.
5. Using social media, identify three recent fake news stories about the pandemic. Write and source fact check briefs to debunk about the fake news.

References

Branson-Potts, H., Reyes-Velarde, A., Stiles, M. & Campa, A.J. (2020 May 17). *The price of being 'essential': Latino service workers bear brunt of coronavirus. Los Angeles Times.* https://www.latimes.com/california/story/2020-05-17/latino-essential-workers-coronavirus

Brodie, M. (2021 September 28). KFF COVID-19 vaccine monitor: September 2021. *KFF.* https://www.kff.org/coronavirus-covid-19/poll-finding/kff-covid-19-vaccine-monitor-september-2021/?campaign_id=9&emc=edit_nn_20210928&instance_id=41490&nl=the-morning®i_id=83666512&segment_id=70082&te=1&user_id=f7edae9562d9964e6c2c1282d2446fac

Centers for Disease Control. Covid Data Tracker. Retrieved September 27, 2021. https://covid.cdc.gov/covid-data-tracker/#datatracker-home

La Conversación. Greater than Covid. UnidosUS. Retrieved September 27, 2021. https://www.greaterthancovid.org/theconversation/latinx-community-en-espanol/

Coronavirus disease (COVID-19) advice for the public: Mythbusters. (2021 May 5). World Health Organization. Retrieved September 27, 2021. https://www.who.int/emergencies/diseases/novel-coronavirus-2019/advice-for-public/myth-busters

California Department of Public Health. (2021) COVID-19 and Race and Ethnicity Data. Retrieved September 27, 2021. https://www.cdph.ca.gov/Programs/CID/DCDC/Pages/COVID-19/Race-Ethnicity.aspx

COVID 19. Centros para el Control y la Prevención de Enfermedades. Retrieved September 27, 2021. https://espanol.cdc.gov/coronavirus/2019-ncov/index.html

Fighting the Infodemic: The #CoronaVirusFacts Alliance. Poynter. Retrieved September 27, 2021. https://www.poynter.org/coronavirusfactsalliance/

Infodemic. World Health Organization. Retrieved September 27, 2021. https://www.who.int/health-topics/infodemic#tab=tab_1

Jacobson, A. (2020 March 19) *Hispanic Media Does Its Part To Offer COVID-19 Info.* Radio+Television Business Report. https://www.rbr.com/hispanic-media-does-it-part-to-offer-covid-19-info/

Kendi, I.X. (2020 April 6). *What the racial data show. The Atlantic.* https://www.theatlantic.com/ideas/archive/2020/04/coronavirus-exposing-our-racial-divides/609526/

Mays, J.C. & Newman, A. (2020 April 8). *Virus is twice as deadly for Black and Latino people than Whites in N.Y.C. New York Times.* https://www.nytimes.com/2020/04/08/nyregion/coronavirus-race-deaths.html

Mejia, B. (2020a March 15). *As coronavirus spreads, housekeepers in L.A. declare staying home 'a luxury.' Los Angeles Times.* https://www.latimes.com/california/story/2020-03-15/coronavirus-pandemic-disease-housekeepers-westwood

Mejia, B. (2020b December 27). Christmas in the ICU: Prayers, pain, few miracles. 'Jesus is holding your hand. Don't let go.' *Los Angeles Times.* https://www.latimes.com/california/story/2020-12-27/not-many-miracles-but-plenty-of-pain-in-an-orange-county-icu

Mejia, B. (2021 January 29). *When coronavirus invaded their tiny apartment, children desperately tried to protect dad. Los Angeles Times.* https://www.latimes.com/california/story/2021-01-29/how-overcrowded-housing-led-to-covid-death-la-family

Meyer, R. & Madrigal, A.C. (2021 March 15). *Why the Pandemic Experts Failed. The Atlantic.* https://www.theatlantic.com/science/archive/2021/03/americas-coronavirus-catastrophe-began-with-data/618287/

Mora, G.C. & Schicker, E. (2020 May 6) *Racial minorities more at risk in the workplace and the economy.* IGS Polls, University of California, Berkeley, Institute of Governmental Studies. https://escholarship.org/uc/item/1kd7h0sc

Pratt, T. (2021 September 19). *Covid vaccinations among US Latinos are rising thanks to community outreach. The Guardian.* https://www.theguardian.com/world/2021/sep/19/covid-vaccinations-latinos-rising-community-outreach

The Pulitzer Prizes. Finalist: Jack Dolan and Brittny Mejia of the Los Angeles Times. The 2021 Pulitzer Finalist in Local Reporting. Retrieved September 27, 2021. https://www.pulitzer.org/finalists/jack-dolan-and-brittny-mejia-los-angeles-times

Tips for reporting on Covid-19 and slowing the spread of misinformation. (2020 March 10). First Draft. https://firstdraftnews.org/articles/tips-for-reporting-on-covid-19-coronavirus-and-slowing-the-spread-of-misinformation/

Tompkins, A. (2020 March 4). *How newsrooms can tone down their coronavirus coverage while still reporting responsibly. Poynter.* https://www.poynter.org/reporting-editing/2020/how-newsrooms-can-tone-down-their-coronavirus-coverage-while-still-reporting-responsibly/

Villafañe, V. (2020 March 19) *EstrellaTV adds newscasts for COVID-19 coverage. Media Moves.* https://www.mediamoves.com/2020/03/estrellatv-adds-newscasts-for-covid-19-coverage.html

Zamudio, M.I. (2020 May 6). *Testing Lags In Latino Communities Hit Hardest By COVID-19 In Chicago. WBEZ Chicago.* https://www.npr.org/local/309/2020/05/06/851291931/testing-lags-in-latino-communities-hit-hardest-by-c-o-v-i-d-19-in-chicago

8

Reporting on Immigration

Teresa Puente

In August 2015, Univision journalist Jorge Ramos challenged the then-presidential candidate Donald Trump on a campaign stop.

> He stood up at a press conference and started asking questions about immigration.
>
> "You weren't called," said Trump. "Sit down."
>
> Ramos persisted with his questions and Trump told him to sit down again.
>
> "Go back to Univision," Trump eventually said.
>
> Ramos, originally from Mexico and today a U.S. citizen, refused to sit down. Security personnel then escorted him out of the room.
>
> Ramos was, a short time later, allowed to go back into the room and ask questions about immigration.

This dramatic exchange illustrates the challenges journalists face when reporting on immigration. Journalists must ask the hard questions especially when one immigrant community is negatively targeted or vilified. Too often immigration is framed as an issue of criminality, and the economic, political and humanitarian reasons why people leave their homelands is not given the proper context.

There are more than 62.1 million Latinos in the United States according to the 2020 U.S. Census, around 19 percent of the national population (Lopez et al., 2021).

Immigration as it pertains to the Latinx community has been a major news story for decades and even the dominant media narrative.

But what many people don't realize is that most U.S. Latinos are not immigrants. Around 79 percent of the Latinos in the United States were U.S. citizens

DOI: 10.4324/9781003212331-8

as of 2019 (Noe-Bustamante, 2019). The vast majority of those are native born but this also includes naturalized immigrants, those born in Latin America and who went through a process to become U.S. citizens.

The ten largest Latin American ethnic groups in the United States are Mexican, Salvadoran, Cuban, Dominican, Guatemalan, Colombian, Honduran, Ecuadorian, Peruvian, Nicaraguan, Venezuelan and Argentine (Noe-Bustamante, 2019). Puerto Ricans are the second largest Hispanic ethnic group but note they are not immigrants and U.S. citizens. Too often Latinx immigrants are not portrayed in a diverse light.

There also are regional differences in terms of where Latinx people live. Mexicans make up more than two-in-three Hispanics in the Los Angeles and Houston metro areas. Puerto Ricans are the largest group in the Orlando, Florida, metro area. Salvadorans are the largest in the Washington, D.C., metro area. Cubans are the largest origin group in the Miami metro area (Noe-Bustamante, 2019).

Data also shows that immigrants are a declining share of the Latinx population.

The number of Latinos in the United States who are immigrants declined to 33 percent in 2017, down from 37 percent in 2010, as immigration has slowed in recent years (Noe-Bustamante, 2019).

Latinos have always shaped this country. Under the Treaty of Guadalupe, Mexico ceded 55 percent of its territory, including parts of present-day Arizona, California, New Mexico, Texas, Colorado, Nevada and Utah, to the United States (National Archives).

When covering immigration, always be sure to include this history and context. Many immigration stories about Latinos have negative framing, focusing on crime and/or border crossings and showing Latinos as others or a threat (Chavez, 2008). The news media can't ignore the challenges of immigration, but it's important to also cover stories about the contributions that immigrants make to the U.S. economy and society.

Immigration issues are complex and immigration laws often change creating confusion for immigrants themselves. It's essential to consult experts such as immigration attorneys or nonprofit groups working with immigrants.

Also bear in mind when looking for sources on immigration that you verify the source and consider who funds them and their origin story. Some anti-immigrant groups such as FAIR, the Federation for American Immigration Reform, have been described as hate groups by the Southern Poverty Law Center. This organization has identified 19 different anti-immigrant hate groups across the United States.

Here are some important historical events surrounding immigration and highlights of journalistic coverage:

Great Depression: As many as 1.8 million people were deported to Mexico. By some estimates as many as 60 percent were U.S. citizens. The raids by local

FIGURE 8.1 Photo of immigration protest in Long Beach, CA by Teresa Puente

authorities occurred across the United States. One such raid in 1931 rounded up more than 400 people at La Placita Park and deported them to Mexico (Little, 2019).

Journalist Vicente Serrano made a documentary about his grandmother's deportation from the United States called "A Forgotten Injustice" (WBEZ, 2008). Another key resource is the book *Decade of Betrayal, Mexican Repatriation in the 1930s* (Balderrama & Rodriguez, 2006).

The Bracero Program: This government program from 1942 to 1964 allowed Mexicans to come to the United States with short-term contracts to work in agriculture. With more than 4.6 million contracts signed, it was considered the longest U.S. contract labor program (Bracero History Archive).

It was created to help stem labor shortages anticipated from WWII. The program resulted in an influx of undocumented and documented laborers, 22 years

FIGURE 8.2 Photo of border at Nogales, AZ by Teresa Puente

of cheap labor from Mexico and remittances to Mexico by Braceros (Library of Congress).

Some of these workers were never fully paid and this resulted in a lawsuit in 2001 that was covered by several U.S. media outlets, including the Dallas Morning News, the L.A. Times and the New York Times (Belluck, 2008). An investigation by Dallas Morning News reporters found that both the U.S. and Mexican governments kept records of what each bracero was owed, and both governments recorded countless complaints about missing savings (Corchado & Sandoval, 2002).

Operation Wetback: This was a mass deportation campaign by President Eisenhower in the mid-1950s. This is an extremely offensive slur that was used by the government and even some media at this time. The INS claimed that 1.3 million Mexican immigrants were deported (Koestler, 2005) from the Southwestern states, but other sources put the number at around 300,000 (Blakemore, 2019). It was a militarized effort, and people were packed into trucks, trains and planes and sent back to Mexico. A congressional investigation described conditions on one cargo ship as a "penal hell ship" and compared it to a slave ship on the Middle Passage (Lind, 2015).

The Los Angeles Times republished some of its coverage of that time period and acknowledged how offensive the word "wetback" is. Some of the headline from the 1950s included "1259 More Wetbacks Deported in a Single Day," "Wetbacks Herded at Nogales Camp" and "U.S. Patrol Halts Border Invasion" (Ballinger, n.d.).

In 2013, the Los Angeles Times released new guidelines for covering immigration (Edgar, 2013). "Do not use 'illegal alien,' 'an illegal' or 'illegals' except in rare cases in direct quotes; they should not be used in headlines or other display type." Many other news organizations also follow this policy.

The National Association of Hispanic Journalists has long advocated for the elimination of this term (Tenore, 2011). They also have published a Cultural Competency Handbook (NAHJ, 2020). The Associated Press recommended no longer using the word illegal to refer to immigrants or people in 2013 (Constantini, 2013).

Proposition 187: This was a ballot proposition that passed in California in November 1994 that sought to limit services to undocumented immigrants. It would have required that police, healthcare professionals and teachers to verify and report the immigration status of all individuals, including children. Immediately after it passed, a federal court found that it violated the U.S. Constitution. It was tied up in the courts until 1998 when it was declared unconstitutional because only the federal government can set immigration laws (ACLU, 1999).

Los Angeles Times columnist Gustavo Arellano wrote a column on the 25th anniversary of Proposition 187. He recalled that on November 2, 1994, over 10,000 teenagers across California walked out to protest Proposition 187 (Arellano, 2019).

> What 187 did is spawn a new generation of politicians," Kevin de León, told Arellano. The former president pro tem of the California Senate was in his early 20s when he helped to organize a rally outside Los Angeles City Hall that drew more than 70,000 people. "There's no question about it. There's no ambiguity. There's no vagueness. There's no room for misinterpretation.

Immigration protests: In 2006 and 2007, millions of people across the U.S. protested proposed restrictive immigration laws. The protests were sparked by H.R. 4437, the Border Protection, Anti-terrorism and Illegal Immigration Control Act of 2005. It would have criminalized undocumented immigrants and charged anybody with aiding them with a felony. This would have included providing food, housing or medical assistance. There were a series of protests with more than 139 protests in 39 states (Engler & Engler, 2016). The largest demonstrations were in Chicago and Los Angeles. Spanish-language radio hosts also helped mobilize the protests. The bill failed but so did efforts to achieve comprehensive immigration reform.

In March 2006, NPR did an interview with Rafael Pulido, aka "El Pistolero," the host of a morning talk show for Chicago's WOJO's La Que Buena. He was one of the lead voices organizing the protests (Block, 2006).

"This is the first time that we've all come together for this same cause. And at one point or the other, we have been on the air simulcastly (ph), you know, broadcasting to the L.A., to the Bay Area, to Houston, to Dallas, to Denver and Atlanta and various other cities. But this has been the only event that has brought us together," Pulido told NPR (Block, 2006).

Family Separations: The Trump Administration policy to separate children from their parents garnered additional national attention when ProPublica obtained audio from inside a U.S. Customs and Border Protection Facility (Thompson, 2018). In the audio, one can hear sobbing children begging for their parents and a Border Patrol agent disparaging them. There also were protests nationwide in more than two dozen cities against the family separations (Rose, 2018). The Biden Administration identified more than 3,900 children separated from their parents at the U.S.-Mexico border under Trump but the ACLU put the number of separated children at more than 5,500 (Spagat, 2021).

El Paso hate crime: A white supremacists killed 22 people at an El Paso, Texas Walmart on August 3, 2019. Patrick Crusius published a manifesto (Ura, 2019) in which he indicated the crime was motivated by hatred toward Hispanics and immigrants. He drove ten hours from his home in Allen, Texas to kill Mexicans and claimed there was an invasion of Hispanics in Texas. Few news articles gave context to counter that Hispanics are part of Texas history and that it used to be Mexico.

Two Latinx journalists wrote opinion articles criticizing the coverage by mainstream media. They argued that Latinos were not adequately covered.

On August 9, 2019, a few days after the El Paso shooting, journalist Lulu García-Navarro published this article in The Atlantic, "The Media Erased Latinos From the Story: It was the deadliest attack targeting Latinos in recent U.S. history. Why wasn't that the headline?" (Garcia-Navarro, 2019).

She chronicled how she walked by the Newseum in Washington, D.C., that displays front pages from across the country in its windows and the headlines reinforced this idea. Garcia-Navarro wrote, "And yet the headlines in our largest papers and the cable-news chyrons omitted or downplayed the historic nature of the carnage in El Paso. Instead, they gave top billing to calls for unity by a president who has for years used angry rhetoric that dehumanizes and maligns Latinos."

Another Latino journalist, Adrian Carrasquillo, weighed in with another opinion piece on August 10, 2019 published in Politico. He argued that the anti-Latino angle was downplayed in media coverage and that anti-immigrant rhetoric by current and past political leaders played a role in fomenting the hate (Carrasquillo, 2019).

> But the media's desire to erase the shooter and his ideology ended up erasing his victims and their community, too. While the news media successfully portrayed this shooting as part of a national epidemic of mass killings, we failed to accurately convey how this one was different. The visceral emotions of the Latinos I spoke with should have been—and should still be—front and center," Carrasquillo wrote. "This killer expressly traveled to a city filled with Mexicans and immigrants. This is new territory. The El Paso shooting isn't just a sad moment that will pass, but the culmination of an anti-immigrant four decades in politics that ratcheted up in the 1990s and 2000s and has become only louder, emboldened and unchecked by American leaders, led by the president but certainly not just by him. Of the 49 victims three years ago at Pulse, a gay nightclub in Orlando, 90 percent were Latino. Almost half were Puerto Rican. Others were Colombians, Mexicans and Dominicans. But what makes El Paso different is that people were targeted, not by someone pledging themselves to ISIS, but to white supremacy.

Immigrants are often dehumanized by political leaders and this must be examined more often in the media. In times of crisis, the immigrant stories are told as dramas and we don't often hear the voices of the impacted. Rarely do we see in the media stories of the contributions made by immigrant business owners, medical professionals, teachers, artists and more.

A Closer Look: DREAMers and DACA

One of the biggest immigration stories of the 21st century has been the story of the DREAMers and later DACA (Deferred Action for Childhood Arrivals). These are the terms that have been used for immigrant youth who arrived in the United States as minors and had no pathway towards permanent residency. The DREAM Act and DACA were efforts to find a solution for this group of immigrant youth.

Since 2001, at least 11 versions of the DREAM Act have been introduced in Congress (American Immigration Council, 2021).

This legislation was aimed at immigrant youth who were brought to the United States before the age of 16 and were undocumented. In 2021, an estimated 1.9 million immigrants would have a pathway to stay permanently in the United States under the DREAM Act (fwd.US).

Over the last 20 years, various versions of the DREAM Act have been introduced in Congress but they did not pass. It has received bipartisan support and also opposition.

The various versions of the legislation have contained key differences. But they all would have provided a pathway to legal status for undocumented people who came to this country as children. Some versions have garnered as many as 48 co-sponsors in the U.S. Senate and 152 in the House of Representatives. Among key sponsors of the legislation were former Congressman Luis Gutierrez, a Democrat of Illinois and U.S. Senator Dick Durbin, a Democrat of Illinois, former Sen. Orrin G. Hatch, a Republican from Utah and Sen. Lindsey Graham, a Republican from South Carolina.

There has been bipartisan support for each version of the bill, but none have become law. To date, the 2010 bill came closest to full passage when it passed the U.S. House of Representatives but fell just five votes short of the 60 needed to proceed in the Senate. Among those who voted against the DREAM Act in the Senate in 2010 were five Democrats (Loop, 2017).

When Barack Obama was elected president in 2008, he faced considerable pressure to work on immigration reform. Since the Congress had failed to pass the DREAM Act, his administration issued a memorandum to create DACA (Deferred Action for Childhood Arrivals).

There were around 650,000 immigrants with DACA, but the DACA eligible population is 1.9 million (Benenson, 2020).

There are several advocacy groups that have worked to support immigrant youth. Among them are United We Dream, an immigrant and youth-led community founded in 2008. United We Dream has more than 100 local groups in 28 states.

Also, some universities have centers or offices on their campuses to support DACA students. California is a leader in this area with the California Undocumented Higher Education Coalition that has a map of statewide resources including at the campuses of the University of California, California State University and the California community college system. More than 15 states also offer in-state tuition for undocumented students (CAPPEX).

In 2017, The Trump Administration announced that it would end DACA. It could not cancel current DACA recipients but for a period new applications were not allowed.

DACA was tied up in the courts and in February 2018, the U.S. Supreme Court declined a request to hear a lower court ruling on DACA effectively upholding lower court rulings to continue DACA.

Joe Biden became president in January 2021 and he has vowed to support DACA and to seek a permanent solution for immigrant youth and also for their parents.

The DREAMers and DACA has been one of the most covered news stories related to immigration. Many of the immigrant youth have come forward and spoken publicly in the media and also organized protests and sit-ins across the country. These youth have held sit-ins, protests, press conferences and more using the phrase "Undocumented and Unafraid" (Puente, 2011).

Many journalists have covered DREAMers for close to 20 years (Puente, 2001, 2016). More recent coverage has highlighted the progress that some youth have made with DACA in advancing their educational and career goals

(Carcamo et al., 2019). But even with the new Biden Administration there is still no permanent solution or pathway to citizenship.

In Conversation with Dianne Solis

Dianne Solis covers immigration, the border, U.S.-Mexico relations and justice issues for the Dallas Morning News. She earned her bachelor's degree in journalism at Freso State, a master's degree in journalism at Northwestern University and has completed a Nieman Fellowship at Harvard University. She started her career in broadcast journalism as a reporter trainee at a television station in Fresno, California. She also was a correspondent for The Wall Street Journal.

She served on the board of directors at Radio Bilingüe, a bilingual public radio station that became a network. She has worked as a journalist for more than 35 years.

What inspired you to become a journalist?

Solis: My father was pushing me towards writing and toward being a journalist because his father had been a part-time journalist for a Spanish-language newspaper in Fresno called El Faro. It was one of those times I actually listened to my father. And I really liked reading and writing and listening to people's stories. And I knew that those stories weren't being told or that they were undertold, and I wanted to correct that. There was sort of an erasure of our names and our voices in media, all forms of media from conventional cinema to books and news sites.

What is your approach to covering the beat of immigration?

Solis: I think it's important to approach it with humility and treat people with lots of respect. They come from different cultures and they merit that kind of respect. You'll get a richer story that way.

Because my grandparents came from another Mexico. There was a familiarity with that and I'm very comfortable. I see other journalists who are more brash and I've seen them stumble.

Over the three decades what are some of the most important stories you have covered?

Solis: I did a story three decades ago about Central American children who were arriving into Brownsville unaccompanied without parents or a guardian. They were 14 to 17, and the city was stunned. In Cameron County down at the border they were stunned. The children were coming in search of a childhood. They were largely being inscripted into the military or the guerilla movement. At that time the U.S. government reacted and created housing or what would become a shelter system for these children. I was deeply moved by three children I wrote about. I didn't use their surnames. I don't have their last names and of course I would love to find them. Of course, I have written many more stories about unaccompanied children and teens who have come to the United States largely to Texas.

The other big story that impacted me was a series of stories, more than a dozen, on the murder of a 12-year-old boy named Santos Rodriguez by a Dallas place officer. He was trying to extract a confession from the boy in a game of Russian roulette with a pistol to his temple … It blew Santos' brains out. There has been a search for justice for this boy for 48 years. He died on July 24, 1973.

At the 40-year mark, I found the mother, who was very much alive and living in poverty. I convinced her to talk to me and we developed a relationship through the years. I told that story and many more as community groups tried to find different ways to honor that child.

What is our responsibility as journalists when we interview immigrants who are undocumented?

Solis: Back at that time they were so young and I didn't speak to their parents. I don't know what became of them. The feeling was because of their youth and their undocumented status was that we would not use their last names.

But I have used last names before and we talk through the circumstances of their cases. They can decide and their attorney can decide.

Those who have DACA who want their voices and faces seen and heard and feel it's almost as a sign of respect. You hear the slogan "undocumented and unafraid." That's their choice and not everybody makes that choice.

You have a discussion with the source and each case is different. If they're minors, it's important to bring in the parents. Some parents don't want that exposure for the child but they do want the story told or the collective story told.

How do you report on immigration in a way that is fair to all sides?

Solis: A subject as cinematic as immigration benefits from a camera that is trying to do 360s and taking in many views, and many sides of the story, and literally on the Mexican side and the U.S. side, and Guatemala and the U.S. side, or on the Cameroonian and the U.S. side. I think you have a richer story as a result.

When you center immigrants in the story, you are showing their value and the respect that people should have for them. Just as you would for anybody in public policy as well. The voices that we respect and elevate speaks volumes. These kinds of stories that are rich in humanity penetrate people's defenses and get them thinking. That's really what I'm trying to do.

What advice would you give to a journalism student just starting out?

Solis: It's going to take a lot of tenacity to stay in the business. It is such a rewarding one. The examined life is just fabulous. You are always learning and that's really exciting.

Socrates said the unexamined life was not worth living, the younger me had that written somewhere on a sticky paper somewhere.

Journalism really is about the examined life and it's about going where few others have license to go and asking questions about them, their struggles and their triumphs. It's been really really rewarding.

Note: This is an edited interview transcript.

Trade Tools and Tips

It's important to discuss with a source if they want their immigration status to be public. Some sources have used their full names and others have chosen to remain anonymous. It's up to the source to decide and also discuss with your editor your media outlets guidelines. However, one policy may not apply in all situations.

The language one uses to describe immigrants should also be considered carefully. Avoid slurs, stereotypes and derogatory language.

In 2013, the Associated Press stopped using the term "illegal immigrant" (Constantini, 2013) that many in the Latinx community found offensive. Here is the recommendation from the AP, the style book that is widely used in newsrooms across the United States.

Illegal immigration *Entering or residing in a country in violation of civil or criminal law. Except in direct quotes essential to the story, use illegal only to refer to an action, not a person: illegal immigration, but not illegal immigrant. Acceptable variations include living in or entering a country illegally or without legal permission.*

Except in direct quotations, do not use the terms illegal alien, an illegal, illegals or undocumented.

Do not describe people as violating immigration laws without attribution.

Specify wherever possible how someone entered the country illegally and from where. Crossed the border? Overstayed a visa? What nationality?

People who were brought into the country as children should not be described as having immigrated illegally. For people granted a temporary right to remain in the U.S. under the Deferred Action for Childhood Arrivals program, use temporary resident status, with details on the program lower in the story.

The National Association of Hispanic Journalists (NAHJ) advocated for this change since 2006 (Carmichael & Burks, 2010) and has continued to hold news organizations accountable when using offensive terms. NAHJ cut ties with FOX News over the use of this term (Tarlo, 2019) and other inflammatory language. In 2021, NAHJ also applauded the Biden Administration for removing the word "alien" and replacing it with "non-citizen" in U.S. immigration laws.

In 2020, NAHJ released a cultural competence handbook with guidance on reporting on immigration and other issues impacting the Latinx community.

Phrases such as "illegal immigrant" and "illegal alien" replace complex and ever-changing legal circumstances with an unspecified assumption of guilt. Living in the U.S.

without legal authorization (unlawful presence) is a civil offense, while improper entry (crossing the border), is a misdemeanor. It should be noted that because many undocumented immigrants arrived legally, they have not committed a crime.

NAHJ suggests avoiding other terms such as "chain migration," used by anti-immigration groups to refer to the well- established legal process of issuing "Family-Based Immigrant Visas."

It also recommends avoiding terms like "anchor baby" "used to refer to a child born to a non-citizen parent, under the false assumption that the child will provide them a pathway to securing naturalization."

NAHJ suggests some alternative terms. "Terms that have been used to properly humanize newest Americans, newcomers, undocumented citizens, unauthorized immigrants, families who have moved from one place to another, and people who weren't born in the United States."

Dos and Don'ts

Dos

1. Do include immigration status only if it is relevant.
2. Do make sure you have permission and explain what it means to an undocumented source if you publish their name.
3. Do look for a balance of opinions and a diversity of sources on a topic.
4. Do look for stories about the challenges immigrants face and the contributions they make in the United States.
5. Do give context to the complicated subject of immigration.

Don'ts

1. Don't stereotype or generalize.
2. Don't use the word "illegal" as it refers to immigrants or people, per AP style.
3. Don't assume all Latinos are immigrants.
4. Don't assume all Latinx immigrants are of Mexican heritage.
5. Don't report on immigration as a problem.

Discussion Questions

1. Where can you look for sources on immigration? How can you seek out community sources, legal sources and government sources?
2. What are some examples of stories about the challenges that immigrants face in the United States? How can you also report on the solutions?

3. What are some of the contributions that immigrants make to the United States? How can you document and or quantify these contributions?
4. How can you portray the diversity of Latinx immigrant sources?
5. What are some of the regional or statewide differences in Latinx immigrant communities in the United States?

Assignments

1. Develop a list of ten local sources you could contact on immigration. Look for nonprofits, activists, academic experts, community and political leaders in your local community. Use databases, social media and community networks to identify sources.
2. Do a profile of a Latinx immigrant owned business. Contact your local chamber of commerce or walk around a neighborhood and find a Latinx business owner to interview.
3. Profile a Latinx immigrant who became a U.S. citizen or an immigrant who does not have permanent status. Interview them about their journey to the United States and the legal barriers or challenges they faced.
4. Interview an immigration attorney or a legal expert who can explain the difference between an immigrant, a refugee and the process for political asylum, becoming a legal permanent resident and a U.S. citizen. Ask them to explain the process for family-sponsored immigration, waiting periods and how employer-sponsored immigration works.
5. Interview a student who is an immigrant. This could be an international student and ask them about the process for obtaining a student visa. This also could be an immigrant student who came to the United States as a minor, such as a DACA recipient.

References

1942 Bracero Program (n.d.). *A Latinx Resource Guide: Civil Rights Cases and Events in the United States*. Library of Congress. Retrieved September 24, 2021. https://guides.loc.gov/latinx-civil-rights/bracero-program

Arellano, G. (2019 October 29.) *Prop. 187 Forced a Generation to Put Fear Aside and Fight. It Transformed California, and Me. Los Angeles Times*. https://www.latimes.com/california/story/2019-10-29/proposition-187-california-pete-wilson-essay

Balderrama, F.E. & Rodriguez, R. (2006). *Decade of Betrayal: Mexican Repatriation in the 1930s*. University of New Mexico Press.

Ballinger, M. (n.d.). *From the Archives: (1954-55, June) How The Times Covered Mass Deportations in the Eisenhower Era. Los Angeles Times*. Retrieved September 24, 2021. https://documents.latimes.com/eisenhower-era-deportations/

Belluck, P. (2008 October 15). *Settlement Will Allow Thousands of Mexican Laborers in U.S. to Collect Back Pay. New York Times*. https://www.nytimes.com/2008/10/16/us/16settle.html

Benenson, L. (2020 October 16). *Fact Sheet: Deferred Action for Childhood Arrivals (DACA)*. National Immigration Forum. https://immigrationforum.org/article/fact-sheet-on-deferred-action-for-childhood-arrivals-daca/

Block, M. (2006 March 28). *Spanish D.J. Organizes Immigration-Reform Protests*. NPR https://www.npr.org/templates/story/story.php?storyId=5307593

Blakemore, E. (2019 June 18) *The Largest Mass Deportation in American History*. History. https://www.history.com/news/operation-wetback-eisenhower-1954-deportation

Bracero History Archive (n.d.). Retrieved September 24, 2021. http://braceroarchive.org/about

California's Anti-Immigration Proposition 187 is Voided, Ending States Five Year Battle with ACLU, Rights Groups. (1999 July 29). ACLU. Retrieved September 24, 2021. https://www.aclu.org/press-releases/cas-anti-immigrant-proposition-187-voided-ending-states-five-year-battle-aclu-rights

Carcamo, C., Castillo, A., Watanabe, T. & Kohli, S. (2019). *DACA Changed a Generation of California Immigrants. These are Some of Their Stories. Los Angeles Times*. https://www.latimes.com/california/story/2019-11-12/daca-supreme-court-dreamers

Carmichael, K. & Burks, R.A. (2010 December 17) *Undocumented or Illegal?* AJR. https://ajrarchive.org/Article.asp?id=5002

Carrasquillo, A. (2019 August 10). *This is what Latinos think Everyone got Wrong about El Paso. Politico*. https://www.politico.com/magazine/story/2019/08/10/el-paso-shooting-227612/

Chavez, L. (2008). *The Latino Threat: Constructing Immigrants, Citizens, and the Nation*, Stanford University Press. https://doi.org/10.1017/S0022216X10000404

College Options for Undocumented Students (n.d.). Cappex. Retrieved September 24, 2021. https://www.cappex.com/articles/match-and-fit/college-options-undocumented-students

Corchado, A. & Sandoval, R. (2002 January 27). *Braceros Want an Old Promise Met. Dallas Morning News*. http://www.latinamericanstudies.org/immigration/braceros1.htm

Constantini, C. (2013 April 2.) *Associated Press Drops 'Illegal Immigrant' From Stylebook. ABCNews*.https://abcnews.go.com/ABC_Univision/press-drops-illegal-immigrant-standards-book/story?id=18862824

Cultural Competence Handbook. (2020 August) National Association of Hispanic Journalists (NAHJ). Retrieved September 24, 2021. https://nahj.org/wp-content/uploads/2020/08/NAHJ-Cultural-Competence-Handbook.pdf

The Dream Act. An Overview. (2021 March 16) American Immigration Council. https://www.americanimmigrationcouncil.org/research/dream-act-overview

Dreamers by the Numbers. (2021 March 21) fwd.Us. https://www.fwd.us/news/dreamers-by-the-numbers/

Edgar, D. (2013 May 1). *L.A. Times Updates Guidelines for Covering Immigration. Los Angeles Times*. https://www.latimes.com/local/readers-rep/la-me-rr-la-times-guidelines-immigration-20130501-story.html

Engler, M. & Engler, P. (2016 March 4) *Op-Ed: The Massive Immigrant-Rights Protests of 2006 are Still Changing Politics. Los Angeles Times*. https://www.latimes.com/opinion/op-ed/la-oe-0306-engler-immigration-protests-2006-20160306-story.html

Federation for American Immigration Reform. Southern Poverty Law Center (n.d.). Retrieved Sept. 24, 2021. https://www.splcenter.org/fighting-hate/extremist-files/group/federation-american-immigration-reform

A Forgotten Injustice. (2008 October 2). WBEZ. https://www.wbez.org/stories/a-forgotten-injustice/9f08c7da-57e5-4fa5-a7ad-e4c33332df52

Garcia-Navarro, L. (2019 August 9) *The Media Erased Latinos From the Story. The Atlantic.* https://www.theatlantic.com/ideas/archive/2019/08/we-must-recognize-hispanics-were-targeted/595783/

Koestler, F.L. (1995, December 1) *Operation Wetback.* Texas State Historical Association, Handbook of Texas. https://www.tshaonline.org/handbook/entries/operation-wetback

Lind, D. (2015 November 11) *Operation Wetback, the 1950s Immigration Policy Donald Trump Loves, Explained. Vox.* https://www.vox.com/2015/11/11/9714842/operation-wetback

Little, B. (2019, July 12). *The U.S. Deported Millions of its Own Citizens to Mexico During the Great Depression.* History. https://www.history.com/news/great-depression-repatriation-drives-mexico-deportation

Loop, E. (2017 September 5). *Five Democrats Voted Against the Dream Act in 2010. Now Moderates are Fighting Trump. Buzzfeed.* https://www.buzzfeednews.com/article/emmaloop/some-senate-democrats-used-to-shy-away-from-dreamers-but

Lopez, M.H., Krogstad, J.M. & Passel, J.S. (2021 September 23) *Who is Hispanic?* Pew Research Center. https://www.pewresearch.org/fact-tank/2021/09/23/who-is-hispanic/

NAHJ Applauds Biden Administration's Immediate Focus on the Impact of Language in Proposed Immigration Bill. (2021 January 21). NAHJ.org. https://nahj.org/2021/01/21/nahj-applauds-biden-administrations-focus-on-language/

Noe-Bustamante, L. (2019 September 16) *Facts about U.S. Hispanics and their diverse heritage.* Pew Research Center. https://www.pewresearch.org/fact-tank/2019/09/16/key-facts-about-u-s-hispanics/

Puente, T. (2001 June 5). *Illegal Immigrants Face Barrier in Pursuit of College Education. Chicago Tribune.* 2C.1.

Puente, T. (2011 March 11). Undocumented and Unafraid. *Chicanísima Chicago. Chicago Now.* https://www.chicagonow.com/chicanisima-latino-politics-news-and-culture/2011/03/dream-act-youth-rally-in-chicago/#image/1

Puente, T. (2016 November 10). *The Nightmare of Donald Trump's Deportation Promise. Time.* https://time.com/4566512/donald-trump-deportation-promise/

Rose, J. (2018 June 1). *Protesters Across The U.S. Decry Policy Of Separating Immigrant Families.* NPR. https://www.npr.org/2018/06/01/616257822/immigration-rights-activists-protest-trump-administration-child-separation-polic

Spagat, E. (2021 June 8). *US Identifies 3,900 Children Separated at Border Under Trump.* Associated Press. https://apnews.com/article/az-state-wire-donald-trump-immigration-lifestyle-government-and-politics-54e2e5bbff270019d8bda3c81161c7c7

Tarlo, S. (2019 August 23) *Nation's Largest Hispanic Journalist Group Cuts Ties With Fox News Over Migrant "Invasion" Rhetoric.* Salon. https://www.salon.com/2019/08/23/nations-largest-hispanic-journalist-group-cuts-ties-with-fox-news-over-migrant-invasion-rhetoric/

Tenore, M.J. (2011 November 7) *Despite Criticism, AP Stylebook Dictates that Journalists use 'Illegal Immigrant'. Poynter.* https://www.poynter.org/reporting-editing/2011/despite-criticism-ap-stylebook-dictates-that-journalists-use-illegal-immigrant/

Thompson, G. (2018 June 18). *Listen to Children Who've Just Been Separated From Their Parents at the Border. ProPublica.* https://www.propublica.org/article/children-separated-from-parents-border-patrol-cbp-trump-immigration-policy

Treaty of Guadalupe Hidalgo (n.d.). National Archives. Retrieved September 24, 2021. https://www.archives.gov/education/lessons/guadalupe-hidalgo

Ura, A. (2019, August 5) *A Racist Manifesto and a Shooter Terrorize Hispanics in El Paso and Beyond. Texas Tribune.* https://www.texastribune.org/2019/08/05/hispanics-terrorized-after-el-paso-shooting-and-racist-manifesto/

9

Reporting on the Latino Vote and the Diverse Latino Electorate

Mercedes Vigón and Alejandro Alvarado Bremer

With the approach of every election cycle, presidential or midterm election, a debate on the potential impact of the Latino vote intensifies, especially in the mainstream media. Most of this reporting highlights the potential impact of the vote.

Here were some of the headlines about the Latino vote:

> Latino Voters Moved Toward Republicans. Now Biden Wants Them Back.
>
> (New York Times, Medina & Lerer, 2021)

> New data helps explain Trump's gains among Latino voters in 2020.
>
> (Vox, Narea, 2021)

> The New Swing Voters.
>
> (The Atlantic, Brownstein, 2021)

Latino residents represented 19% of the total population in 2020, compared to 16% in 2010 and 13.5% in 2000.

Despite the complexities that we´ll discuss during this chapter, the 2020 presidential election provides a clear example of the influence of the Hispanic electorate in the United States.

While many of the headlines indicated more Latinos were turning Republican, actual data showed the Latino vote is still solidly Democratic.

DOI: 10.4324/9781003212331-9

After analyzing 13 key states with 80% of the nation´s Latinos, an UCLA report concluded that the Latino electorate was responsible for tipping the power balance in this presidential election. Their findings showed Latinos´ votes aligned with the Democratic candidate, Joseph R. Biden, by very wide margins across the country.

The results were clear: in Arizona, a state who has consistently voted for a Republican candidate since 1996, the size of the Latino electorate, mostly supporting Biden, flipped the state to Democrat. The difference between one candidate and the other was smaller in Georgia and Wisconsin, but again the growth in Latino voters and their support for Biden, helped tip the state in favor of Biden (Domínguez-Villegas et al., 2021).

To understand the significance of Latino Hispanic, or Latinx vote at a national level, especially in the battleground states, it's important to consider the role of the U.S. Electoral College. Its role is to choose the president, but its members are not allocated proportionally to the number of people who vote for a political party in each state. The winner of each state by a simple majority (half + one) gets all the electoral votes in most of the country (Tacher Contreras, 2020).

During the presidential election, the U.S. candidates concentrated their campaign efforts in the battleground states. To identify them, it is useful to review each state voting record for at least 20 years. From 2000 to 2016, 38 states have voted for the same political party. Those states are known as the "blocked states," and hardly ever change party affiliation. There are exceptions: in 2016 President Donald Trump was able to win Michigan, Pennsylvania and Wisconsin, which had been blue or Democratic states since at least 1992. In 2020, President Biden recovered them, and also won Arizona and Georgia, which last voted for a Democratic presidential candidate in 1996 and 1992, respectively. Still, the candidates organized their campaigns knowing that the presidential elections are decided by the margins, a handful of states, the battleground states, which might shift from one election to the next.

The Diversity of the Latino Vote

When reporting on elections, it is imperative to examine the U.S. population by demographic factors. In the case of the Latino vote in addition to segmenting them state by state, reporters must identify Latinos' immigration status and their generation/s since their arrival to the country. They also should focus on Latino voters who are eligible to vote as U.S. citizens and also why those who may be eligible for citizenship haven't applied for it.

Latinos have different levels of political integration and a varied sense of belonging to this country. Recent immigrants without voting rights have limited access to political participation or representation; some naturalized or permanent citizens might have not registered to vote, or might not have developed

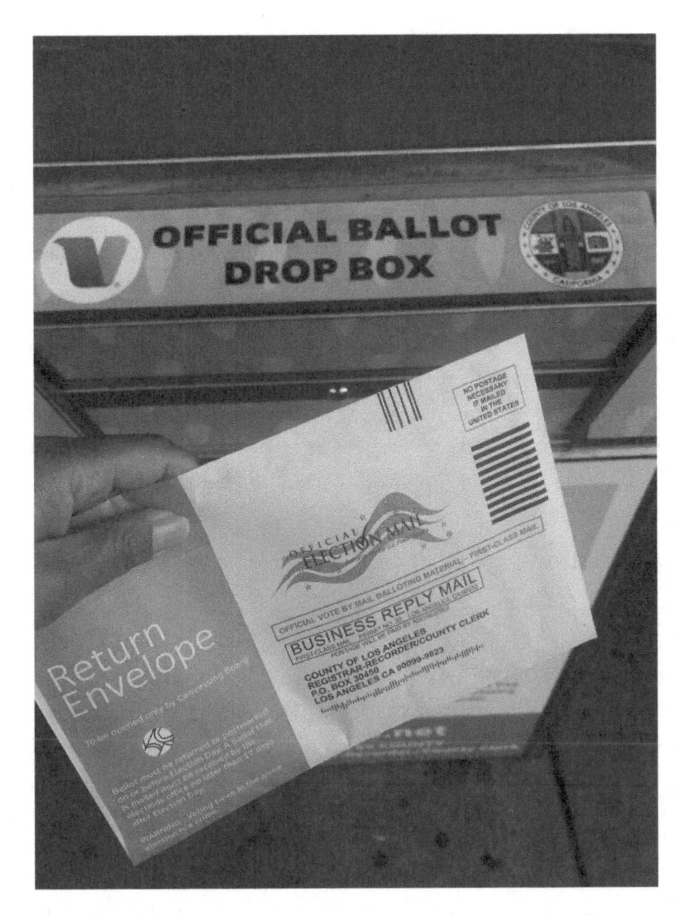

FIGURE 9.1 Photos of voting booth by Teresa Puente.

an interest in participating or choosing elective officials. Other Latinos, who have been seen multiple generations since their ancestors arrived, might be more prone to register to vote, participate, or even to become elected officials. Some Mexican-Americans from California, Nevada, Utah, New Mexico, Texas, Colorado, parts of Arizona, Wyoming, Kansas and Oklahoma lived in American territories long before they were part of this country. When Mexico gave up half of its territory to the United States, after losing the war in 1848, Mexicans living in these areas were invited to become U.S. citizens. They now might be considered founding members of the United States of America.

These different levels of integration and experience in the fabric of the society help explain why the growth of Hispanic population in the United States has not translated into a similar growth in political participation or political representation. However, Latino political representation in the United States has constantly increased during the last decade reaching 6,882 elected officials in 2019, reports the National Association of Elected Officials, or NALEO Still, this figure accounts for a little more than 1% of all local and federal officials in the United States. New Mexico and Florida have the nation's highest percentage of Latino political representation. Elected officials of these states represent 48.8% and 26%, respectively, of their total population. Florida has benefited from decades of political activism in Cuban, Puerto Rican, Venezuela and other Hispanic communities. But Latinos do not always choose their own ethnicity as representatives. For example, in Central Florida, the Puerto Rican community of Orange and Osceola counties have chosen three county commissioners from their island, but they have yet to elect one representative or senator for Tallahassee. A Politico survey reported that Florida Puerto Ricans, half of them from these counties, considered corruption as one of their main concerns and they also distrust many of the Puerto Rican public figures from the island.

Voter Participation

Several factors help to explain why the growth of the Latino population never translated into a similar growth of the Latino electorate.

First, as we already mentioned, many Latinos are immigrants. And around 20% of these immigrants have no citizenship. Second, the Latino population includes a high share of minors, not yet eligible to vote.

Still, researchers point out that the power of the future Latino vote could also be found in the youth population. There are more than 18 million Latinos under 18, roughly 30% of the Latino population. It is estimated that 800,000 Latinos who are U.S. citizens turn 18 every year (Axios, 2020).

And finally, a decisive factor is the turnout: even when Hispanics are eligible, they still need to register and be able to go and vote or mail their ballot.

Latino turnout during past elections has been low compared with other racial and ethnic groups in the country, reports the Pew Research Center, a nonpartisan fact tank dedicated to following these types of trends with data-driven social science research. During the 2020 election, when Latino turnout drastically improved, "Hispanic adults were 10% of the voters but 20% of the nonvoting citizens." This contrasts with African Americans who were 11% of the voters and only 14% of the nonvoters, or Asian Americans which made 4% of the voters and an identical share of nonvoting citizens (Igielnik et al., 2021).

Still on the bright side, during the 2020 presidential election, Latino turnout drastically changed: more than 60% of Hispanic citizens registered to vote, and 88% of them, or 16.6 million, voted. This represented more than a 30% increase, the largest 4-year increase in Latino vote ever (Domínguez-Villegas et al., 2021; Igielnik et al., 2021).

So Why Do We Use Latino/Hispanic or Latinx If We Are So Different?

The U.S. Census started to use the term Latino or Hispanic in the 1960s, as a pan-ethnic group tracing their origin to Latin American and Spain. Despite recriminations that this homogenous term hides Latino communities' richness and diversity, the use of the term endures (Taylor et al., 2012). Scholars, such as Tacher Contreras (2020) and Mora (2014), argue that these terms have proven useful not only as self-awareness, but also to increase the spaces and opportunities for political participation and representation. Cadava (2020) and other researchers have argued that preferences cut across class, political views, being native born or immigrant, or from older or younger generations. According to them, Hispanic would be chosen more often among wealthy/middle class, conservatives, native born and older generations, while Latino would be used more often among working-class, liberals, immigrants or younger generations. Still, most studies suggest that it is actually based on regional use (Lopez, 2013; García, 2020).

Nowadays, the Pew Research Center refers to "Hispanics" or "Latinos" interchangeably. The Census Bureau prefers the term "Hispanic." The classical explanation is that the term "Hispanics" refers to people from Spanish-speaking countries in Latin America and in Spain, excluding Brazil; while "Latinos" are people from all Latin American countries (including Brazil, but not Spain (García, 2020; Igielnik et al., 2021).

This chapter will use the terms Latino or Hispanic interchangeably, following the finding of the Pew Research Center: a 2015 survey identified that "32% of Hispanics prefer to use the term 'Hispanic,' 15% prefer the term 'Latino' and the rest (51%) have no preference" (Lopez et al., 2020). These researchers concluded that Latinx, a label created more recent as an alternative to Hispanic or Latino, is used only by 3% of the Latino population, according to the previously mentioned survey from the Pew Center. Most of the adult Latino population has never heard of it (76%), and the other 20% of the Hispanic population have heard of Latinx but do not use it (Noe-Bustamante et al, 2020).

The Census and the Pew Center are key primary sources when reporting on Latino issues. They release information periodically, updating it continuously. To keep up with their newest findings, you can subscribe to them:

- https://www.census.gov/newsroom/subscriptions.html
- The Pew Center published surveys and reports on Latino issues/trends constantly:
- https://www.pewresearch.org/about/follow-us/

What Issues Do Latino Voters Care About?

During the electoral cycles, news directors and managing editors balance the day-to-day campaign coverage, with the in-depth reporting. Among the immense wealth of information and the demands of continuous updates, reporters confront the challenge to produce more than horse race stories. These are daily stories which focus on pooling data and public perception. Despite the criticism of many scholars, they serve a purpose, but they must be complemented with other stories covering candidate policies, campaign finance, advertising expenditures, fact-checking, election explainers and of course, the issues and priorities of the public.

To overcome this difficulty, reporters start by identifying Latino communities with the demographic labels provided by the Census and different surveys. Armed with this data, they are equipped to gain a clear understanding and map the issues that specific Latino communities confront.

Also, it's important for reporters to focus on what are the top issues that concern Latino voters when developing story angles. For Latino voters, the economy (80%), healthcare (76%), the coronavirus outbreak (72%) and racial and ethnic inequality (66%) were the top election issues (Krogstad & Lopez, 2020). Latino voters were concerned but less so with the following issues: Supreme Court appointments (64%), violent crime (63%), climate change (60%), immigration (59%), gun policy (58%), foreign policy (57%), economic inequality (52%) and abortion (41%).

Reporting on other election issues open up to different subtopics. For example, a reporter inquiring on access to housing could gather information about affordability, safety or quality of life. She could ask the following questions: can your kids play outside the house, or drive their bikes around the block? Can they go to parks nearby? Does the neighborhood have good lighting at night? How is the public transportation or the traffic in the area? Is their housing threatened by climate change, fire or flooding? How is the quality of their air, soil, water? Is there any source of pollution close by? Do they have easy access to fresh products? And access to entertainment?

As these issues constantly evolve, a reporter taps into the communities to follow them.

Political News Coverage for U.S. Latinos

A group of news directors defining excellence in journalism agreed that the best electoral coverage needs to minimize the horse race reporting and focus more on issues. This strategy has been successful in facilitating a better understanding between local candidates and their Latino residents. It also allows reporters to change the dynamic of their delivery from only following the daily events to a more substantial coverage (Rosenstiel & Al, 2007).

FIGURE 9.2 Photos of election win 2020 by Teresa Puente

Local news directors send their reporters to comb the Latino communities and evaluate the changes of Hispanics worries and desires. During election times, these news media invite random Latinos residents to participate in focus groups, or other informal meetings, and gain a better understanding of the complexity and evolution of the Latino in their regions or nationwide. This allows reporters to identify disconnects and address contractions between proposed representative campaigns and their Latino constituencies. In these cases, reporters can act as bridges requesting politicians to give concrete answers on complex or oversimplified Latino issues and asking candidates and Hispanics alike to square up contradictions.

A Closer Look: NALEO and Latino Elected and Appointed Officials

The National Association of Latino Elected and Appointed Officials or NALEO, is a non-profit, non-partisan membership organization of more than 6,800 Latino elected and appointed officials in the United States.

They also collect data on the growth of Latino elected officials in the United States regardless of the political party.

In the 117th (2021) Congress there are currently 46 Latinos. There are 40 U.S. representatives and 6 U.S. senators (Schaeffer, 2021).

In 2021, only one governor, Michelle Lujan Grisham was Hispanic, a Democrat in New Mexico. In U.S. history, 15 Hispanic people have served as U.S. governors, the greatest number – seven – from the state of New Mexico.

NALEO was founded by U.S. Representative Edward Roybal in 1976, and he served as NALEO president until 1999. The original name was the National Association of Latino Democratic Officials. The name changed in 1978 to represent all Latino elected officials regardless of party.

In 1981, the NALEO Educational Fund was established with the aim to increase Latino political representation across the country.

In 2020, NALEO and other Latino organizations advocated for President-elect Joe Biden to appoint at least five Latinos to cabinet-level positions (Isaad, 2021). Among the Latinos in Biden's top team are Dr. Miguel Cardona, Secretary of Education; Isabel Guzman, Small Business Administrator; Xavier Becerra, Health and Human Service Secretary; and Alejandro Mayorkas, Homeland Security Secretary.

Arturo Vargas, chief executive of NALEO Educational Fund, said the new 2020 U.S. Census numbers should persuade state officials to put Hispanics at the forefront when forming policies and drawing districts.

The results of the 2020 Census showed the overall Hispanic population in the United States grew by 23%, to a total of 62.1 million. Since 2010, 51.1% of the total U.S. population growth came from the Latino population (Krogstad & Noe-Bustamante, 2021). In the 2020 Census, more than 20 million Latinos identified with more than one race on the 2020 census, up from just 3 million in 2010.

As of 2019, 12 states had Hispanic populations of at least 1 million – Arizona, California, Colorado, Florida, Georgia, Illinois, New Jersey, New Mexico, New York, North Carolina, Pennsylvania and Texas (Portela, 2021).

"People haven't recognized that Latinos are changing the face of the nation," Vargas told The Washington Post. "There is a meaningful and significant Latino population in virtually all states, except maybe Vermont, New Hampshire and Maine. … What I would hope is that policymakers begin looking at their decisions about resource allocation and other policies through a Latino lens."

A Conversation with Daniel Coronell, News President at Univision from 2011 to 2021

Coronell covered the last three presidential elections: 2012, 2016 and 2020.

Telemundo and Univision are the two Hispanic media with the highest audience and economic power in the U.S. Hispanic market. They have been on the market for at least 30 years each, with programming that includes entertainment and news.

How Diverse are Latinos Politically?

Coronell: They are very diverse. Their decisions are marked by structural aspects of their affiliation but also circumstantial. In the last presidential election, in Zapata county in Texas, a Democrat ended up voting for Donald Trump. The reason? They were afraid of Biden's response from the oil industry. There are things that they tend to identify. Every four years someone discovers Hispanics. We must start from diversity. We are at a crucial moment. We are at the center of the controversy. We are not all equal, there is little in common with a Mexican immigrant from Texas with a Cuban from Miami. It is important that the political class understands the diversity of the Hispanic voter. It is important to increase the representativeness of Hispanic voters. We should be 19 and we have 4 (U.S.) senators. And those four do not represent the demographic composition of the United States either.

Are Univision Journalists Liberal or Conservative? How do You Deal with it?

Coronell: Univision journalists are first and foremost journalists. Certainly the newsroom is not a homogeneous group, in the same way that Hispanics are not a uniform community. We, reporters, have different ways of seeing life but a common purpose: to provide citizens with reliable information. Our journalistic duty to report impartially must always be above our political preferences as individuals. At the same time, journalists everywhere must be clear that we work for the citizens, that we are public servants above corporate employees. Univision's historic commitment to the Hispanic community is its greatest asset and should go beyond any political or business juncture.

What is the attitude of conservative Latino voters towards the media, particularly Telemundo and Univision?

Coronell: Unlike entertainment, news is not primarily intended to flatter audiences. As journalists, we have a duty to tell people what they like and what they don't like. This example that I am going to give you is exaggerated. Imagine if the Warsaw Jewish newspaper put victims and perpetrators on the same front page. Donald Trump attacked Hispanics. He made an unfair generalization pointing to Hispanic as criminals, thieves and rapists. The job of a journalist is not to be a passive actor, but to be a critic. Reporters are not a simple transmission belt of what the powerful say. We must diligently differentiate what is true from what is not. These types of speeches are reported clarifying that they are based on false arguments. It is a duty that we have to fulfill, even if a part of the audience dislikes it. Journalistic credibility is built by seeking the truth, not popularity.

Is there a difference between the first-generation Latino voter and the second and third generation?

Coronell: There is a difference, and it is very noticeable in Florida and California. The first-generation voter looks for what is happening in his country by identifying what is happening in the United States. In the second generation, they have no historical frames of reference. We all carry cultural and educational loads that create a particular perspective for us. In many members of the Cuban community, issues cross generations. U.S.-Cuba relations. Many members of the Hispanic community are economic or political exiles. It is impossible that this does not mark the historical heritage of a family.

How does it affect content production?

Coronell: (Some) 48% are first and second grade immigrants, and 46% of the third and fourth. There are some people in the audience studies who don't feel they speak fluently but see Univision for cultural identity. Hispanics represent 18% of the U.S. population, (but) the media in English only dedicates 2% of programming on topics that interest Latinos.

What are the main issues that concern Latinos in campaign times?

Coronell: There have been big changes. I have covered three elections. In the reelection of President Obama, the immigration issue was not a priority. In the Trump campaign, it went from third to first, with employment and the economy. And with Biden, the issue of health, economy, employment, migration became fourth. But it is still important. And even more it is a determining matter.

A Conversation with Manuel Aguilera

Aguilera is director of ChapinesUSA, founder and CEO of HispanoPost, former executive director of Diario Las Americas, and former director of programming at Univision Interactive Media. Aguilera covered the 2008 presidential elections for the Spanish newspaper El Mundo; the 2012 elections for Univision Digital and the 2016 and 2020 elections for HispanoPost.

How diverse is the Latino community in the United States?

Aguilera: The Hispanic community in the United States is totally diverse. What many times they want to sell by the big media or by the big agencies, which have commercial interests, homogenize the entire Latino community. It is a very easy speech for advertisers, to get investment, and also politically. In reality, there are thousands of Hispanic markets and thousands of behaviors, and I think there is a tendency to homogenize the idea, the Latino community politically. There is practically no difference between the editorial line of Univision and Telemundo. I think that because they start from the premise that the Latino community can only be offered information from that point of view.

So, do you think that, for example, the conservative voter is left out?

Aguilera: Well, I think it is not conceivable, that is, I think there is a stereotype, which is the Latino who has immigration problems, if not him, a relative, and is very interested in migration. They tend more toward Democrats than Republicans, who in theory are enemies of migrants. Most Latinos should perhaps be conservative because of their past, often religious Catholic (background). They come from countries where they have suffered from crises caused by the left or by excesses of populist governments. In the end, this interpretation is made that the majority of Latinos in the United States would have to be of Democratic tendency.

But in reality, there is a difference in Latino voters even by country of origin.

Aguilera: Yes, of course, that's what the first thing I said, that is, diversity is total. What does the reality of a Cuban who arrived with the Adjustment Law have to do with that of a Guatemalan who entered the border on foot? They really have in common the language, some cultural traits, but their vital, personal and social adventures do not have much to do with it. That is why I think it is a mistake to insist on talking about a monolithic bloc among Hispanics.

And what is the reason for this eagerness to try to homogenize the Latino voter?

Aguilera: I think it is also a question of poorly understood survival. I believe that the large Hispanic media think that if they fail to impose that perception that Latino is homogeneous, the business is going to collapse. Ultimately, you depend on attracting as many Spanish-speaking people as possible.

In your experience, on the one hand, is there an agenda of topics that interest the media? Perhaps there is another agenda of issues that concern Latinos in campaign times. What would those themes be?

Aguilera: The great motivation of the Latino does not differ much from that of the non-Latino, of the American. In the end I think the economy is the big issue. In this last election, COVID has been crossed, which also has an economic component. The most important thing for the voter is if you are going to find a job, if you are going to be able to pay the mortgage, if you are going to be able to pay for your children's university. For example, regarding immigration, not that it is an issue that all Latinos have. Too many people are very settled in this country, no matter Latin origin, it is not that it is an issue that matters to them because they have already resolved it. We are talking about first generations of Latinos but also second.

Do you think that the coverage of the elections gives the same space to the preferences of conservative Latino voters as to those of liberals and progressives?

Aguilera: I do not think so. A number of interests within the Latino community are taken for granted that make the debate revolve around some Democratic issues. There is a perception that Democrats are softer on immigration issues, that they provide more facilities. In reality, for example, President Barack Obama was the president who deported the most immigrants in history. Yes, I think that a nod is made more to the themes that favor the Democratic Party.

If you could locate Telemundo and Univision in the ideological political geography of the left, center, right, where would you locate them?

Aguilera: I think center-left. If I see them with a tendency more towards what the Democrats can be. But I think that in the case of CNN en Español, much more. However, the inside of the organizations themselves, especially Telemundo and Univisión, are in the affiliates, and they have different political views with respect to the national media. But, for example, América TV, a local Miami station, has an even more conservative line closer to the Cuban community, and it has worked for them.

Should the journalist become an activist, lose his neutrality?

Aguilera: Not totally. That scares me a lot and I think that the activists must be others, right?

We, precisely, what we must tell is all the faces of one truth. I remember the 2016 election, when Trump won. The Univision show looked like a funeral. Regardless, we all have a political tendency, it is undeniable. You cannot tell people that journalists are pure souls, that we have no ideology or preferences. But when it comes to giving information, we should be impartial, and we must give the same importance to one candidate as to another and really that a candidate wins, and I changed my face, or another seems inappropriate. I believe that the exercise of journalism is based on independence, objectivity and above all, on the differentiation of journalistic genres. When information is made, information is made, another thing is opinion.

Note: These are edited transcripts of the interviews

Trade Tools and Tips

When reporting in the diverse Latino vote, there are different approaches depending on the objectives:

- To evaluate the demographic increase on Latino residents in the United States highlighting the impact that the Hispanics might have on the election results. The main sources used in these stories are polls, surveys, experts and analysts who make predictions. Some journalists and scholars discard this coverage as horse race reporting. Others argue that this approach increases national interest in Latino issues, which can result in a more nuanced coverage.
- To follow individual candidates, or political parties, appearances and the outreach efforts towards the Latino communities. The main sources are political personalities, who might pledge allegiance to some of the Latino issues.
- To provide accurate information about the candidates and the options to the public so they can make an informed decision. This type of coverage, key to guaranteeing a healthy democratic system, also allows the audience to evaluate the campaign promises alignment with their most prevalent issues. When done well, it also counters election misinformation and propaganda.

Essential Resources for the U.S. Election

Not-for-profit organizations, media groups and academics have created an immense wealth of information to help journalists and the general public to analyze the election data. The Global Investigative Journalism Network compiled an extensive online roundup of the best resources for the 2020 Elections. It is organized by topics such as Analysis, Polls, and Roundups, Campaign Finance, Advertising Expenditures, Fake News and Fact-Checking, Election Coverage How-To's, Election Security, Election Explainers, Legal Issues and Dirty Tricks, and Speeches, Transcripts, Tweet and Videos, Voter Data, Voting Rights and Rules and Voting Results.

- https://gijn.org/essential-resources-for-the-us-election-a-field-guide-for-journalists-on-the-frontlines/

Another type of service coverage, prevalent in the Spanish-language stations, is to explain the American democratic system to the recently arrived Latino immigrants from A to Z. The objective is informing their audiences on the necessary steps to become a naturalized U.S. citizen, and also to be able to vote.

National campaign coverage tips (Provided by Lourdes Torres, Senior Vice President of Political Coverage and Special Projects at Univision.)

Torres has covered seven presidential elections, Bill Clinton's was the first she covered in 1996.

1. The main objectives of political news coverage are:
   - Report so that voters can exercise their vote with knowledge.
   - To educate the audience about a complex electoral system, very different from that of their countries.
   - Encourage civic participation in a democratic process.
   - Make Latinos take responsibility for their destiny.
2. Electoral coverage includes the elimination processes of both parties, or primaries, in what is an effort to educate and also arouse electoral interest among Latino voters.
3. The electoral process in the United States is complex, the result of the electoral college and of being a democratic republic in which power is shared between the federal and state governments. Therefore, electoral processes vary from state to state. Understanding this helps to understand this country intimately from a political, social and even cultural point of view.
4. Politicians, in general, really do not know the Latino community. They tend to show up during their campaigns and say things to ingratiate themselves with the voters. As a medium we have a responsibility to inform about the candidates and their positions on issues vital to Latinos beyond their speeches. As a medium and as Latinos living in this country, we must reclaim our political space and not give our vote to a candidate who does not support his speeches with facts.
5. Keep pressure on the candidates to get the same access that the non-Latino media has. Campaigns tend to put Latinos in a second or third category. Latinos are commonly assigned to "work" by Spanish-language media that do not have a high level of access to candidates. Insist that they give us space and recognition and that we have access to the people who make decisions. This translates into getting interviews and debates with candidates and then presidents.
6. Ultimately, the imperative is that the Latino voter casts their vote in an informed manner. Part of our job is to inform ourselves. The use of surveys is very important. They are expensive, complicated and not very "sexy" in the television ratings. However, it provides us with information on the issues of most concern. This helps us pinpoint questions for candidates and decide which stories to ask reporters for. In addition to surveys, being connected to community organizations is vital to know empirically what editorial orientation we give to coverage.
7. Political specials are usually community forums and/or political debates. The topics of interest are put by the participants. It might come as a surprise,

but Latinos are not only interested in immigration (as many politicians understand). Latinos are NOT a monolithic community but they are united by the diversity of opinions and experiences.

8. One of the many tools to control the fulfillment of these objectives is the editorial meeting, before, during and after the coverage. And it has to be multiplatform. You should plan coverage giving space and space to digital, social, local and radio platforms. In each medium, Latinos from different social profiles are found and each one is vital. Each platform has its art and beauty. But the goals are the same for all of them.

Discussion Questions

1. How diverse is the Hispanic electorate nationwide? How diverse is your state? Does your state have adequate Latinx political representation?
2. Do you think the mainstream media painted an accurate picture of Latino voters in the 2020 presidential election? What did they get right or wrong? What did they miss?
3. Who was the first Latino elected official in your state? How many Latino elected officials are there in your state from the local to statewide level?
4. What new ideas can you bring to election coverage?

Assignments

1. Analyze some recent election stories. Can you identify any political bias or preference for a political party?
2. Check the U.S. Census data on Latinos in your state. Identify: national origin, ideology (liberal, progressive, centered), level of education, geography, or any other data that you find relevant. What story ideas can you develop about diverse Latinos voters?
3. Identify the issues most relevant to Hispanics during election times. Differentiate the issues nationwide, from those in your state, and in your neighborhood.
4. Watch some of the election stories from Spanish-language networks. What differences do you notice in coverage compared to English-language network news?

References

Axios. (2020, October 20) Voting Rights Activist: 800,000 Latino citizens turn 18 every year. https://www.axios.com/latino-voters-eligible-citizens-815d44bf-9040-48b7-9a2c-fc57af4eda8b.html

Brownstein, R. (2021, April 22.) *The new swing voters*. *The Atlantic*. https://www.theatlantic.com/politics/archive/2021/04/can-biden-win-over-latinos-he-lost-trump/618669/

Cadava, G. (2020). *The Hispanic Republican: The shaping of an American political identity, from Nixon to Trum*. Haper & Brothers.

Domínguez-Villegas, R., Gonzalez, N., Guitierrez, A., Hernández, K., Herdon, M., Oaxaca, A., Rios, M., Roman, M., Rush, T., & Vera, D. (2021, January 19). *Vote choice of Latino voters in the 2020 presidential election*. Latino Policy & Politics Initiative, UCLA. https://latino.ucla.edu/wp-content/uploads/2021/01/Election-2020-Report-1.19.pdf

García, I. (2020, May). Cultural insights for planners: Understanding the terms Hispanic, Latino, and Latinx. *Journal of the American Planning Association*, 86 (2) 393–402. https://doi.org/10.1080/01944363.2020.1758191

Igielnik, R., Keeter, S., & Hartig, H (2021, June). *Behind Biden's 2020 victory. An examination of the 2020 electorate, based on validated voters*. Pew Research Center. https://www.pewresearch.org/politics/2021/06/30/behind-bidens-2020-victory/

Isaad, V. (2021, January 21) *President Joe Biden's diverse cabinet includes four Latinx members*. HipLatina. https://hiplatina.com/biden-latino-cabinet-members/

Krogstad, J.M. & Lopez, M.H. (2020). *Hispanic voters say economy, health care, and COVID-19 are top issues in the 2020 presidential election*. Pew Research Center. https://www.pewresearch.org/fact-tank/2020/09/11/hispanic-voters-say-economy-health-care-and-covid-19-are-top-issues-in-2020-presidential-election/

Krogstad, J.M. & Noe-Bustamante, L. (2021, September 9.) *Facts about U.S. Latinos for National Hispanic Heritage Month*. Pew Research Center. https://www.pewresearch.org/fact-tank/2021/09/09/key-facts-about-u-s-latinos-for-national-hispanic-heritage-month/#:~:text=As%20of%202018%2C%20about%2080, who%20have%20become%20naturalized%20citizens

Lopez, M. H., Krogstad, J. M. & Passel J. S. (2020, September 15). *Who is Hispanic?* Pew Research Center. https://www.pewresearch.org/fact-tank/2020/09/15/who-is-hispanic/

Lopez, M. H. (2013, October 28). *Hispanic or Latino? Many don't care, except in Texas*. Pew Research Center. https://www.pewresearch.org/fact-tank/2013/10/28/in-texas-its-hispanic-por-favor/

Medina, J. & Lerer. L. (2021, July 27). *Latino voters moved toward Republicans. Now Biden wants them back. New York Times*. https://www.nytimes.com/2021/07/27/us/politics/latino-voters-biden-democrats.html

Mora, C. (2014). *Making Hispanics. How Activists, Bureaucrats, and Media Constructed a New American*. The University of Chicago Press.

NALEO, The National Association of Latino Elected and Appointed Officials Educational Fund. *2019 Directory of Latino Elected Officials*. https://naleo.org/2019-national-directory/.

Narea, N. (2021, May 19). *New data helps explain Trump's gains among Latino voters in 2020. Vox*. https://www.vox.com/policy-and-politics/22436307/catalist-equis-2020-latino-vote-trump-biden-florida-texas

Noe-Bustamante, L., Mora, L. & Hugo, L. M. (2020, August 11). *About One-in-Four U.S. Hispanic Have Heard of Latinx, but Just 3% Use It. Young Hispanic women among the most likely to use the term*. Pew Research Center. https://www.pewresearch.org/hispanic/2020/08/11/about-one-in-four-u-s-hispanics-have-heard-of-latinx-but-just-3-use-it/

Portela, P. (2021 September 20.) Hispanic Heritage Month: What the U.S. Census report confirms about the Latinx Population and what it means to Today's Communicators.

Business Wire. https://blog.businesswire.com/hispanic-heritage-month-what-the-u.s.-census-report-confirms-about-the-latinx-population-and-what-it-means-to-todays-communicators

Rosenstiel, T., & Al, E. (2007). *We interrupt this newscast: how to improve local news and win ratings, too.* Cambridge University Press.

Schaeffer, K. (2021, January 28). *Racial ethnic diversity increases yet again with the 117th Congress.* Pew Research Center. https://www.pewresearch.org/fact-tank/2021/01/28/racial-ethnic-diversity-increases-yet-again-with-the-117th-congress/

Tacher Contreras, D. (2020). Voto latino y su influencia electoral en los Estados Unidos. *Norteamérica*, 15(2) 233–250. https://doi.org/10.22201/cisan.24487228e.2020.2.441

Taylor, P., Lopez, M. H., Martínez, J. & Velasco, G. (2012, April 4). *When labels don't fit: Hispanics and their views of identity.* Pew Center. https://www.pewresearch.org/hispanic/2012/04/04/when-labels-dont-fit-hispanics-and-their-views-of-identity/

10

Covering Latinos in Business and the Economy

Melita M. Garza

On CNBC, news anchor Carl Quintanilla ran through the numbers. Only 4 percent of Fortune 1000 company executives were Latino. When it came to the corporate boards of these companies, 75 percent lacked a single Latino director. Quintanilla then turned to Oscar Muñoz, the former CEO of United Airlines, and asked: "Do you see 2020 as a catalyst year, as a stair-step year, when it comes to inclusion?" Munoz, a Mexican American and a native Californian, gave a short and provocative reply: "No, it won't be" (CNBC, 2020).

At *La Opinión* in Los Angeles, bilingual reporter Jacqueline Garcia reported on Chamba, a free employment app in Spanish and English. Two Denver, Colorado-based Latino entrepreneurs, Diego Montemayor and David Ruiz, started Chamba to help match workers with jobs as the economy largely shut down during the pandemic. "We are in high demand for construction jobs, restaurants, cleaning and warehouses," Montemayor told Garcia. By May 2021, the app, which was publicized via TikTok, had more than 30,000 users nationwide (Garcia, 2021).

Meanwhile, another bilingual journalist, Claudia Torrens, a New York-based Associated Press writer, reported on the impact of COVID-19 on Latino immigrants, noting that unemployment for this group had jumped to 8.8 percent in February 2021 from 4.8 percent in January 2020. The story made the link between Hispanics losing jobs and Hispanics losing homes (Torrens, 2021).

From executive suites and corporate boards to tech start-ups and low-wage and industrial workers, the role of Latinos in the economy and business, whether native-born or immigrant, is a significant, yet often overlooked news story.

This chapter helps demystify often complex business topics concerning the economic and financial status of Latinos and the nation, showing you how to

DOI: 10.4324/9781003212331-10

write about both engagingly and with clarity and precision. Business news has a far-reaching impact on society, providing information that can help readers, viewers and listeners learn about such things as job opportunities, whether and where to buy an affordable home and how to avoid business scams. Business news also informs the public about consumer safety issues and product recalls, as well as the latest tech gadgets and apps that make life easier, among many other things.

Business journalism is one of the news industry's prime growth areas, and the skills needed to tell these stories are relevant across all platforms and all beats. Understand that business news is Latino news. Equip yourself to report on business and you will be able to fill in enormous gaps in coverage of Hispanic issues. Latinos play a central role in the nation's economic life, contributing $2.6 trillion to the nation's economic output, known as GDP, in 2018, according to a report published in 2020 (Hamilton et al., 2020). To understand the scale of the economic impact of the Latino community, consider this: If Latinos were a separate nation, they would have the eighth largest GDP in the world, behind France and India (Hamilton et al., 2020). This chapter will focus on selected news topics that are particularly relevant to Hispanics, including entrepreneurship, jobs and consumer issues. Consider this chapter a jumpstart into learning about business journalism.

New angles on the Latino business story can develop quickly. For instance, the COVID-19 pandemic, which led to business and industry shutdowns beginning in March 2020, shone a spotlight on Latinos, a group disproportionately represented in the category "essential worker." Although some states established their own definition of "essential worker," typically these included food and agricultural workers, healthcare workers, as well as laundry, housekeeping and transit workers, among others. And these workers aren't just concentrated in Southwest and border states but found throughout the country (Jong, 2021). But this is not the only Latinx business story. Hispanics are also starting small businesses at a faster rate than other demographic groups. Between 2009 and 2019, Latino small business grew at a rate of 34 percent, versus 1 percent for all others combined (Orozco et al., 2019). By comparison, white-owned small business declined 6 percent in this period, underscoring the importance of reporting with nuance (Orozco et al., 2019).

To understand how Latinx-related financial news fits into the broader U.S. economy and business news picture, you'll want to familiarize yourself with helpful resources. The best overview for understanding business reporting is *Show Me the Money: Writing Business and Economics Stories for Mass Communication* by Chris Roush (Roush, 2017). This book will walk you through every facet of business and financial journalism, from large public and private companies to small business, Wall Street and the Federal Reserve and other regulatory agencies. Another useful tool for every reporter, whether a business journalist or not, is *Math Tools for Journalists*, 2nd edition, by Kathleen Woodruff Wickham, which provides everything you need to know about numbers as a business reporter (Wickham, 2003). If you know how to add, subtract, multiply and divide, you have sufficient math skills to shine as a business reporter. The rest is knowing the simple formulas and putting your skills into practice. To find more story ideas, strategies and helpful tips, explore the website at Arizona State University's Donald W. Reynolds Center for Business Journalism. The Reynolds Center is a one-stop shop for primers on how to cover many aspects of business and financial news. Join the Society for Advancing Business Editing and Writing (SABEW) for access to webinars, workshops and job news. Student memberships are only $25.

You don't need to wait to get specialized training to begin reporting and writing about business news, however. This chapter will give you some ideas about where to look for stories that will set you apart as a journalist, and most importantly, matter to your readers, viewers and listeners.

Case Study: Reporting on Latinx Workers with Government Statistics

Some of the best business stories are available via a free giant tip sheet – U.S. government data. Let's consider one example. Each May, a federal agency releases the annual report "Labor Force Characteristics of Foreign-Born Workers" (BLS, 2021). Unfortunately, many reporters never find their way to the data, which is posted on the Bureau of Labor Statistics website (BLS.gov). Yet, this report, and many others issued by the government, contains a wealth of information for reporters trying to shed light on the U.S. Latino experience. These reports might look daunting, with numerous tables of numbers, but if you know how to analyze the data, you can zero-in on insightful story ideas that you can localize for your community.

Pamela Ortega, a reporter for Gaylord News, an Oklahoma news service, found one data point in the BLS press release particularly striking. She zeroed in on the fact that for every dollar a U.S.-born Latino earned, an immigrant made a fraction over 86 cents. To bring the story to life, Ortega called numerous contacts to identify workers who would go on the record about their experiences with pay disparities. In Kevin Palomino, a 20-year-old native of Ciudad Juarez, Mexico, she found an interviewee who agreed to tell his story, provided his current employer was not identified by name. Palomino is a recipient of the Obama-era program, Deferred Action for Childhood Arrivals, widely known as DACA. Palomino proved a potent example for Ortega's story, since being paid less than his U.S. born colleagues had typified his experience in a series of jobs.

Ortega, however, went beyond interviewing workers affected by differences in pay. Through her interview with Miriam Campos, Ortega turned what could have been a story of Hispanics as victims into a story of a marginalized group's efforts to empower itself. Campos is a banker and a founder of the OKC Latino Young Professionals, a grassroots group that provided interview, salary negotiation, and other training for Hispanics trying to boost their careers. "I wanted to help others, not just be a great candidate with a great degree but go in there and get the opportunities," Campos told Ortega.

Ortega's story angle is one that might easily be localized for any community. But there are many other stories the BLS news release can help you tell. Let's look at three potential story ideas from this single press release. Looking at table 1 of the report, you can get a snapshot of the percentage and number of Latinos, native-born and immigrant, in the workforce. Table 4 shows the occupations of immigrants and the native-born; although it doesn't separate out Latinos, this chart suggests leads about where to look for workers to interview for your stories. Table 5 might be the most important for journalists reporting on the Latinx communities, not only because it lets you follow the money, but also breaks the data out by immigrant and U.S.-born Latinos. Use this information to find out who makes more, native-born Latinos or foreign-born Latinos. How does that compare to U.S.-born and foreign-born of other races and ethnicities? This enables you to write a human-interest or policy story backed up by data. Now let's walk through these three tables and how to develop stories from them.

Starting with table 1, Employment Status of the Foreign-born and Native-born Populations by Selected Characteristics, 2019–2020 Annual averages, you need to understand how to look at the table. First, tucked under the title you will find a notation that says [numbers in thousands]. That is a clue to readers to add three zeroes to any number in the table. Numbers are often written in "thousands" or "millions," meaning the last three or six zeroes, respectively, are deleted. For example, in row 1 and column 1 of table 1, find the number 259,175. Since the chart is in thousands, add three zeroes to report the correct value, that is, 259,175,000. In AP style, this would be rounded and written as 259.2 million.

Note that the other figures in the chart under the headings Participation Rate and Unemployment Rate may look like numbers but they are percentages. To understand those figures, add a percent symbol to the figure. Thus, the participation rate shown for 2019 in row 1 would be 63.1 percent. For example, you would then write: "The U.S. labor participation rate stood at 63.1 percent as of May 31, 2019, according to the federal Bureau of Labor Statistics (BLS)." The same explanation applies to the Unemployment Rate. Lastly, we need to make sure that readers understand what is meant by the "civilian noninstitutional population," a term the government uses to refer to people that are not in prison or in the military.

The BLS breaks out the ethnicity of workers, with foreign-born worker information in the first row of the table and native-born worker data in the second row. You might use the data to add depth to the story or to drill down on a population group within your city using census data.

Or you could compare employment rates between foreign-born and native-born Hispanics. The data shows, for instance, that in 2020, when the COVID-19 pandemic raged across the United States, unemployment among foreign-born Hispanics rose to 9.4 percent from 3.4 percent in 2019. Meanwhile native-born unemployment rose 11 percent in 2020 from 5.4 percent a year earlier. Then the question becomes why was unemployment among native-born Hispanics higher than for the foreign born?

Turning to table 4, you find that many foreign-born workers in 2020 held service jobs, particularly in food preparation and related occupations, as well as in building and grounds cleaning and maintenance. Among foreign-born men, 15.2 percent held jobs in construction, according to the table.

Table 5, depicted here as Table 10.1, shows the wage disparity between foreign-born and native- born Hispanics. Foreign-born Hispanics were the lowest paid among all foreign-born workers of any racial or ethnic background in both 2019 and 2020. And a foreign-born Hispanic made only 86.7 percent of what a native-born Hispanic made, as you can see in the last column. To make this clear in your story, you might say that for every dollar a Latinx native made in these years, a Latinx immigrant made only 86.7 cents.

As the U.S. raced to recovery from the pandemic, however, workers were increasingly in the driver's seat on wages. Many industries, including the restaurant industry, began paying bonuses to lure workers. In the warehousing industry, Amazon was offering $1,000 signing bonuses and promising to pay as much as $20 per hour, far higher than the minimum wage U.S. workers have had to accept for many years.

Another report from the Bureau of Labor Statistics also deserves mention. Unlike the annual labor force characteristics report, the Employment Situation report is issued monthly. Within that report is a separate report on Hispanics. The Employment Status of Hispanic or Latino population by sex and age, in table A-3 lets reporters dig into detailed and compelling information. For instance, you can find the unemployment rate for men and women over 20 years of age and a separate breakout of both sexes ages 16–20. The impact of the pandemic on Hispanics is clear when you see the unemployment rate of women ballooned to 18.6 percent in May 2020, but by May 2021 had fallen to 7.1 percent as many were again working. Whether that is by choice or necessity, the BLS doesn't say. That's a story for you to investigate by speaking to social service organizations, public policy experts and agencies serving Latinas. Table A-2 in the same monthly report gives you similar information for whites, Blacks and Asians.

TABLE 10.1 Median Usual Weekly Earnings of Full-Time Wage and Salary Workers for the Foreign Born and Native Born by Selected Characteristics, 2019-2020 Annual Averages [Numbers in Thousands]

	2019					2020				
	Foreign born		Native born			Foreign born		Native born		
Characteristic	*Number*	*Median weekly earnings*	*Number*	*Median weekly earnings*	*Earnings of foreign born as percent of native born*	*Number*	*Median weekly earnings*	*Number*	*Median weekly earnings*	*Earnings of foreign born as percent of native born*
Total, 16 years and over.................	21,007	$800	96,576	$941	85.0	18,674	$885	91,713	$1,000	88.5
Men..................	12,584	863	52,423	1,042	82.8	11,301	941	49,610	1,115	84.4
Women..................	8,423	719	44,154	841	85.5	7,373	798	42,103	903	88.4
AGE										
16 to 24 years..................	987	564	9,778	583	96.7	816	596	8,548	607	98.2
25 to 34 years..................	4,682	797	24,894	854	93.3	4,004	885	23,657	907	97.6
35 to 44 years..................	5,704	864	21,078	1,083	79.8	5,117	963	20,524	1,130	85.2
45 to 54 years..................	5,491	815	19,899	1,102	74.0	4,833	926	18,981	1,165	79.5
55 to 64 years..................	3,293	815	16,773	1,065	76.5	3,107	869	15,910	1,137	76.4
65 years and over.................	850	749	4,155	964	77.7	797	772	4,093	1,034	74.7
RACE AND HISPANIC OR LATINO ETHNICITY[1]										
White non-Hispanic or Latino............	3,203	1,141	68,143	1,016	112.3	2,840	1,230	64,924	1,075	114.4
Black non-Hispanic or Latino..................	2,089	749	12,353	735	101.9	1,882	837	11,299	794	105.4

(*Continued*)

TABLE 10.1 Median Usual Weekly Earnings of Full-Time Wage and Salary Workers for the Foreign Born and Native Born by Selected Characteristics, 2019-2020 Annual Averages [Numbers in Thousands] (*Continued*)

	2019					2020				
	Foreign born		*Native born*			*Foreign born*		*Native born*		
Characteristic	*Number*	*Median weekly earnings*	*Number*	*Median weekly earnings*	*Earnings of foreign born as percent of native born*	*Number*	*Median weekly earnings*	*Number*	*Median weekly earnings*	*Earnings of foreign born as percent of native born*
Asian non-Hispanic or Latino............	5,466	1,198	2,218	1,168	102.6	4,858	1,347	2,268	1,277	105.5
Hispanic or Latino ethnicity.................	10,008	658	11,219	759	86.7	8,867	704	10,691	812	86.7
EDUCATIONAL ATTAINMENT										
Total, 25 years and over.................	20,020	819	86,798	999	82.0	17,858	909	83,166	1,057	86.0
Less than a high school diploma........	4,038	577	2,972	617	93.5	3,210	601	2,489	655	91.8
High school graduates, no college[2].................	4,950	675	21,806	766	88.1	4,183	702	19,970	801	87.6
Some college or associate degree......	3,093	779	24,185	868	89.7	2,715	829	22,698	910	91.1
Bachelor's degree and higher[3]...........	7,939	1,418	37,834	1,360	104.3	7,750	1,492	38,009	1,409	105.9

1. Data for race/ethnicity groups do not sum to totals because data are not presented for all races.
2. Includes persons with a high school diploma or equivalent.
3. Includes persons with bachelor's, master's, professional and doctoral degrees.

Note: Updated population controls are introduced annually with the release of January data.

Source: Bureau of Labor Statistics, "Labor Force Characteristics of Foreign-born Workers," Table 10.5, May 18, 2021, https://www.bls.gov/news.release/forbrn.toc.htm

In Conversation with Nancy Rivera Brooks, Assistant Business Editor, *Los Angeles Times*

After graduating from Cal State Northridge in 1979, Nancy Rivera Brooks began working as a business reporter at the El Paso Times. In this interview excerpt, Rivera Brooks, part of a team of Latino journalists at the *Los Angeles Times* that won the Pulitzer Prize in 1984, discusses her career trajectory, offers career advice and highlights the importance of Latinx perspectives in business news coverage. This interview has been edited for space. Find the full transcript and a video of the interview in this textbook's web resources.

How and where did you get your start in journalism and business journalism?

Rivera Brooks: While I was in college, I worked at KLCS-TV, Channel 58, which is a PBS station that still exists, owned by the Los Angeles Unified School District. And I worked in their news department as an assistant part-time working on a system-wide student news program, 15 minutes in English, 15 minutes in Spanish, called 'Student News Noticiero Estudiantil' that brought high school kids from around the district to produce the news. It was a great program. And I'm sad it no longer exists.

And my first job in journalism was at the *El Paso Times* in El Paso, Texas. I was hired as a business journalist. I knew nothing about business journalism. This was 1979, so I had three other offers, if you can believe that. And this was the best job I was offered. And as an LA girl [who] never really had been away from home, it was kind of scary for me to go to El Paso. They told me they didn't

FIGURE 10.1 Photo of Nancy Rivera Brooks (Photo by Mark Potts)

care that I knew nothing about business that all I had taken was one economics class in which I got a "C," I will admit. And they said they liked the way I wrote. They liked my clips. They said it was easier to teach someone who knows how to write about business than it is to teach a businessperson how to write. So, we took it from there. And I learned a lot on the job and made some really dumb mistakes, which I learned a lot from. And three years later, I was hired at the *Los Angeles Times* as a business reporter, covering small and minority business. The field was booming then, and they were hiring a lot. And the previous reporter covering smaller minority business, a Latina, apparently, you could have just one Latina and one person covering small minority business. She was going to go to the *New York Times*. So, that was my job opening. And I've been at the paper since then, in the business department as a reporter and now an editor for 40 years come next June.

So, what did you tell yourself about jumping into this topic that seemed perhaps – did it seem alien to you or how did you overcome any trepidation about business itself?

Rivera Brooks: Yes, I had some, but my boss was really great. And he taught me a lot. My dad (William Rivera) taught me a very important lesson. He started out as a reporter in sports, and then went into public relations. And he taught me when I was in college: "Say yes. Say yes to anything, any assignment anyone gives you, even if you don't think you can do it. Any new duties they want to give you even if you don't think you have the skills. Fake it till you make it." And so that was my plan. And that's been my watchword of my career. Ever since. Don't let them see you sweat. Fake it till you make it. And you can do it.

Okay, so after three years, you went to the *Los Angeles Times*. Did that play a role in motivating you to stick with business journalism? Why did you stick "with business"?

Rivera Brooks: I really enjoy business journalism. I like being good at something that other people think is difficult. And you're being a specialist in an area that others think "Oh, well, that's math. That's hard." And business journalism is really like any other journalism, it's people doing things to other people; people doing things with other people. Great crime. I've written some great crime stories in the guise of business journalism. Any story is a business story if you squint hard enough, that's been one of my sayings. And currently we find that our readers really respond to character driven business stories to stories about local institutions that something's happening with. And those are stories that sometimes Metro used to do; sometimes we do. There's been a lot of crossover. But I just really enjoy the coverage of business. Putting it in plain English, in words people can understand. The *Los Angeles Times* has never been a jargony business section. So, we just always find the story behind the story. Back when we used to do earning stories, it was always, "What is the story in the earnings?" Not "this revenue, and this earning, this profit, and the net income and operating profit." It's always, "what made this happen?" So that has always drawn me to business and kept me in business. And business has always been a very warm pool for me, a very collegial place. So, I have never wanted to leave this section. Even though other opportunities have opened up. Recently, I was asked to apply for a job. And I said, "You know what? I'm good."

So just to back up on your last anecdote for those students who may not be familiar with it, can you briefly explain what an earnings story is?

Rivera Brooks: An earnings story was the bread and butter of any business section, not just the *Wall Street Journal*, or the *New York Times*. It's when a public company every three months, every quarter, tells the world how much money it made, how much money it lost, how it made that money, how it lost that money, and what their sales were. And then other things – their expenses, the big things that happened that quarter that affected everything. There is a phone call with analysts and investors; there's a news release; there's a very detailed filing with the Securities and Exchange Commission.

Why is it important to have more Latinos in business journalism?

Rivera Brooks: We were publishing a series of photos online for a story for the general Hot Property column, which was mainly just celebrity listings and luxury listings. And it was an actress (a TV actress mainly, she had a Ranchero house and in the garden, she had a big concrete statue of the Sleeping Mexican, which I could not believe. And I said, "Okay, pull that photo, it's not going online. It's not going in the paper." I said, "That offends me. And I think it's gonna offend a lot of our readers." And so that photo was out. So, it's important, the perspective, the voices, the sources, the keeping your colleagues honest. And it isn't all about – because I know Latino reporters get really worked up about 'I don't want to be stuck. I don't want to be pigeonholed in a certain kind of beat. And I only do the Latino stories and I want to do the stories that are the big story of the day.' But even when you do those stories, you bring your own special flavor, your own secret sauce that someone who isn't Latino would not bring. So, we need more (Latinos).

Trade Tools and Tips

1. Don't use more than two numbers in the lead of your story.
2. Don't pile a lot of numbers and statistics into the rest of your story – use only the number(s) needed to highlight the story's point and serve as a news peg.

3. Do contact public information officers listed on government releases – they are willing to help you sort through numbers.
4. Do spend at least 20 minutes each week on inclusive source development. Check in with a source you haven't connected with lately, work on adding new sources, and send a thank-you email or snail mail note to those who helped you with stories that week.
5. Do use LinkedIn, Facebook, Twitter and other social media to look up the backgrounds of people you interview or to find past or current workers at businesses you cover. Don't accept all the dates and job titles you find on social media as fact but use them to double-check what your interviewees tell you about themselves. Clear up any discrepancies.

Discussion Questions

1. The case study focuses on the employment status of Latinx immigrants compared to native-born Latinos and other groups. What are the key reasons for making these distinctions in a Latinx-oriented business story? In other words, what does your audience gain from including this context in a story?
2. The case study walked you through how to read a chart from a government economic news release. Discuss why identifying key data points should guide your interviewing and not the other way around. In this case, how would identifying news pegs from the numbers help shape the interviews you do with workers?
3. Discuss how Nancy Rivera Brooks built her career as a Latina focusing on business journalism. What does this tell you about the twists and turns you might encounter in your own career?
4. In the introduction to this chapter, you learned about how the number of Hispanic small businesses increased between 2009 and 2019, while the number of White-owned small businesses fell. This information is likely surprising to many, possibly even to you. Discuss ways you might improve coverage of Latinx small business issues and why such coverage matters.
5. Discuss what the chapter author meant by this quote from the introduction: "Business news is Latino news."

Exercises

1. Contact your local Hispanic Chamber of Commerce or the closest Hispanic chamber in a neighboring town. Explain that you are developing story ideas on local Latino businesses and ask if they have a membership directory and/or data on the different kinds of businesses represented in the chamber. Based on what you learn, establish an agenda for covering various sectors of the Latino business community. For instance, which are more numerous, bakeries, bodegas, or small insurance, law, or accounting firms?

2. Consumers are a key driver of the economy, accounting for approximately 70 percent of economic growth. To fuel that spending, consumers need to be on a sound economic footing. That's why surveys of "consumer sentiment," that is, how consumers feel about the economy, are a closely watched barometer. The University of Michigan conducts such a survey (Survey of Consumers) for the general population that is often reported on in the mainstream media. However, Florida Atlantic University conducts a quarterly Hispanic Index of Consumer Sentiment, which gauges how optimistic the Latinx community is about economic issues. Look up the most recent survey and develop a solid approach for creating a local story around this topic. Who would you interview? After reading the news release, what questions would you ask?
3. Get a student digital subscription to the *Wall Street Journal*, which is available to students at a nominal cost per semester. It may also be available through your university library. For this exercise, study the front pages for a month, and make a daily notation about the number of Hispanics quoted as sources or as the subject of news stories. Not all Hispanics have Spanish-language surnames, so this would only be a rough estimate. That said, given the significant role Latinos play in the U.S. economy, what does this exercise tell you about the number of untold stories there are about Latinx business and economic issues?
4. Create a "source map" to use for a feature on a Latinx small business. Too often reporters think of just interviewing the owner and possibly a manager. Both are necessary. But they aren't enough. You'll want to interview customers and competitors too, just for starters. For a feature on a popular new taco truck, research the competition within a two-mile radius of the truck. What's the size of the competition? How are these trucks' offerings different or similar? Ask the competitors to talk to you about the challenges in the business. You want to be as informed as possible about the business landscape before you focus on the main subject of your feature story.
5. Identify a minimum of three Latinx business reporters and follow their Twitter feeds. What stories do they link to? Which journalists do they follow? Study the work of these Hispanic business reporters for at least a month. Look up terms you don't understand and document the word, the definition and the sentence in which you first encountered the word. One good source for business term definitions is Investopedia.

References

CNBC. (2020, December 10). "Diversity and Inclusion: The Next Generation of Latino Leaders." https://www.youtube.com/watch?v=AD0oc3oPH4c

Garcia, J. (2021, May 28). "Latinos Create Job App for Spanish," *The Daily (Woodland, California) Democrat.*

Hamilton, D., Fienup, M., Hayes-Bautista, D. and Hsu, P. (2020, September 24). *"2020 LDC U.S. Latino GDP Report: Quantifying the New American Economy,"* Latino Donor Collaborative (LDC). https://diversity.ucdavis.edu/sites/g/files/dgvnsk731/files/inline-files/2020_LDCLatinoGDP_final.pdf

Hispanic Index of Consumer Sentiment. Florida Atlantic University. https://business.fau.edu/departments/economics/business-economics-polling/bepi-hics/

Jong, Z. (2021, May 27). *"The Latino Community Stepping Up for America: And How They Will Drive America's Recovery."* Latino Donor Collaborative (LDC). https://www.dropbox.com/s/n53ivrhh9fdlfcl/Report-%20The%20Latino%20Community%20Stepping%20Up%20for%20America.pdf?dl=0

Orozco, M., Tareque, I.S., Oyer, P. and Porras, J.I. (2019). "State of Latino Entrepreneurship." Stanford Graduate School of Business, Latino Entrepreneurship Initiative. https://www.gsb.stanford.edu/sites/gsb/files/publication-pdf/report-slei-state-latino-entrepreneurship-2019.pdf

Roush, C. (2017). *Show Me the Money: Writing Business and Economics Stories for Mass Communication*, 3rd edition. New York: Routledge.

Survey of Consumers. University of Michigan. https://data.sca.isr.umich.edu/reports.php

Torrens, C. (2021, May 4). *"Some Immigrants, Hard Hit by Economic Fallout, Lose Homes,"* Associated Press. https://apnews.com/article/immigration-health-coronavirus-business-07183bf8f43b078efbc8a67fd3f9ba2a

U.S. Department of Labor, Bureau of Labor Statistics BLS. (2021, May 18). "Labor Force Characteristics of Foreign-born Workers." https://www.bls.gov/news.release/forbrn.toc.htm

Wickham, K. (2003). *Math Tools for Journalists*, 2nd edition. Portland, OR: Marion Street Press.

11

Dispatches from the Frontlines

Foreign Correspondents Cover the World and Beyond

Jesús Ayala Rico

Foreign correspondents are some of the bravest and most influential people I know. Through their informed reporting, they shape our understanding of the world by highlighting growing issues in specific countries, regions and the world at large. They can promote cross-cultural knowledge, understanding and can even influence political outcomes (Hannerz, 2012). A foreign correspondent is a journalist who reports for a publication or media network from a foreign location. Depending on what region they are reporting from, foreign correspondents will have different reporting beats. War correspondents, for example, report on the quickly evolving state of armed conflict in places like Afghanistan, Iraq and Syria. Political correspondents cover elections, trade deals, bilateral relations and human rights. Many U.S. outlets now have correspondents who cover the U.S.-Mexico border full-time and who specialize in issues like family separation, border militarization, child sex-trafficking and NAFTA. And some correspondents will go wherever the story takes them. The lengths of assignments can vary from a few days or weeks to months, years, or even permanent posts overseas.

Thanks to foreign correspondents, we've witnessed the fall of the Berlin wall, understood the political nuances of the cold war and the Cuban missile crisis, learned about the killing of Osama Bin Laden, and have experienced the dramatic saga of 33 miners trapped inside a mine in Chile and the adrenaline of countless Olympics games.

DOI: 10.4324/9781003212331-11

A Closer Look: Covering Authoritarian Regimes in Latin-America

While some foreign correspondents work in what may be considered media-friendly countries with access to government officials, other journalists are challenged by assignments in areas of the world where journalists are often perceived as the enemy (Dahlby, 2014). In 2017, Reporter Hatzel Vela of WPLG-TV in Miami became the first local television journalist in the country to cover Cuba from the inside. For Vela (pictured in Figure 11.1), becoming a full-time correspondent in Cuba was a dream job. Vela was the first American journalist to report the death of Fidel Castro on November 25, 2016. Hours later, he was on the ground in Havana covering how Cubans were reacting to the news of losing their longtime president and commander-in-chief. Being able to live and work in Cuba afforded Vela the unique opportunity to cover some of the most significant stories in a post-Fidel Castro Cuba – from the mysterious attacks on American embassy workers to the devastation caused by Hurricane Irma in September 2017. But Vela quickly learned to manage his expectations as an American journalist (Ceballos, 2018). "This is a one-party system here, there's only the communist party," Vela said. "There are no candidates, no political ads, no campaigning, so the coverage here is vastly different." Covering an authoritarian government like Cuba can be particularly challenging for American journalists. "There are definitely roadblocks, and it gets challenging when trying to get any kind of information from the government about any issue," Vela said.

FIGURE 11.1 Reporter Hatzel Vela of WPLG-TV reporting from Havana, Cuba. Photo Courtesy: Hatzel Vela

On the one hand, Cuban officials desperately want to host American journalists like Vela since foreign coverage legitimizes the position as an important player on the world stage, but the problem is that they also don't believe in freedom of the press and therefore want to monitor reporting and control the messaging to ensure it fits only their narrative. I know this from personal experience. From the moment my ABC News team and I arrived in both Cuba and China in 2012 and 2017, respectively, both regimes – which just happen to be communist – assigned "tour guides" to highlight some of the "points of interest." But make no mistake, these "guides" were in fact government-appointed minders who were instructed to carefully watch us to ensure our reporting didn't stray too far from their government's agenda. While in Havana, it was common for me to come back to my room at the Hotel Nacional after a long day of reporting only to find out that officials had looked through my luggage – this happened during three of the four nights we were there. As an American journalist, there isn't much you can do when this happens, and there isn't anyone you can really complain to. You simply learn to deal with it and move on. I am not exactly sure what my Cuban minders expected to find since we were invited to cover the arrival of the American Ballet in Cuba as "cultural ambassadors." I suppose they were nervous that our reporting might somehow embarrass them or bring them dishonor; so while some might say that the Cold War ended, there still appears to be a mutual mistrust on both sides.

By the time I traveled to Beijing in 2017, I already knew the drill. In China officials also looked through my belongings, but this time I was better prepared – I knew not to take any notes and I also knew not to use the internet or landlines since both are usually monitored by officials. There are times, however, when governments are outright hostile toward American journalists. In Caracas, Venezuela, the national police pepper sprayed our entire team when we covered civil unrest in 2014. Our cameraman was injured and he was very lucky that they were merely rubber pellets (see Figures 11.2a and 11.12b).

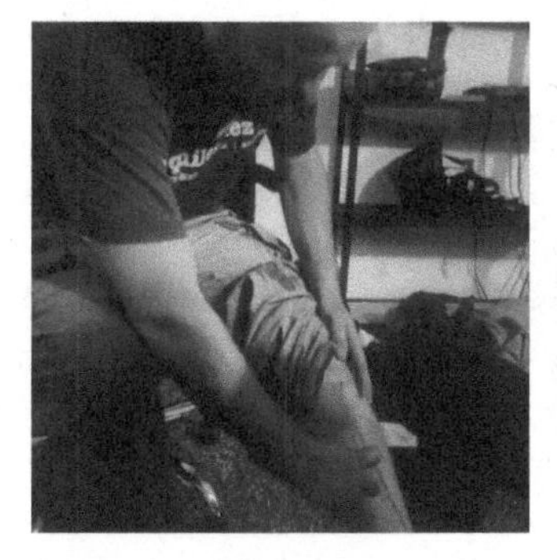

FIGURE 11.2 (a) and (b) Freelance cameraman César Fuentes cleans blood from his leg after being injured by Venezuela's national police force while covering demonstrations in Caracas on February 19, 2014.

A day prior, President Nicolas Maduro ordered that CNN be expelled from the country (BBC, 2014). "They want to show the world that there is a civil war in Venezuela," Maduro said. "I do not accept propaganda against Venezuela. If they do not rectify things, get out of Venezuela, CNN, get out," he said.

I spent over a decade covering foreign news in countries like Mexico, Cuba, Venezuela, El Salvador, Guatemala, Peru, Chile, Haiti, China, Japan, Malaysia, Italy, Spain, Israel, Egypt and Australia. The world's stories can be yours to share too, but you'll need some essential skills first. Below I give you some of my trade tools to begin your international journey.

Study Abroad: Preparing the Next Generation of Foreign Correspondents

I didn't realize it then, but my training as a foreign correspondent began while I was still in college. The number prerequisite for becoming a foreign correspondent is being a highly skilled traveler. I spent a year studying abroad in Spain my junior year in college. During that year, I traveled all throughout Europe, northern Africa and the Middle East. My year abroad was the best preparation for becoming a foreign correspondent – I learned to read maps in foreign languages and not get lost, how to quickly convert currency and how to hone my instincts and stay safe while traveling. Traveling is a skill and my time abroad allowed me to become a skilled traveler.

Have you ever watched the *Amazing Race* on CBS and marveled at how the most skilled players are able to make it from one country to the next so effortlessly? Would you be able to do that? If you answered yes, then you may have a shot as a foreign correspondent. If you know you would likely get lost, then there's still hope for you, but you have some work ahead of you. One of the biggest regrets that students often have about their collegiate experience is not participating in a study abroad program.

If you are serious about a career as a foreign correspondent, then taking the time to immerse yourself in a foreign culture through a study abroad program should be an essential part of your journey. This can happen either while earning your degree or after graduation. While studying overseas, students learn to adapt to new experiences, expand their understanding of global issues and learn a new language (Bebawi and Evans, 2014). For students who aspire to become foreign correspondents specifically, it is important to find an immersive journalism program that will give you a taste of what it's really like to report from a foreign country.

Studying abroad or participating in an overseas journalism program or course will without a doubt be one of the most transformational experiences you can ever aspire to be a part of as an aspiring journalist. For Xochilt Lagunas, now a reporter at KVEO-TV, reporting about the arrival of the migrant caravan in Tijuana, Mexico during her senior year in college turned out to be more

FIGURE 11.3 Student Dominic Torres reporting from Valencia on the crisis of Venezuelan refugees arriving in Spain.

overwhelming than she could have ever imagined. "Seeing so many families with young children proved to be much harder than I could have ever imagined," Lagunas said. "There were a few times where I couldn't even hold back the tears no matter how hard I tried. There's nothing that can prepare you for how you are going to react when you are out in the field."

His study abroad experience found Dominic Torres (pictured in Figure 11.3), now a production assistant at CNN, reporting about Venezuelan refugees seeking asylum in Valencia, Spain. "Field reporting has been essential to my learning process of becoming a field producer. Getting lost overseas and having a story fall through was a benefit to me because now I understand transit, can produce on the fly, and understand how to communicate in a foreign language," Torres said. "Sure, students might understand technology, but putting those muscles to work in an environment unfamiliar is a different monster."

While many traditional journalism assignments are hypothetical and geared toward in-class learning, study abroad courses provide students with a first-hand experience of how it feels to be a foreign correspondent reporting on deadline (Kanigel, 2021). Like Lagunas and Torres, you will be thrown into real life reporting situations – this will no longer just be a class exercise and you will walk away from your study abroad experience with a better idea of what it takes to succeed as a journalist while gaining critical real-world experience that pushes you to improve your skills by taking you out of your comfort zone and honing your professional development.

For more study abroad resources, visit your university's study abroad office or https://studyabroad.state.gov/.

PREPARING YOURSELF TO REPORT ABROAD

Consider a Minor

All foreign correspondents are expected to command a broad knowledge of foreign affairs and be an expert on many aspects of the region they cover (Purdey, 2011). If you are still enrolled in school and are very serious about an international career, it would be to your advantage to pursue a double-major or minor in political science or international relations. If you are interested in cultivating a beat reporting about a specific region, then you might also want to consider learning as much as you can about the region you intend to cover – many universities offer courses in specialized studies like Latin American studies or Middle Eastern studies, etc. Finally, don't forget that speaking a foreign language is invaluable if you want to excel as a reporter overseas. Presently, there is a global demand for professionals who can fluently speak and translate Spanish, Arabic, Chinese and Russian. The key here is fluency – being able to order tacos in Spanish is not the same as interviewing the President of Mexico about bilateral relations. Hone your language skills even if you think you are already proficient.

Intern for a News Outlet with a Global Presence

Growing up I wanted to be a lawyer because I wanted to make a difference in my community. In fact, I decided to attend U.C. Berkeley solely because I wanted to attend their prestigious law school. But that all changed one night when I was writing a paper in the middle of the night and looked up and saw Christian Amanpour running for cover in war-stricken Sarajevo. I was captivated by her bravery, her commanding knowledge of international politics and her ability to make Americans care about foreign affairs. I spent the entire next week obsessed with Amanpour and her trajectory – her story as a woman, an immigrant and Iranian refugee inspired me so much that I decided to apply for an internship at ABC News in their Washington D.C. bureau. It was the best decision I ever made – I realized that I could make an even bigger impact through journalism and my background in political science was in fact a huge asset. I spent the next summer getting a taste of D.C. politics and was able to shadow correspondents at the White House, Congress and the Pentagon. After completing my internship, I was hired full-time and the rest was history – although I would not travel abroad as a journalist for many years. Nonetheless, I spent the next five years reading and absorbing as much as I could about international affairs. When the call finally came and I was asked if I could travel overseas on assignment, I was not nervous at all because I was ready. It would not have happened, however, without a combination of the right education and the right internships.

Read, Always

The most important lesson to take away is that your preparation as a foreign correspondent begins many years before your first reporting trip. In order to truly become an expert on the foreign affairs of a region you intend to cover, you must always be reading and learning. This important work begins well before you even get on a plane. To be a foreign correspondent, you'll need to become a subject-matter expert. You can start this process by crafting out a beat for yourself – don't wait for your editor to give you a beat, just commit to a subject that intrigues you and start reading as much as you can. I've been reading *The Economist* since I was a sophomore in college – I would make weekly trips to the library to check out a copy and I eventually asked my parents to gift me a subscription as a birthday present. It was a wise investment. After you read a complex article, maybe a story about territorial disputes over the South China Sea or England leaving the European Union, translate your thoughts in a way that makes sense to a general audience – this will train you to break down complex topics into reports that are clear, concise and compelling. I credit my broad base in Latin American politics to Andrés Oppenheimer, a syndicated foreign affairs columnist with The *Miami Herald* – his weekly column about Latin American politics is a must for anyone who wants to cover that region. Anytime I came across an interesting article, I'd print it even if I didn't have time to read it at that very moment. Eventually, I'd amass a folder with several articles which made for perfect reading materials once I was dispatched on a story. The East-West Center is a great resource for journalists who aspire to cover Asia. The U.S. State Department also provides country reports about numerous topics like human rights practices, terrorism, religious freedom, etc. You can view those reports here: https://www.state.gov/department-reports/.

The department also issues travel warnings about every single country and region in the world: https://travel.state.gov/.

Be Ready

If you are truly serious about reporting abroad, you always want to make sure that you have a valid passport. Again, a big part of preparing happens before you even leave. Some countries even require you to have a valid passport for at least two years to be able to request a visa. I almost missed out on covering the devastating quake in Haiti in 2010 because I had an expired passport (see Figure 11.4). It was totally

FIGURE 11.4 Cameraman Jim Sicile and Producer Jesús Ayala Rico cover the devastating earthquake in Port au Prince, Haiti in 2010

my fault because I just did not keep track of the expiration date. I was extremely lucky that I was able to place a rush order and get it on time, but it was much more expensive than it needed to be. If you slack you will pay the price, literally!

Be Patient

You should also keep in mind that when you are reporting overseas, the pressure is amplified. Your news director just spent thousands of dollars to send you overseas, so the expectation is that you will deliver and there is very little room for error. It's for this reason that most journalists who are sent overseas are usually veteran-level reporters. If you are a younger reporter and have the travel itch, you must learn to be patient. Your time will come. In the meantime, keep reading and preparing yourself so that you are in fact ready when the time comes. You might also want to identify who runs the foreign desk and your organization and introduce yourself. I introduced myself to the director of foreign at ABC News about two years into my career. I expressed my interests and he listened and appreciated my incentive, and while I was not dispatched on any overseas assignments for several years, I was occasionally asked to help translate interviews and do research for our foreign correspondents. That was great training because I was able to learn immensely by working besides colleagues who were more seasoned.

PRACTICAL TIPS FOR REPORTING OVERSEAS

Travel Smart

Most international flights are red-eyes, or flights that depart overnight. If you know you are going to need to sleep on the plane, then pick a window seat. There is nothing worse than trying to sleep and not being able to because you need to get up to allow your aisle mates to get through. Also, it is very important to stay hydrated on flights. However, if you really want to get a good sleep onboard, then limit your liquid intake before to avoid getting up to use the restroom. Do your hydrating hours before the flight and stop drinking liquids about 3 hours before your flight. I am not a fan of sleeping pills. Most of my colleagues relied on sleeping pills to ensure they were able to sleep, but overusing sleeping pills can lead to dependency. Not to mention that I once had a colleague who spent most of the flight sleep-walking and doesn't even have any recollection. A better strategy might just be to exercise before the flight to ensure that you are tired by the time you are departing.

Know Your Time-Zone

Once you make it abroad, always make sure that you calculate the time difference correctly. If you are expected to go live for the 6 p.m. newscast, then what time would that be where you are at now? Several journalists have missed air or their deadline because they did not calculate time zone changes correctly. Your world clock on your phone can be very useful, but I've been in situations where my phone also displayed the wrong time. When I was in Beijing, China my mobile device showed that it was 14 hours ahead, but in reality Beijing is 15 hours ahead of Los Angeles. A simple phone call to someone back home to confirm the time and some old-fashioned math conversions will save you some heartache.

Get Ahead of Jetlag

The most common complaint when traveling overseas is jet lag. The best tip to avoid jet lag is to get to your destination's time zone while traveling. If my flight leaves at 11 p.m. from Los Angeles, I might be tempted to sleep as soon as I board my flight. But 11 p.m. in Los Angeles is really 2 p.m. in Beijing, so sleeping as soon as I board the flight is actually not a great idea. A better idea would be to power through and stay up for at least 6–7 hours before falling asleep. This will reduce jet lag upon arriving in China. You also want to make sure you are staying hydrated since travel tends to dehydrate your body. If you are still struggling with jet lag once you arrive at your destination, then it is essential to get at least one hour of direct sunlight exposure to help regulate your sleep-wake cycle. If you are feeling tired, avoid taking a nap and instead go sit in the sun.

Manage Your Expectations

I want to make it abundantly clear that when you travel overseas, you give up all your rights as an American journalist. As I've already discussed, some foreign correspondents are lucky enough to work in media-friendly countries, but many others are challenged by assignments in areas of the world where journalists are often perceived as the enemy. You should learn to expect the unexpected. Facilities may be modern or rundown, working or out of order, clean or dirty. In many countries you may have to lower your standards a bit when it comes to facilities like hospitals, restaurants, hotels, public bathrooms and public transportation. You should also not expect to find the same foods in restaurants or supermarkets. If you have a food allergy or intolerance, then plan accordingly and bring any essentials with you. Many foreigners have a very negative opinion of American tourists. The last thing you want is to come across as spoiled or entitled. Basically, you take what you get and deal with it.

Draft a Carnet

If you are traveling with expensive production equipment, I highly recommend that you take the time to draft up a *carnet* (pronounced car-nay). A carnet is an international customs and temporary export-import document, which is used to clear customs. It's essentially an itemized list of your production gear which proves to customs officials that you entered the country with your gear upon entry, and that you are leaving the country with the same gear and are not trying to export it without paying duties and import taxes. Think of carnets as a "merchandise passport" for your equipment. There is debate about whether carnets are truly essential when traveling, and it all really depends on how much equipment you are traveling with. If you are perhaps only traveling with a DSLR camera, then it may not be a huge deal since most tourists now travel with cameras. But things can get dicey and complicated if you are traveling with gear that is reaching an estimated value of, say, $10,000 U.S. dollars. That may seem like a lot, but if you are a broadcaster your equipment can actually add up pretty quickly when you factor in the cost of your video camera, your audio equipment, you also need to itemize every single adapter, battery and accessory, and if you are traveling with a drone or eve editing software chances are that customs officials will want to investigate your items further. To be clear, as a news producer I always traveled with about $10,000 U.S. dollars worth of broadcast equipment and I almost always cleared customs without any issues. But in Israel, Cuba and Venezuela, custom officials were much stricter – not only did they demand that I have a carnet, but they also looked at it very meticulously. In Cuba, officials even made a copy of my carnet on the way in, and they looked over the same copy on the way out to ensure that I hadn't "smuggled-in" any equipment and left it behind. It took me well over an hour to clear customs in La Havana, so if you are traveling with gear it is worth your time to draft up a carnet since the burden falls on you to prove the gear is yours and was not purchased while on your trip.

Below is an example of the carnet I always traveled with during my tenure at ABC News (see Figure 11.5). It is important that every piece of equipment be clearly marked and labeled with serial or asset numbers. Most equipment has a factory serial number on it, or chances are that your school or newsroom likely also labels equipment with asset numbers and you can also use those, or include both as I do.

abc NEWS

PRODUCER: JESUS AYALA KIT #8
CONTACT #
Firmware: v1.20

Equipment	Make/Model	Type	SERIAL#	ASSET#	QUAN
Camera Bag	PETROL	Cam Accessory			1
Camera	Sony PMW-100 HD XDCAM	SxS Cam	120005	584066	1
Sony Mic	SONY ECM-XM1	Audio			1
Shotgun Mic	RODE NTG-2	Audio		576295	1
Sony Mic	Sony ECM-XM1	Audio			
Wide Angle Lens	SONY VCL-HGO737K	Cam Accessory		107430	1
Handheld Stabilizer	FREZZI SG-HH	Cam Accessory	1157	576277	1
JESUS(A)	SONY SBS-32G1A	Accessory	EFFR1024	105498	1
JESUS(B)	SONY SBS-32G1A	Accessory	EFFR1025	105499	1
JESUS©	SONY SBS-32G1A	Accessory	EFFR1022	105501	1
Battery Charger	SONY BC-U1	Cam Accessory	12063002084	583697	1
Battery	SONY BP-U30	Cam Accessory	271232	105454	1
Battery	SONY BP-U60	Cam Accessory	1222217	105895	1
Battery	SONY BP-U60	Cam Accessory	1222214	105892	1
Cam Light	LITE PANELS LP-MICRO-PRO	Accessory	60540	579396	1
Plug on Wireless TX	SENNHEISER SKP-100G3/B	Audio	4061004459	579401	1
Wireless TX	SENNHEISER SK-100G3/B	Audio	4071034976	579400	1
Wireless RX	SENNHEISER EK100G3/B	Audio	4061014280	579399	1
Lavalier Mic	SENNHEISER	Audio			1
Wireless RX Input Cable	SENNHEISER	Audio			1
Foldable Headphones	SENNHEISER PX-100-II	Accessory		107736	1
Misc. Cables	Audio	Cables			1
12" Mic XLR	Audio	Cables			1
Tripod Head	MANFROTTO 701-HDV	Accessory	C2636375	584296	1
Tripod	MANFROTTO 547B	Accessory	A2975406	105694	1
Monopod	MANFROTTO 694CX	Accessory	A3136260	105326	1
Rain Cover	PORTA BRACE	Cam Accessory			1
Bureau Drive		Accessory			1
Travel Drive		Accessory			1

FIGURE 11.5 It is essential to carry a carnet if you traveling with gear or equipment to facilitate clearing customs without any issues

Bank Access

You will need to call your bank before you travel with a detailed itinerary of what cities and countries you plan to travel to. If you fail to inform your bank of your travel plans, you may find yourself overseas with blocked bank cards. Taking the time to call your financial institutions before your departure will ensure you have access to your money. One of the most useful tips I ever received before traveling overseas was to take pictures of the backside of all of my credit cards and print out multiple copies. This allows you to still be able to know where to call to cancel credit cards if they are stolen. Printouts are essential in case your phone is also stolen and having immediate access to the information is crucial to minimize fraud damage.

Visas

Most countries allow Americans who hold a valid U.S. passport to travel overseas without a Visa as long as the trip is less than six months (U.S. Department of State, 2021). However, some countries do require U.S. tourists to have a valid visa to be able to visit including Russia, India, China, Vietnam and Turkey. Visit https://travel.state.gov/ to determine whether you will need a visa to travel.

Understand Local Laws

In the United States, you are presumed innocent until proven guilty, but in other countries you are actually presumed guilty, and the burden of proof falls on you to prove that you are in fact innocent. Not knowing local laws can get you into serious trouble. Just because something is legal in the United States doesn't mean it is legal in another country. Most people who run into legal woes abroad don't break the law on purpose – they often end up doing something illegal without knowing it. Ignorance will not be a valid excuse. The bottom line is that you must obey all local laws. If you find yourself in legal trouble, the U.S. Embassy or Consulate may only be able to assist you by visiting you in jail, giving you a list of local attorneys and notifying your family. You will be financially responsible for your legal representation as well as any legal proceeding brought against you. Do yourself a favor and avoid getting into any legal trouble overseas.

Have an Emergency Plan

Once you become an experienced traveler, you come to understand that trips don't always go the way you'd hope. You need to have a backup plan or an exit strategy in case this happens. Some unpredictable emergencies that could occur abroad include natural disasters like earthquakes and hurricanes, traffic accidents, violent crime, acts of terrorism and a serious illness or injury. The first step in crisis management is being prepared before a crisis even occurs (Moseley, 2017). The more prepared you are for emergencies, the better able you will be to respond under pressure. Where will you go if you need to leave the country? What will you do if you are a victim of a crime or are injured? You want to take the time to figure out the answer to these important questions and how you would get out of harm's way if you needed to. It's essential that you know step-by-step instructions for more than one way to get to the U.S. Embassy or a safe meeting point for your entire team. You should register with the U.S. Consulate or Embassy a few weeks before your departure. The Smart Traveler Enrollment Program (STEP) is a free service that allows U.S. citizens and nationals traveling or living abroad to enroll their trip with the nearest U.S. Embassy or Consulate. The STEP program allows the U.S. Embassy to contact you in an emergency. It is very important to follow all instructions from local authorities about security and evacuation. Doing so could save your life. If you are staying in a hotel, talk to the staff to be sure you know the hotel's emergency plan for a variety of crisis events including fires, floods, electrical outages, storms and other relevant scenarios.

Health and Insurance

Prior to departure or immediately upon arrival, you should identify appropriate medical facilities in case of injury abroad. It is important to know whether your travel insurance will pay in advance for care, or whether you will need to apply for reimbursement. In the case of injury, the U.S. Bureau of Consular Affairs can assist your family in sending you the necessary funds to pay for your medical care.

Protecting Your Mental Health: Tips for Trauma-Informed Journalism

Whether you are covering a full-blown war, or reporting from a hazardous natural disaster, or simply covering a papal conclave, reporting overseas is not easy. The travel alone can be hard on the body and a source of stress, and that is only exacerbated by the pressure that foreign correspondents are under to ensure they can return home with a compelling story.

As an award-winning veteran journalist who spent a lot of my career covering international news, I know journalism and I know trauma, and I know the devastating toll they can both have on our minds and bodies. I've spent nearly two decades of my journalism career covering tragedy, devastation and human suffering – from riots and mass shootings, to airplane crashes and train derailments and even every type of natural disaster imaginable including earthquakes, mudslides, wildfires, tsunamis and hurricanes. I've basically seen it all and I have witnessed more human suffering that any journalist should ever have to. Sadly, I am not alone. Journalists often cover traumatic events, but we receive very little trauma training. Despite having a solid journalism education, I was never taught how to emotionally prepare to cover a tragic event or how to recognize the symptoms of emotional distress.

Often, overseas events share a common denominator: Victims dealing with unimaginable grief and despair and the tragedies rock their communities forever. I now consider myself an expert on journalism and trauma, but only after having done everything completely wrong. In fact, I spent most of my career taking great pride in my ability to cover these gut-wrenching news stories without being emotionally affected, not realizing that this should have actually been a dire warning. But in my case, there was no warning whatsoever, so I coped as best as I could with absolutely no trauma training. I'd spend most of my career parachuting into traumatic events and all the while numb to my own emotions. I never actually realized that I had been insulating my psyche from secondary trauma for most of my career.

The news industry has created a culture of silence with unhealthy expectations for journalists to be "strong" and show no signs of fatigue or emotional distress. Consequently, we often build a wall to insulate ourselves from survivors, witnesses and the first responders we interview. Insulating ourselves allows us to do our jobs under enormous pressures and during moments marked by extraordinary grief. But this ultimately prevents healing from the secondary trauma that we are exposed to. It's important that you understand that stories that involve human suffering are likely to be upsetting, but if a story starts to feel overwhelming then that is your cue that you need to go into self-care mode and seek better balance.

For more trauma informed journalism techniques visit the Dart Centre's website: https://dartcenter.org/resources/dart-center-style-guide-trauma-informed-journalism.

A Conversation with Mandalit del Barco, Correspondent for National Public Radio: Covering the 2021 Tokyo Olympics During the COVID-19 Pandemic

Due to a global pandemic, the 2021 Olympic Games are unlike any other. No fans or families in the stands to cheer competitors on. Journalists wishing to cover the games also had to quarantine for weeks and undergo very strict health clearance requirements imposed by the Japanese government. They were only allowed to leave their hotels for 15 minutes a day. Mandalit del Barco (pictured in Figure 11.6), a veteran correspondent with National Public Radio, has covered breaking news across the world. Del Barco traveled to Haiti to report on the

FIGURE 11.6 Mandalit del Barco (National Public Radio)

aftermath of the devastating earthquake in 2010. She has chronicled street gangs exported from the United States to El Salvador and Honduras, and in Mexico. From China, del Barco contributed to NPR's coverage of the United Nations' Women's Conference. She also traveled to Tokyo to cover the unprecedented 2021 Olympics and shares her insights.

Ayala Rico: Out of all the stories you've covered overseas, which one has stuck with you the most?

Del Barco: Well, there's a lot that have stuck with me. In Haiti, I did a story about the national orchestra. They performed in one of the poorest "barrios" in Port au Prince for whoever was left, who wasn't killed during that earthquake. They gathered their instruments from the rubble, and they performed a concert for the people who were in the tent cities. And it was the most beautiful thing because they had lost their colleagues after the stage crumbled on top of them in the earthquake. And they rescued their instruments that were banged up and they were able to play this beautiful music to honor them. It was just so profound. I always try to find some bit of culture or humanity to bring out so that people can feel what it's like to be there as well. So that's what I look for.

Ayala Rico: Let me go back a little bit. Many students want to report abroad and want to see the world. I remember right out of the gate at ABC, I wanted to go overseas but it didn't happen right away. I had to be very patient and get on the radar of the right people. How did that unfold for you? At what point did you say, hey, I want to go overseas? And at what point did you actually get on the right people's radar so that you could actually make it happen?

Del Barco: Earlier in my career at NPR, I just had this idea that I wanted to do a documentary about Spain. It was 1992, that's how long ago it was. And there were all these things happening like the World Expo, the Olympics in Barcelona. And I want to report from there, so I kind of made it happen for myself. I created this documentary. And I was like, I'm going to do this. I probably paid for everything. I don't remember. Or maybe NPR did pay a little bit of it. But anyway, I had to create that opportunity for myself at the beginning. And then later, I went back to Peru, where I was born. I got a Fulbright Fellowship and I combined it with this fellowship from the International Center for Journalists. So, I stretched it out to a whole year. I spent that year going back to Peru and teaching and helping a feminist radio station and it was the presidential election. I got my year of living dangerously, you know, going through the streets, were there tear gas canisters flying and the police were there. And it was just like out of a movie, right? Just what you think of when you imagine being as foreign correspondent. And I was there to be there to witness and to be a reporter and it was so exciting. I mean, as long as you don't get hurt, but it was like exciting and thrilling to do that. Sometimes I had to create those opportunities myself at the beginning.

Ayala Rico: Out of all your training in your toolbox. What do you think prepared you best to be able to report abroad?

Del Barco: Having a kind of global view of the world is one thing that I think is really important if you're going to go anywhere abroad. So being prepared to think globally and being prepared to know where you're going and understand the culture of a place and try to get to know people first who are from there. A lot of journalists get parachuted down into a country and they're kind of like fish out of water. And that can be fun and interesting sometimes, but I think it's even more deep if you can if you know about a place or a culture, or you can understand it and appreciate a place and how it works. Then you can do a story about presidential politics anywhere in the world. If you are open to that kind of global viewpoint, global points of view and like being very open minded.

Ayala Rico: What would be your best tip for students? I know for me I spent my free time reading a lot. I'd read the Miami Herald and The Economist because like you said sometimes you get parachuted in and

you don't have time to really do the research. And you kind of need that institutional knowledge. So, for me that's my best tip to students. What would be your best tip?

Del Barco: Reading is definitely essential. But you can also listen to the music, watch a movie from another country. You know, understanding who the players are, understanding a little bit of the culture because that's really super important. You can't just be expected to just go in and know anything. You have to do your homework first. You don't always have time. But even when you're there, get to know people. Tell me about your life, what is it like to be you? What is your life all about?

Ayala Rico: Okay, let's switch gears and discuss the Olympics. When you found out that you were going to cover the Tokyo Olympics in the middle of a pandemic, what was your reaction? And how many hurdles did they make you jump through to get clearance?

Del Barco: When they first told me, I was like, "oh my god, that's great." My next thought was, wait we're in the middle of a pandemic. How is this gonna work? Can I even go? Are they even having this Olympic Olympics? Because that wasn't for sure. Nothing was for sure. And then how are they going to have this? Are we going to get to do anything? Also, I was thinking, oh god I have to find somebody to take care of my daughter for a month because I'm a single mom. Once I figured all that out, which was very last minute and nerve-racking, they had all these COVID tests that we had to take, before we left. Then another test right before we left at the airport. And then again when we got to the hotel, and we were quarantined for four days and couldn't leave the hotel, except to the convenience store right next to the hotel. I thought, how am I going to survive being in this tiny room where I couldn't even stretch my arms out? Because it was not big enough, you know? And then we were in the bubble of the Olympics for two weeks, which meant we could only go to the media center or any venue that was holding the competition. And then finally after two weeks [of quarantine], I got to go out and finally do what I wanted to do, which was to talk to the Japanese people, because like they weren't allowed to go watch the Olympics in their own country. Most people there were not vaccinated because they didn't get the vaccine in time. In addition to that, we had so many restrictions on what we could do as journalists. There are always restrictions, but it seemed to be much more heightened this time. There's a television network that had the rights for everything, so we were not allowed to record anything. Oh my God, as a radio person, I can't even record the sound of the soccer game where I'm at? And we were not allowed to even interview people as they were coming off their field or their competition. We could only record press conferences. Do you know how boring coverage is if it's only press conferences? So, I had to get very creative.

Ayala Rico: Did you feel that the safety protocols were justified? Or do you think that they were exaggerated?

Del Barco: I can appreciate that they were trying to protect everybody, and I totally agreed with that. And that's not a problem. But I thought some of the protocols were a little bit absurd. For example, at the airport, they had us do a spit test. And we then all got on a bus together to go to the media center. After we got off the bus, they put us in individual taxis for five minutes to go to our hotel where we all met up again together. So, we had to take individual taxis but then we were together before and after that taxi ride? And then the spit test, how do they know who's spitting into the vile? There was nobody watching us. They just handed us some plastic tubes. We had to do it back in our hotel, and then anybody could in theory take the test. So, it was a little bit theatrical, you know, and that's why I say in my blog. I'm glad that they wanted all of us to be vaccinated before we went out there. I had to be vaccinated and all my team was vaccinated. But I don't think that all the athletes were vaccinated. In some countries, they didn't have a vaccine yet. Even the Japanese government had not rolled out their vaccinations. They knew this was happening even a year ago, so why didn't they vaccinate everybody just to at least give people some peace of mind in Japan? Those poor people couldn't even go see the games in their own cities. I talked to people that lived across the street from the gymnastic center. They had tickets but they could not go to see Simone Biles because they were not allowed. It was a little absurd.

Ayala Rico: That's unfortunate. So back to some of the logistics. One of the things that is so hard when traveling overseas is just getting there with all the equipment, and then having to clear customs. Have you ever had issues?

Del Barco: As a radio reporter, we do have tiny little recorders that need batteries. So you gotta like be able to be able to either stock up on batteries or have them available. When I was in Peru actually my little recorder broke. And I was in Ayacucho where my dad's from in the up in the Andes Mountains. There's no Sony store there. I found a guy who worked on transistor radios, and fans, and stuff. And I was like, can you do anything with this? And I was like, oh my god. I'm just basically giving up this little equipment to this guy that probably has no idea. I remember going back there one time and I looked at, peered in and every little piece was laid out with every screw and like, oh my god. It never really worked out. So if something breaks down, it's really an issue. I brought two of everything. I brought two laptops, two recorders, two mics, lots of cables and wires, tons of batteries. It's very heavy to bring all that gear even for a radio person. Then I brought in this big Pelican case for our bureau that we set up there. I don't even know what all they had in there. NPR packed it for me and they sent it to me. So I didn't know what was in there. So when the customs agent was like, did you pack this yourself? I'm like, no but my company did. You know, I didn't want to lie. But there's always issues with equipment for sure. You have to anticipate that something's gonna break. So you need a second one or third one of everything!

Ayala Rico: So, in retrospect, given everything you went through at the Tokyo Olympics, Was it worth it? Would you do it again?

Del Barco: Yes, I would definitely do it again. Even under the same circumstances. Just because it was kind of a fun challenge. Like how do I create interesting radio stories without being able to record anything? Hmm, let me see. Let me just like, think what I can do. It forced me to be really creative. I did a story, and I couldn't interview Sky Brown, a 13-year-old skateboarder because they didn't let me interview her. So, I did a story with sound of her on YouTube videos. And she had recorded a song, so I had the song and I had archival interviews. So, I mixed some of that stuff. It was a challenge. And also, being able to be there to watch the Olympics was really cool. I got to see Simone Biles super close and nobody else was there. You know, it was a very privileged position to be in. Most of the world could not see this. And Allyson Felix, I saw her win her gold medal. And skateboarders for the first time; surfers for the first time. When you're a journalist, you're in the middle of history, and that's amazing. It's an amazing life.

Discussion Questions

1. Not all foreign correspondents will work in media-friendly countries with access to government officials. In some countries, journalists are even perceived as enemies of the state. Discuss some of the challenges that reporting from an oppressive or undemocratic country might pose. How might your expectations as an American journalist need to change, and how would you prepare for such assignments?
2. Most foreign correspondents are veteran reporters with many years of experience. It's highly unlikely that you will report overseas within the first five years of your career, but that does not mean you cannot start grooming yourself to report abroad. What are some techniques you can develop early in your career to start grooming yourself for a career as a foreign correspondent?

Class Exercises

1. Many foreign editors don't cover foreign news because they say that American audiences do not care about news happening overseas. Partner up with a class-mate. Each of you will pick one foreign affair or incident that

has been in the news recently. Take turns pitching the story – one of you will be the journalist while the other pretends to be the editor. Be persuasive and try to convince your "editor" that an American audience will care about your story.

2. To be a foreign correspondent, you'll need to become a subject-matter expert, but you'll need to be able to break down complex topics in a way that makes sense to a general audience. Pick a foreign affairs article and read it, then practice crafting a report about a complex issue that is clear, concise and compelling.

References

BBC News. (2014). Venezuela threatens to expel CNN over protest coverage, BBC News. Retrieved July 25, 2021 from https://www.bbc.com/news/world-latin-america-26283971

Bebawi, S., & Evans, M. (2014). *The Future Foreign Correspondent*. Palgrave Macmillan, 13–19.

Ceballos, J. (2018). FIU alum talks covering Cuba as a foreign correspondent. Retrieved July 25, 2021 from https://panthernow.com/2018/11/28/fiu-alum-talks-covering-cuba-as-a-foreign-correspondent/

Dahlby, T. (2014). *Into the Field: A Foreign Correspondent's Notebook*. University of Texas Press, 16–25.

Dart Center for Journalism and Trauma at Columbia University. (2021). Retrieved July 25, 2021 from https://dartcenter.org/resources/dart-center-style-guide-trauma-informed-journalism

Hannerz, U. (2012). *Foreign News: Exploring the World of Foreign Correspondents*. University of Chicago Press, 7–12.

Kanigel, R. (2021). 10 Tips for Training the Next Generation of Foreign Correspondents in Media Shift. Retrieved July 25, 2021 from http://mediashift.org/2014/06/10-tips-for-training-the-next-generation-of-foreign-correspondents/

Moseley, R. (2017). *Reporting War: How Foreign Correspondents Risked Capture, Torture and Death to Cover World War II*. Yale University Press, 20–29.

Purdey, H. (2011). *International News Reporting: Frontlines and Deadline*. Wiley Publishers, 72–79.

U.S. Department of State. International Travel. (2021). Retrieved July 25, 2021 from https://travel.state.gov/content/travel/en/international-travel.html

12

Broadcast TV News

Reporting and Producing for El Noticiero

Jesús Ayala Rico

Univision and Telemundo have been competing to win over Latina/o/x viewers in the United States for decades. Together, both networks reach the vast majority of Spanish-speaking audiences – Univision reports they reach 99 percent (Univision, 2021) while Telemundo states they reach 93 percent (NBC Universal, 2021). Telemundo was long considered the underdog and struggled to compete against Univision's steady imports of Mexican telenovelas and entertainment programming, but the network secured its place as one of the Latino media giants when the network was acquired in 2001 by NBC Universal for $2.7 billion (Oppelaar et al., 2001).

The history of Spanish language television in the United States, however, finds its roots in the very creation of Telemundo's main competitor, Univision Communications Inc. In 1955, KCOR-TV in San Antonio, Texas became the first broadcast station to begin broadcasting in Spanish (Subervi-Vélez et al., 1993). In 1961, the station was sold to Emilio Azcárraga, a Mexican television tycoon who owned a broadcasting empire known as Televisa (Subervi-Vélez et al., 1993). Under Azcárraga's ownership, the station was rebranded as KWEX, and in 1961 became the headquarters of the United States' first Spanish language network Spanish International Network (SIN); that network would later become Univision. Telemundo was originally known as NetSpan and was formally created in 1984.

Up until the mid-1980s, the three major American networks – ABC, CBS and NBC – did not see any value of the purchasing power of Latinos. This is ironic considering that both Univision and Telemundo eventually became self-sustained and extended their reach across the entire country. Telemundo owns 25 television stations in the United States, while Univision owns

DOI: 10.4324/9781003212331-12

29 stations. Telemundo was created in 1984 when WKAQ-TV and WSCV in Ft. Laureldale-Miami-West Palm Beach merged with WNJU in Linden, New Jersey and KSTS in San Jose, California to form NetSpan (NBC Universal, 2021). By 2000 Univision was grossing $501 million (Wentz, 2001). But despite the potential for profits, the "big three" were apathetic about covering Latino communities in a meaningful way and refused to provide positive portrayals of Latinos. It's no coincidence then that both Univision and Telemundo were able to consolidate their influence over Hispanic audiences in the United States. More importantly, both networks filled the void left by indifferent English language networks, becoming watchdogs and advocates on behalf of the Latino communities they serve by engaging in civic journalism to ensure that Latinos are covered fairly and accurately. It's a commitment that does not go unnoticed by Latina/o/x viewers who are loyal and hold a special emotional bond to Spanish language TV because it keeps them culturally connected with relatives back in Latin America.

Loyal Latinx/a/o families spent many hours glued to the T+-V screen watching *Chespirito*, *Sabado Gigante*, *La Copa de Oro* and countless telenovelas, Moreover, your family likely learned about the most important news impacting your community from broadcast veterans like Jorge Ramos and Maria Elena Salinas (Figure 12.1), or Maria Celeste Arraras and Enrique Gratas. You probably even wondered what it would be like to report and anchor *Noticiero Univisión*, *Primer Impacto*, or *Despierta América*; or if you were like me, you probably wondered what it would be like to work behind the scenes at one of these newscasts.

FIGURE 12.1 Veteran anchors Jorge Ramos and Maria Elena Salinas anchoring Univision's flagship newcast Noticiero Univision. Credit: Courtesy Univision Communications Inc.

Veterans like anchor Jorge Ramos maintain that the future of journalism will only be bright if we train more Latina/o/x students to bet on journalism. "My only advice is, follow your dream and do whatever you like to do the most," he advises. "I chose journalism because I wanted to be in the places where history was being made," he adds (Ramos, 2016). Like Ramos, you too can be a part of that rich history if that is what you are truly passionate about. It was my own passion that afforded me the opportunity to travel around the world covering breaking news as a producer for ABC News. It was a privilege to be able to have a front row seat to so many historic events – think about it, you are literally getting to witness and cover history as it happens! I was fortunate to cover Hurricane Katrina, the devastating earthquake in Haiti, the Pope's visits to Cuba, civil disturbances in Venezuela, the rescue of 33 trapped miners in Chile, and the historic presidential campaign of Barack Obama. I've learned from some of the best in the industry and had the immense privilege to work with news icons like Diane Sawyer, Ted Koppel and the late Peter Jennings. It wasn't an easy journey – more on this shortly – but it was certainly a rewarding one. In this chapter, you will find some of the trade tools that I've honed during my 20-year tenure as a news producer, and which allowed me to rack up a few Emmys and Murrow awards along the way. I will also include some of the advice that I wish someone would have given me early on in my career about being a Latino in mainstream news and tips to overcome the eventual self-doubt that some may surely have. It is my sincere hope that these *consejos* will serve you as you embark on your career in the broadcast industry.

A Closer Look: How a Team of First-gen Latinx Students Overcame Imposter Syndrome to Win an Emmy

Breaking into the competitive world of broadcast news as a Latina/o/x is certainly doable but it isn't always an easy feat. For decades now, Latinos have been severely underrepresented in TV News. According to the Radio Television News Directors Association's annual newsroom employment survey, in 2020 the number of Latinos and Latinas working in television newsrooms fell by 0.7 percent, making up only 10.9 percent of all newsroom employees working at local English-language television stations (Papper, 2020).

Being a person of color and working in a TV newsroom comes with its own set of challenges. It's very common for many of us to feel isolated or like we "don't belong." I wish someone had told me early on that these feelings are quite normal – it would have allowed me to prepare mentally for some of the microaggressions that journalists of color often face in newsrooms. In television, those feelings may be even more amplified since the industry tends to promote European standards of beauty and even frowns down upon accents or regional dialects.

TABLE 12.1

Television news work force - 1995 - 2020									
	1995	2000	2005	2010	2015	2017	2018	2019	2020
Caucasian	82.90%	79.00%	78.80%	79.80%	77.80%	75.60%	75.20%	74.10%	73.40%
African American	10.1	11	10.3	11.5	10.8	10.9	11.7	12	13.3
Hispanic/ Latino	4.2	7	8.7	5.8	8.2	10.5	10.8	11.6	10.9
Asian American	2.2	3	1.9	2.3	2.9	2.6	2	2	2
Native American	0.6	<1.0	0.3	0.5	0.3	0.4	0.3	0.3	0.4

Source: RTDNA's Newsroom Diversity Report

I was elated after being hired at ABC News right out of college, so imagine how demoralizing and gut-wrenching it was when my first boss, a hard-core Republican from Georgia, openly said I was "speaking in tongues" when he overheard me speaking in Spanish to an intern. After my boss' racially insensitive comment, I personally had to overcome a crushing bout of imposter syndrome – a strong feeling of inadequacy and chronic self-doubt that persists leading many of us to feel like frauds (Clance, 1985). You should find some comfort in knowing that even legendary journalists like Ruben Salazar battled through isolation and self-doubt (Salazar, 1996).

I've seen the "inner-saboteur" still at play even among some of my brightest students. In 2020, California State University, Fullerton celebrated a momentous milestone. For the first time ever, eight of my students joined the ranks of those who have won the prestigious College Television Award. The award, otherwise known in the television industry as a "student Emmy," is awarded by the Academy of Television Foundation, the same body of judges which awards the primetime and daytime Emmys. The winning team traveled to Tijuana to report on the arrival of the migrant caravan at the U.S.-Mexico border, and other border issues including the plight of deported veterans, family separation, border militarization and child sex-trafficking (see Figure 12.2). It is an outstanding achievement when you consider that over 374 entries were submitted from 112 colleges and universities nationwide, but it is even more remarkable because the CSUF team was entirely composed of first-generation Latinos who represent the largest university in California's public education system. Further, CSUF just happens to be a Hispanic-serving institution – approximately 44 percent of its 40,235 students are Latino.

Winning an Emmy is certainly an occasion for celebration, but it's a moment that almost never happened. In the Fall of 2019, I assembled the first cohort for a new class, *Reporting on Minorities of the Southern Border.* My goal for the course

FIGURE 12.2 First-generation Latinx students from CSUF reporting from the U.S-Mexico border for *Al Día: A Border Emergency*, winner of the 2020 College Television Award for Best TV Newscast

was simple yet highly ambitious – I would supervise an advanced border reporting seminar and would push students to their absolute limits hoping some would produce award-winning work. I never had any doubts I could train my students to be "Emmy worthy." After all, winning awards is what I was groomed to do during my tenure as a Producer at ABC News. As the recipient of four national Emmys and seven Edward R. Murrow awards myself, competitive journalism is where I thrive. My students, I was certain, would also excel given the right training and mentoring.

On the first day of the new class, I shared my vision with an excited although visibly intimidated group of students. After class, one student came up to me and asked "Do you really think we could compete at that level?" "Of course, I do," I replied. "But no one has ever thought of us as winners." His response stopped me in my tracks. I realized in that very moment just how daunting this would be, and the uphill battle we were now facing. The primal ingredient in any competition is believing you *can* win. But we were entirely off the mark.

Unbeknownst to them, I understood all too well. I, too, once was a Latino student, often dismissed and underestimated, and just like them, I once sat in a newsroom terrified and wondering whether I had what it took to succeed and wondering if I even belonged knowing that I was openly being looked down upon for speaking my native language. I eventually found a way to cope with my own fear and self-doubt. Whenever I felt insecure, I often thought about why my parents risked their lives and migrated to this country to begin with – "*para que mis hijos tuvieran un mejor futuro*," my mother still says. Throughout my career

I've allowed that to be the armor that gives me courage and allows me to persevere even in the face of insecurity.

This feeling of "otherness" in newsroom settings can be particularly hard on journalists of color who are often severely underrepresented in media. It's no coincidence that the National Association of Hispanic Journalists has been advocating for "more Latinos in news" for decades. A 2017 study from the University of Texas at Austin published in the Journal of Counseling Psychology suggests the impostor phenomenon is particularly pervasive for students of color, and "in some cases can degrade the mental health of minority students, who already believe that prejudices and statistics are stacked against them" (Cokley et al., 2017). Minority college students also said they often "faced discrimination and reported higher rates of depression and anxiety than their white peers." The study's findings led its authors to recommend it is vital for school counselors to specifically address how students of color are grappling with these negative feelings which clearly affect their self-image and self-worth.

As Ruben Salazar so eloquently warned us (Salazar, 1996), the only way to truly overcome imposter syndrome is "by continuing to show up." In 2020 all of my students also opted to show up, in a big way! Collectively, they won 40 national collegiate journalism awards, including a Hearst Award, an Edward R. Murrow Award and multiple recognitions from the Associated Collegiate Press, the College Media Association, the Broadcast Education Association, the Society of Professional Journalists and of course the 40th College Television Awards (see Figure 12.3).

My students probably think that creating their award-winning reports was the biggest challenge we have tackled together, but in reality, the biggest obstacle was getting them to believe that they are worthy and do belong. The student who had never been viewed as a "winner" is now working at CNN and has even covered presidential briefings at the White House. Teaching students to believe in themselves, will probably end up being my greatest legacy as a professor.

I am here to tell you too that your dreams are not crazy – they are in fact tangible. I am also here to reassure you that you are worthy, and you do belong – this industry needs journalists just like you now more than ever. If we truly want to see change, we must demand equity and infiltrate as many newsrooms as we can. Our viewers deserve to see a true representation of what their communities look like. You are now at the forefront of creating the newsrooms of tomorrow – because of you the broadcasters of tomorrow will have an easier journey, just as I benefited from the pioneers that came before me. Now that you know your worth, let's do it!

Producing for *El Noticiero*

Producing a *noticiero*, or newscast, is hard work. It requires thoughtful consideration about the news stories that will be included in the news broadcast as well as

FIGURE 12.3 Pictured from left to right: Maricela Perez, Stephanie La Vau, Viviana Borroel, Dominic Torres, Tania Thorne, Xochilt Lagunas and Professor Jesús Ayala Rico attend a journalism awards ceremony in Los Angeles

advanced technical skills to be able to pull-off a seamless show. In this section we unravel what it takes to put together a TV newscast. But before we jump into the practical and technical considerations, we want to look at various production roles to better understand the hierarchy and working structure inside a typical TV newsroom, as seen in Figure 12.4, while paying special attention to the role of the producer.

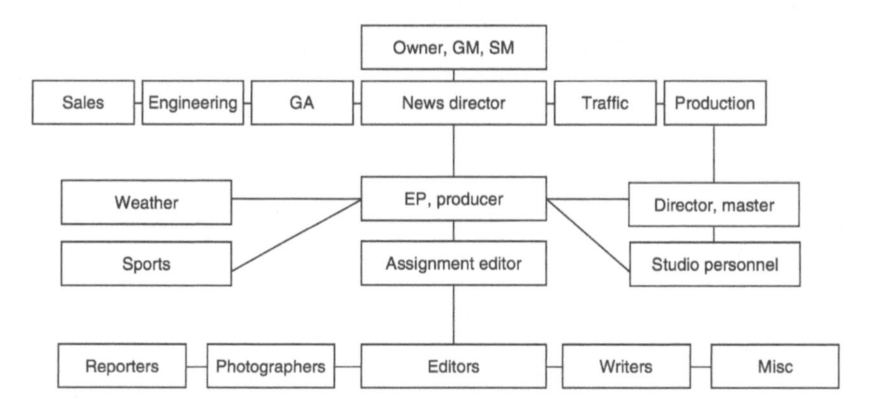

FIGURE 12.4 TV newsroom organization chart

The **News Director** oversees the entire news department and directs the station's editorial content and the news department's budget. In local news, the news director is typically in charge of the entire news staff, including anchors, reporters, producers, photographers, writers and all technical staff. The news director reports to the general manager of the station.

An **Executive Producer** oversees all the staff who work for a specific newscast. In large markets it's common for the morning shows, the midday shows, the evening shows and the late-night shows to all have a designated team comprised of anchors, producers and news staff. EP's are responsible for the overall news content of the newscast they oversee as well as the show's production value, ethical considerations and budget.

The primary role of the **Producer** is to stack the show by determining what news will be covered in a newscast and determining how much airtime will be given to each news story. It is ultimately the news producer who will determine what stories will be just voice-overs and which stories merit more attention or deserve to be covered by a reporter. Good producers have a solid vision for their newscasts and know how to make that vision come to life. Excellent producers have a keen eye for detail and have multiple back-up plans in case problems arise.

The Assignment Desk is the brain of the newsroom and **Assignment Editors** are the ones steering the ship. They are responsible for knowing what events – be it planned events or breaking news – are happening in the entire coverage area. When breaking news happens, Assignment Editors are responsible for determining which news crew is either free or the closest to the news scene and are responsible for dispatching a team for coverage along with appropriate resources, such as a satellite truck, if required.

Reporters and Multimedia Journalists (MMJs) are typically dispatched to the scene of a news event by either an Assignment Editor or a Producer. Reporters usually include all the details they uncover at the new scene in a package (PKG) and often also report live from the scene. Typically, reporters work with a designated camera person while MMJs shoot and edit their own stories.

Other roles in the newsroom include sports and weather anchors, writers, production assistants, graphics artists, video editors, camera operators and a broadcast director and studio crew.

TV Story Formats

Have you ever watched a newscast and noticed that some stories are quite short and meanwhile other stories get a lot more air-time? Have you wondered why? Well, this brings us back to the role of the Producer. Remember, the Producer will stack the newscast and will determine what stories will be included in a

FIGURE 12.5 Broadcast Journalism Studio

newscast and how much air time will be given to each story. Below are some of the most common TV story formats the Producer will consider.

VO (Voice-Over) or Reader

A story in which an anchor reads over pictures. VO's generally run 20–30 seconds and don't include fragments of any interviews. A reader is essentially also a 20–30-second story but readers usually don't have any visual elements – usually because there is no video or photos available for that story. Readers are read entirely on-camera by the anchor without ever dissolving into video.

SOT (Sound on Tape)

Any interview recorded on tape, also called "sound bites" that generally run 7–13 seconds.

VO/SOT (Voice Over + Sound on Tape)

A story in which an anchor reads over pictures and the story ends with a short sound bite from an on-camera interview. Usually 40–45 seconds.

VSV (Voice Over + Sound on Tape + Voice Over)

A story in which an anchor reads over pictures and the story then cuts to a sound bite and returns to more anchor narration over pictures. Usually 50–60 seconds.

PKG (Reporter Package)

A news package is usually the longest type of storytelling found in television newscasts. A package is a self-contained taped news report which contains a combination of reporter narration, recorded interviews (SOTs), and video shot at the scene of a story (broll). Usually, the news anchor will read an introduction live, then the pre-recorded story will be shown. News packages usually run for 1:15 to 2:00 in length. Longform stories for programs like *60 Minutes* or *Dateline* can run from 4:00 to 7:00, and some may even run for an entire show in the form of specials.

Live-Shots (in the field or in studio)

In most medium and large markets, live-shots are the bread and butter of newsgathering. Once upon a time, news stations could only go live with a large satellite truck, an engineer, and a professional camera person, but these days technological advances have made it possible to go live with small digital devices which are powered by numerous cellular air-cards. Most companies like TVU, Dejero and Live-U now make it possible to plug in their units directly into your mobile device and you are live as long as you have cell coverage. The length of your live-shot will vary depending on whether you are doing a live-hit with no video elements at all, or whether you are live simply to toss to a PKG which you already wrote and edited. When a reporter tosses to their own PKG live and then comes back live at the end of the PKG for a tag, this is called a *Donut*.

Keep in mind that all broadcast stories are written in a two-column format. We include all audio elements, including reporter narration, interviews and sound effects in the right column. The left column includes all visual elements including all broll, maps and graphics. Figure 12.6 illustrates what a typical news PKG might look like written in proper two-column format.

Building the Rundown (*la Escaleta*)

Now that you understand the role the Producer plays within the hierarchy of a newsroom, we now can jump into the practical and technical considerations of what it takes to produce a TV newscast. As we have already discussed, the primary role of a producer is to stack the show by determining what news will be covered in a newscast and determining how much airtime will be given to each news story. This process requires thoughtful consideration about the news stories that will be included in the news broadcast as well as some advanced technical skills to be able to pull-off a seamless show. All producers stack their shows by producing a *rundown*.

--FADE IN FROM BLACK--	--CORRIDO MUSIC SOUND FULL--
Full Screen Map: Tapachula, Mexico-Guatemala Border. Effect: Tapachula city in red and flashing. Video pull from "Tapachula." Hugo Tambriz sitting on a bed in an immigrant shelter in Tapachula. He is surrounded by immigrants who have fallen off the train. Hugo is holding a boom box and is listening to music.	ONLY A FEW MONTHS AGO, 14 YEAR-OLD HUGO TAMBRIZ WAS A NORMAL LITTLE BOY. BUT HIS LIFE DRASTICALLY CHANGED IN ONLY A MATTER OF SECONDS. **--NATS HUGO LAUGHING FULL--**
Hugo places the boom box on an old nightstand. He lies down on his bed. Close-up of Hugo's face and eyes. He looks desperate and sad. Kids crossing the Suchiate River on rafts suspended by rubber tires.	HUGO IS A MIGRANT CHILD. HE SAYS HE LEFT HIS TINY VILLAGE IN GUATEMALA LOOKING FOR A BETTER FUTURE. HIS DREAM WAS TO BE REUNITED WITH HIS 19 YEAR-OLD SISTER IN LOS ANGELES, CALIFORNIA. AND LIKE MANY CENTRAL AMERICAN IMMIGRANTS, HUGO AND HIS COUSINS CROSSED INTO MEXICO ILLEGALLY.
On-Camera Hugo	**--SOT HUGO--** *21:27 Les preguntamos a la gente que cuando iba a pasar el tren. Ahora sube pa arriba dicen. 21:48 La gente nos habia dicho que le tren pasaba bien despacio ahi.* We asked people when the train would go by. It will go by today they said. They told us the train went by very slow there. A lot of people have gotten on here and you guys will be able to get on here.

FIGURE 12.6 Broadcast stories should be written in two-column format

A rundown (seen in Figure 12.7) is a list of stories arranged in logical sequence based on their importance. Some might say that a rundown is synonymous with a lineup, or the producer's blueprint for the newscast. The rundown, however, also plays other important roles in a newsroom. A rundown is also your production

AL DIA 9/21/2021 [Archived]

Settings | Print | Create Story | Remove | Approve | Float | Hide Childr

Icon	Page	Slug	Segment	Type	Video
	A	start of show		Broadcast	
	A01	COLD OPEN	PKG	Broadcast	
	A02	SHOW OPEN/ANIMATION	1SHOT	PKG	SOT/ANIMATION
	A03	HELLO	2SHOT	Broadcast	GRAPHICS
	A04	MIGRANT CRISIS	VO/NADINE	Broadcast	CRISIS EN LA FRONTERA
	A05	IMMIGRATION REFORM	PKG/ANDREA E	Broadcast	CRISIS EN LA FRONTERA
	A06	COVID MEMORIAL	VO/MARIO	Broadcast	TRIBUTO A LAS VICTIMAS
	A07	J&J BOOSTER	VO/NICOLE	Broadcast	SALUD
	A08	TOSS TO HEALTH	RDR	Broadcast	SALUD
	A09	HEALTH	PKG/JONATHAN	Broadcast	SALUD
	A10	TRAVEL RESTRICTIONS	VO/JULIAN	Broadcast	MENOS RESTRICCIONES
	A11	TEASE #1	2SHOT	Broadcast	
	B	COMMERCIAL BREAK		Broadcast	
	B01	SPAIN VOLCANO	VO/NICOLE	Broadcast	HOY EN EL MUNDO
	B02	TOSS TO WORLD NEWS	RDR	Broadcast	HOY EN EL MUNDO
	B03	WORLD NEWS	PKG/NATALIA	Broadcast	HOY EN EL MUNDO
	B04	CA DROUGHT	VO/JULIAN	Broadcast	PANORAMA AL TIEMPO
	B05	TOSS TO WX	RDR	Broadcast	PANORAMA AL TIEMPO
	B06	TOO HOT	VO/ANDREA D	Broadcast	SEQUIA EXTREMA
	B07	WX	LIVE/ANDREA D	Broadcast	
	B08	TOSS TO SPORTS	RDR	Broadcast	ACCION DEPORTIVA
	B09	SPORTS	PKG/BRANDON	Broadcast	ACCION DEPORTIVA
	B10	TEASE #2	2SHOT	Broadcast	
	C	COMMERCIAL BREAK		Broadcast	
	C01	TOSS TO ENTERTAINMENT	RDR	Broadcast	ESPECTACULOS
	C02	ENTERTAINMENT	PKG/GABY	Broadcast	ESPECTACULOS
	C03	RUPAUL WINS	VO/JONATHAN	Broadcast	ESPECTACULOS
	C04	CELIA DOLL	VO/MARIO	Broadcast	BARBIE CUBANA
	C05	GOODBYE	2SHOT	Broadcast	
	C06	CREDIT ROLL		Broadcast	
		END OF SHOW		Broadcast	

FIGURE 12.7 Creating a strong rundown is the newscast producer's primary responsibility

road map and helps your team to become organized and set production priorities. Writers will rely on the rundown to determine which stories merit the most attention, graphic artists will use the rundown to know what graphics to create for the show, and the director will not be able to start and end your show on time without a solid rundown.

You will notice that every story has been assigned a slug, or a short name given to every story in the show. More importantly, notice that each story is accompanied by a page number which is in the farthest left column. The page number is very important because most news staff will simply refer to stories by their page number. You might hear a graphic artist say, "Hey the graphics for B10 are now in," or the director may say "Ok, coming to A5 next." To the right of the story slug, you will notice that each story has been designated one of the story formats that we went over. So just by glancing at the rundown we know immediately what stories we are covering and how much airtime the producer has designated to each story. You will also notice that the newscast is divided into three major sections, which we refer to as blocks, and each block is separated by a commercial break. Let us now learn what types of stories go into our three blocks.

The A Block

The first block is called the A block. As you might have already guessed, this is the block where the most important news of the day will go. This block is essential because it usually determines whether a viewer gets invested in the newscast, or changes the channel, or turns off the television entirely and runs off to run errands or heads to the gym. These days we aren't just competing against other channels, we are fundamentally trying to win over the audience's overall attention span and so we are competing against anything that a person can do with their free time. For this reason, it is essential that the beginning of every newscast has a strong *hook* – if you can't win over viewers in the first two minutes, chances are that you've probably lost them for the entire show. So, you must have a strong lead story! If you don't have a compelling story leading your show, you are essentially telling your viewer, "Nothing important happened today, so there's no reason to stay tuned." Picking the lead story is the most important decision a producer will make for their show.

The B Block

The B block will contain more news of the day that may not be as important but still useful. Often, the stories found in the B block were A block stories – say a few days or weeks back – but are no longer as important and merely require a follow up. For many weeks, the COVID-19 pandemic dominated national news and we were certain to see all coronavirus updates in the A block. But if no major developments or health concerns are at play, it would be appropriate to include a story about business reopening or children returning to schools in the B block. You will also find special reports, investigative stories, franchises, or the weather forecast at the end of this block.

The C Block

This block is the appropriate block for "fluffy" news like entertainment segments. Often, producers will also run the sports segment in the last block. If you are a sports enthusiast, you are probably wondering why sports is a low priority in a traditional TV newscast. The simple answer is that most sports fans are not waiting for the 6pm news to get their sports fix – they have probably already looked up the score on their mobile devices or headed over to ESPN's Sport Zone of Fox Sports to get the latest sports news. One of the biggest complaints from viewers is that most news tends to be "negative." So, it is very common to end a newscast with a *kicker,* a light-hearted, funny, memorable story that the viewer is likely to remember. We want viewers to leave the show with a smile on their face and not be traumatized by the state of the news in their communities.

Trade Tools: Working in the Control Room

As a producer, you want your show to feel effortless. The best newscasts are the ones where time just flies by, and you completely lose track of time. There are a few tricks of the trade that can aid you to create better pacing and flow in a show.

- Adding shorter stories into the rundown will create a faster paced show.
- Always group stories based on common topics. Have one anchor read all linked stories.
- If you want to speed up the pace, switch anchors frequently. Just make sure you don't create a "ping-pong effect."
- Not every single story requires an anchor toss or intro. You can go directly to weather and sports segments, for example, without an anchor toss right out of commercials.
- Remember to look for transitions between stories. Just don't use weak transitions such as, "In related news."
- Change anchors when there isn't a logical transition.
- Viewers remember "moments" long after the newscast is over. So, don't forget to create memorable moments. This can be achieved through an interview, a live-shot, show and tell or amazing video (Tomkins, 2017).

Backtiming

Originally, the term newshole referred to the amount of space remaining for news in a newspaper after paid advertisements. In broadcast TV, a newshole is the amount of airtime left for news content within a newscast after commercial spots are purchased (Smith, 2000). If we have three commercial breaks in a show and each break runs for 2 minutes, then that means we have 6 minutes total in commercials. If our newscast is 30 minutes, then that leaves us with 24 minutes of actual news content – keep in mind that we must also include weather, sports and entertainment within our newshole. Once you factor in all your PKGs and voice-overs, live-shots etc. you realize that 24 minutes is actually not that much time.

Writing Teases

As already noted, each block is separated by a commercial break. You will notice that the slug right before each break is called a tease. The fundamental purpose of a tease is to spark the viewer's interest and entice them to stay tuned (Halper, D. & Potter, D. , 2014). The worst mistake you can make is giving the story away. If you did, what would be the point of sticking around for an entire break after knowing the gist of the story? So, it is imperative that teases create and hook and be enticing but don't get to the heart of the story. Think of your teases as riddles that drop hints but keep the viewer wanting or needing more details. Here is an example:

BAD: "*Coming up the 405-freeway will be shut down all week. More details when we return.*"

BETTER: "*Coming up… a busy freeway is getting ready to shut down all week. We'll tell you if it's near you and how you can avoid the traffic nightmare.*"

Notice that the first tease gives away the entire story, so there is no need to stick around for an entire commercial break. The second tease is better for several reasons. It does not give away the exact freeway that will shut down, so I am left wondering if I will be impacted. It also makes a promise to the viewer by informing them that they will get tips on how to avoid the traffic chaos if they stick around.

A Note about Ethics, Video and Reporting on Latinx/a/o Communities

As a Latino journalist, you may run into situations that will require you to handle your interviewees and the video you gather with care. I've covered immigrations for nearly two decades, and I have always been amazed by undocumented immigrants' willingness to share very personal information that could potentially put them in danger – albeit often times this involves recently arrived immigrants who might not fully understand the consequences. While reporting from Tapachula along the Mexico-Guatemala border on the migrant caravan crisis, I was amazed by the number of people who volunteered their full legal names and countries or origin. "We are always very careful when an immigrant volunteers their name and immigration status," states Elizabeth Cotte, the Executive Producer for Univision's flagship newscast *Noticiero Univision*. "Trust is very important and the last thing we would want is to be responsible for someone's deportation or any legal repercussions," Cotte adds. One way to protect an interviewee's identity is by simply omitting any last names. Another common practice is to create a pseudonym – my scripts about undocumented immigrants often have VO's that read something like, "This immigrant, who we will call Maria." What separates Latinx journalists from other cultures is the close ties that we hold to our communities – remember, Univision and Telemundo both emerged as a result of English networks' refusal to cover Latinx/a/o communities. While some critics might contend that our ties to the Latinx/a/o communities make us biased, it's undeniable that we feel an added responsibility to cover our communities accurately; thus, when we report from within our own communities, we will often engage in civic journalism, a form of journalism that promotes civic engagement within Latinx communities and encourages viewers to become a part of the democratic process. "Many Spanish-language media organizations follow the civic journalism model and are likely to offer 'advocate style' news coverage that promotes immigrant interest and encourages political participation by their audience and legalization of their migrant audience" (Rodriguez, 1999).

Additionally, you also want to handle any video that is shot with a lot of care. In 2019, one of my students from Al Día reported from a rescue haven for children who had victims of sexual trafficking. In this case, the director of the shelter gave explicit permission to shoot the children without any restrictions. However, I insisted that we needed to shoot the video in a way that deliberately protected the children's identities. There are numerous ways that one can achieve this. One option would be to only shoot the children from the neck down and focus on shooting tight shots of their hands, eyes, mouths, feet etc. Another option might be to shoot interviews or broll with the children's backs facing the camera. And lastly, one could also place a child in front of a bright background, like a window, and close down your camera's iris until the person you are interviewing turns into a dark silhouette. Any time that you're dealing with victims – be it immigrants, children, battered women, etc. – you want to be careful and handle your interviews and video images with a great deal of care. If you are unsure, always ask yourself how might my reporting impact this person? What might happen once I am gone? Will there be any fallout?

A Conversation with John Quiñones, Anchor for ABC News an Intimate Journey from Migrant Farmworker to Beloved TV Anchor

There are three words that immediately come to mind when I think of Juan Manuel "John" Quiñones (pictured in Figure 12.8). Padrino. Pioneer. Survivor. John was a pioneer and broke down the glass ceiling for Latinos when there were very few journalists of color on television, and he is a survivor because he withered the microaggressions and the blatant racism and is still working in network television news 46 years later. And I'd like to think of John as my *padrino*, or godfather, because John was incredibly generous with his time and advice when I was merely a junior producer at ABC News. In fact, one of my very first high-profile international stories at the network found me in Lima, Peru working beside him. To this day I can still hear John's calm and soothing voice inside my head coaching me and saying, "Jesus, you are the producer, you've got this. Just trust in your abilities and go with your gut. You won't fail. I am here to help and I won't let that happen." Those of us who've had the distinct pleasure of being mentored by *el padrino* are better journalists and better humans for having known him.

Ayala Rico: I want to go back to that time when you were a student. At what point in your trajectory did you decide that you wanted to be a journalist?

Quiñones: I wanted to be a journalist since I was 12. In the barrio, in San Antonio, on the west side, I would watch the news and read newspapers, and

FIGURE 12.8 Quiñones (ABC News)

all the stories that we that were being done about Latinos were negative stories about gangs and violence and illegal immigration, much like it is today. But it really angered me that no positive stories were being reported on because I knew heroes that existed and lived and mentored me and my community, but we have never heard about them. And I felt that I was uniquely qualified to tell those stories. And I loved to dream of traveling. My family have never been out of San Antonio except to pick tomatoes in Ohio and cherries in Michigan as migrant farmworkers. That's the only time. I dreamed of traveling to Africa and to Brazil and to Italy, and I thought journalism was my ticket there.

Ayala Rico: That's amazing. I remember being in Peru with you and one of the things that you said during dinner that I thought was very impressive, and that you just mentioned right now is that you come from a family of migrant workers and your family picked tomatoes and other crops, and you worked in the fields too. So, I'm wondering how that experience shaped your perspective as a journalist?

Quiñones: Well, I knew that I didn't want to do that kind of work for the rest of my life. When you bust your butt doing back-breaking work picking tomatoes on the ground. I mean, I'll never forget being with my father. And there we were, you know, at six in the morning, looking at a row of tomato plants, which seemed to go on for miles and miles. That's what I had to look forward to that day. And my father Bruno said, "do you want to do this kind of work for the rest of your life, or do you want to get a college education someday?" It was a no brainer. I knew that I didn't want to do that kind of work, but no one believed in me when I came back to San Antonio, and I would ask my teachers, how do I prepare for college? How do I take the SAT's that the ACT's or take advanced placement classes? Do you know what my own teachers would tell me? They would say John, it's wonderful that you dream of someday being a television reporter but we think you should try woodshop, or metal shop or auto mechanics. Not that there's anything wrong with those trades. A lot of people make a good hard living doing that kind of work. But I wanted to go to college, and my own teachers and my own counselors did what people do on that show, What Would You Do. They judged me by the color of my skin, and the accent in my voice. But thank God for my mother, Maria. She would say, "It doesn't matter that you have to wear the same clothes to school every day, at least we wash them, right? Don't be embarrassed about having to take bean and tortilla tacos for lunch." She would say, "That doesn't matter. What matters is what's in here, in your *cabeza*, and what's here in your *corazón*."

Ayala Rico: You came up at a time when it was unpopular to be a Latino in journalism. Can you discuss what some of the hurdles you

experienced coming up as a Latino journalist at a time when, frankly, it wasn't acceptable to be a Latino journalist?

Quiñones: There were very few people when I was growing up in the 1970s who had Hispanic last names or were Latino. You could count them in one hand on radio and television. So it was tough to get my foot in the door. And I worked at a radio station. It was a country music station. I wasn't a fan of country music, but man, it was a job. It was an opportunity, right? And I was an intern for $2 an hour. And you know what I did in my first job in broadcasting? The DJs at this country music station had horses that they would use in public appearances and rodeos and parades. Part of my job was to feed the horses in the back of the studios for the disc jockeys. And then at night, I would sneak into the control room and I would practice. At that hour of the night, all the professionals who could help me who could criticize my delivery, were gone. The only one left was the janitor, and his name was Pablo Gonzalez and Pablo's English was worse than my father's. But I would drag him into the control room and I'd ask, "Pablo cómo se oye?," "How does it sound?" And he would go, "mas o menos," "pretty good." And that was my first job.

Ayala Rico: Do you remember any microaggressions once you were in the newsroom or any instances of flat-out racism? Because it was a different time back then?

Quiñones: After I graduated from college, I tried to get a job in television. Everyone would say we already have a Latino. We don't need another one. So, no one would hire me in television, in San Antonio, Houston, Dallas, Amarillo, McAllen, Texas, El Paso, nowhere. And it depressed me. I mean, I was just heart-broken. Early on hiring managers would think I could only do Hispanic stories, or only stories in Latin America. I mean, I took it as an opportunity to get my foot in the door, but I wanted to tell them I'm good enough to be on 20/20. I'm good enough to be on Primetime Live or Nightline. I'm not just the soldier you send out to Latin America because you know you people are getting shot at ... But there were little things, like whenever I would do an English story here in the states, people would presume I was, you know, are you the sound man? Are you the camera man? Nothing against them. But often people did not think I was the correspondent, who would be sitting next to them asking them the questions.

Ayala Rico: One of the things that my students are always so afraid of is rejection. And in this business rejection is inevitable. Tell me about a time when you were rejected and how you handled it?

Quiñones: I can show you 80 letters of rejection that I got when I was trying to get a job in television at the age of 23 years old in Texas, when I was a radio reporter.

Even with promotions within the radio station. My general manager at this station that I worked at kept saying, "You're starting to crawl now. Don't, don't, don't think that you're ready for a raise now." Because I did the overnight news and I wanted to get on during the daytime with everyone else. And he would say, "No, you're not ready. It's not your time." I mean, how many times have our people heard that? It's not your time. That happened to me even at ABC. I wanted to get on 20/20. I wanted to do stories that were not just a minute and a half long on the evening news. I wanted to tell longer stories more like documentaries and investigations on 20/20 like they do on 60 Minutes and on Dateline. There were very few Latinos on those shows. And they would reject me all the time. I was told, "What makes you think you're good enough to be on the big show?" Thank God, there was another producer on this new show called Primetime Live, who took me under his wing and gave me an opportunity. And the first story I did for them won an Emmy award. So, I did another story and another. And finally, they said, "Well, maybe you should... you want to come work for the show." And even then, I don't think I was paid the same amount of money that other people were getting paid. So, it's been a struggle. You just can't take the rejection; you can't let it get you down as much as I was almost on the precipice of giving up. Thank God I didn't, and I learned a valuable lesson there. Don't give up, just keep pushing. And if one door closes, go knock on another one.

Ayala Rico: At what point did you finally realize, OK, I've made it?

Quiñones: I guess, when Oprah invited me on her show, to talk about stories that I had done. When Larry King invited me on to his show to talk about all the stories on polygamy that we were doing in Utah, and in Arizona. And then when I won seven national Emmy Awards, I think I realized, I guess, people like the stories that I've done, and they've had an impact.

Ayala Rico: What's your advice for students who are Latino and who want to follow in your footsteps? What would be your best advice so that they too can pursue a career in broadcast journalism?

Quiñones: Journalism is so competitive, it's incredibly difficult to get your foot in the door. I found that out myself. But you know, if a kid who used to shine shoes in bars and who picked tomatoes, as a migrant farm worker can make it to network television, then, of course, anything is possible! And you do it by just not taking no for an answer. When someone says you're not good enough, blow them off, forget it, go to the next person. Read as much as you can get your hands on. Practice, because you've got to be able to go on the air and not be afraid, right? And not stumble. And the way you learn that is by going to work in smaller stations. Get an internship at a TV station or radio station. Start writing your own blog, get writing samples, record your voice, do a podcast.

You know, now there are so many more outlets than I had. I had to have a little cassette recorder to record my voice and the only one who could listen to it was the person that I played it for. Now you guys have access to social media, and you can get the word out and people can see your work. But just practice! Put in 1000s of hours, it's going to take that long. And in the end, just don't be dissuaded by anyone who says you're not good enough. And remember that if John Quiñones could do it then of course you can too.

Ayala Rico: I'm glad you said that because I think so many students battle with imposter syndrome. I think that the only real way you can overcome it is by not listening to the negative chatter and putting it aside. What do you hope your legacy will be? What does John Quiñones want his legacy to be and how does he want viewers and his colleagues to remember him?

Quiñones: You know, one of my favorite sayings is one by John Quincy Adams who said, "If with your actions or through your actions, you can inspire others, to dream more, to learn more, to do more and to become more, then you are a leader." And I would want that kind of legacy. At a time when too often in this country Latinos are held in such low regard it seems more than ever. I hope that through my work, I have reminded people that we are smart, we're intelligent, we're creative, caring people, and that we have wonderful stories to tell, and we can tell them in a very compelling way if you just give us a chance.

Discussion Questions

1. How is the history of Univision and Telemundo networks a reflection of the wider experience that Latino communities have faced in the United States? Why is it important that Latino communities be covered fairly and accurately?
2. What advantages and disadvantages do bilingual newscasts face in the current media climate? Do you believe it is acceptable for Spanish-language newscasts to be so closely involved in the communities they serve? Is there still a space for civic journalism? Why or why not?
3. You are covering an immigration protest and encounter a young couple who fled gang-violence in Central America. They were denied asylum at the border but managed to enter the country illegally. They agree to be interviewed on-camera and, surprisingly, they even volunteer their full-legal names and cities where they now live. Discuss how you would approach this scenario as a reporter and videographer. Think carefully about the potential legal consequences that this might create for the young couple long after your story has aired. Do you report their legal identities, or do you create a pseudonym? Do you decide to show their faces? Why or why not?

Class Exercises

1. In this chapter, you have learned what a Rundown is and what types of stories go in the different news blocks. Find three stories for each block (nine stories in total) that could go into a TV newscast this evening. Be able to articulate why the stories selected belong in the block you chose.
2. Now, pick one of those stories and write a tease for the story you selected. Remember, a tease should be enticing but should never give the heart of the story away, otherwise the viewer has no reason to keep watching.

References

Clance, P. (1985). *The impostor phenomenon: When success makes you feel like a fake.* Bantam Books, 10–21.

Cokley, K., Smith, L., Bernard, D., Hurst, A., Jackson, S., Stone, S., Awosogba, O., Saucer, C., Bailey, M., & Roberts, D. (2017) Impostor feelings as a moderator and mediator of the relationship between perceived discrimination and mental health among racial/ethnic minority college students. *Journal of Counseling Psychology*, 64(2), 141–154.

Halper, D. & Potter, D. (2014) *Advancing the story: Journalism in a multimedia world.* Sage Publications, 118–132.

Myers, B. (2016). *Where are the Minority Professors*, in The Chronicle of Higher Education. Retrieved July 16, 2021 from https://www.chronicle.com/article/where-are-the-minority-professors/

NBC Universal. (2021). Telemundo network and stations. Retrieved July 16, 2021 from https://together.nbcuni.com/nTelemundoo-station-group/.

Oppelaar, J., & Bernstein, P. (2001). NBC Universal Purchases Telemundo, in Variety. Retrieved July 16, 2021 from https://variety.com/2001/tv/news/nbc-habla-telemundo-1117854168/.

Papper, B. (2020). Newsroom Diversity Report. The Radio Television Digital News Association, Retrieved July 16, 2021 from https://www.rtdna.org/article/2020_research_newsroom_diversity

Ramos, J. (2016). *Sin Miedo: Lecciones de Rebeldes.* Penguin Publishing Group, 16–18.

Rodriguez, A. (1999). *Making Latino news: Race, language, class.* Sage Publications, 19–27.

Salazar, R. (1996). *Border correspondent selected writings*, 1955–1970. University of California Press, 33-37.

Smith, D. (2000). *Power producer: A practical guide to TV news producing.* Radio-Television News Directors Association, 20–43.

Subervi-Vélez, F., et al. (1993). *Hispanic American Almanac: A reference work on Hispanics in the United States.* Gale Research, 17–31.

Tomkins, A. (2017). *Aim for the heart: Write, shoot, report and produce for TV.* CQ Press, 66–72.

Univision. Company Overview. (2021). Retrieved July 16, 2021 from https://investors.univision.net/overview/default.aspx

Wentz, L. (2001). *Univision steps up at Upfronts.* Advertising Age.

13

Radio and Podcasting on the Latinx Community

Vanessa Vancour

The stories and ideas discussed throughout this book reflect the realities and complexities of the Latinx community's diverse lived experiences; it's Latinx media, created with and by Latinx storytellers.

The truth is, when you're working in communities that have historically been marginalized, exploited or stereotyped, doing this kind of work takes time. It means frequenting locally owned businesses to build relationships that are rooted in more *give* than take. This also means the ROI will take time to demonstrate, which is understandably problematic as often projects like this require buy-in from decision-makers, if you aren't one yourself.

While Census data shows more people in the United States are bilingual, media continues to be predominantly monolingual, and bilingual media is reduced to what is known as "ethnic media" (Gerson & Rodriguez, 2018). My wish is for content like this to be woven into the existing fabric, and to no longer be reserved for "special sections."

I spent six years as a journalism educator building a nationally award-winning bilingual Spanish-English language news model that allowed me to experiment with both multimedia production processes, as well as the impact on both students and professionals.

Whether you're a professional journalist, or an emerging one, I hope this chapter will empower you to speak with and to larger, more diverse audiences by way of bilingual audio production. This chapter explores the growth of Spanish-language radio and bilingual podcasting, and lends practical advice for creating your own bilingual audio content.

There are far more bilingual journalists in the United States launching audio content than when I started my program in 2015. The goal of those shows is to

DOI: 10.4324/9781003212331-13

serve listeners who speak *both* languages, and the models break with tradition because the content is delivered en ambos idiomas.

Of course, not all folks who identify as Hispanic or Latinx speak Spanish, but the language is still a central part of the culture. Spanish is, after all, the second most dominant language in the United States.

Recognizing an emerging demographic reality in the United States, formerly English-only news sites including the New York Times, The Washington Post and the New Yorker, have translated their English content into Spanish, and even offered original content in Spanish. In January 2020, USA Today announced a new series in English and Spanish titled *Hecho en USA*, in an effort to deepen connections with bilingual news consumers (Barber, 2020).

And as traditional Spanish language media outlets nationally continue to shut their doors, some like Univision are pivoting to audio-based storytelling to reach the growing Latino podcast audience (Martin, 2019; Univision, 2019)

My favorite Spanish-language podcast is *Radio Ambulante*, which tells uniquely Latin American stories. The founders often describe it as *This American Life*, but in Spanish and transnational. It was founded in 2012 by Carolina Guerrero and Daniel Alarcón, and in 2016 NPR began distributing the show, becoming the first Spanish-language podcast for the network (Pretsky, 2017).

In 2018 I attended the CUNY Latino Media Summit, where Guerrero revealed that 20% of the show's audience did not speak Spanish; they listened to improve their language skills. Since then, *Radio Ambulante* has launched an app to help listeners learn the language while listening to the show (Guerrero, 2018).

While Spanish language radio in the United States has been documented as far back as the early 1920s, the 1970s accounted for an explosion of community radio, primarily among farmworkers. Spanish-language radio has historically been synonymous with advocacy (Casillas & De La Torre, 2019).

An early pioneer in this space is Radio Bilingüe, a non-profit public radio network founded in 1976 by Hugo Morales and Latino activists and farmworkers. It is the only national distributor of Spanish-language programming in public radio in the United States and "owns and operates 13 of its own full-power FM non-commercial stations in California and the Southwest."

Unlike traditional public radio models, podcasting gives journalists and content creators the freedom to create audio in various formats, without guidelines or parameters.

In June 2020, Edison Research released a report on Latino podcast listeners, which found that 25% of Latinos in the United States are monthly podcast listeners, and they listen for 44 more minutes than the average U.S. listener per day (Soto & Castro, 2020).

For the 28% of Latinos who said they had never listened to a podcast, their reason was there weren't any podcasts covering topics they were interested in.

This is where you come in.

As you read through this chapter and begin to form or refine your ideas for a bilingual podcast or radio story, I invite you to draw inspiration from some of my favorite bilingual shows:

- *Latina to Latina* https://www.latinatolatina.com

Host Alicia Menendez interviews remarkable Latinas about "making it, faking it, and everything in between." This show is produced by former NPR employee Juleyka Lantigua-Williams' production company, where you can discover more diverse shows.

- *La Brega* https://www.wnycstudios.org/podcasts/la-brega

It's a bilingual podcast series (Tameez, 2021) about Puerto Rico's history, and is a co-production between WNYC Studios and Futuro Studios, the podcast and programming arm of Futuro Media.

- *¿Qué Pasa, Midwest?* https://www.quepasapodcast.com

Multimedia journalist and bilingual producer Paola Nicole Marizán founded WNIN's first bilingual radio program and podcast in Evansville, Indiana. *¿Qué Pasa, Midwest?* is designed to keep the Latino community informed about local and national news and events.

- *Don't Interrupt Me, Por Favor*

This is a playful interview podcast hosted by three bilingual journalists who go deep with a notable bilingual human about a topic they wish to better understand. Previous guests include World Central Kitchen's José Andrés, the Knight Foundation's Alberto Ibargüen and Latino USA's Maria Hinojosa. It's available on Apple iTunes, Spotify and Stitcher.

- *Tamarindo Podcast* https://www.tamarindopodcast.com

This is a weekly Latinx empowerment podcast that covers topics ranging from politics, culture and "how to keep your calma with well-being practices and self-love, hosted by Brenda Gonzalez and Ana Sheila Victorino."

- *A Donde Media* https://adondemedia.com

Founded by Martina Castro, who also co-founded *Radio Ambulante*, A Donde Media is a globally minded podcast production company worth knowing.

A Closer Look at *Noticiero Móvil*

In 2015, I founded *Noticiero Móvil* at the University of Nevada, Reno, where I worked as an administrative faculty member for six years (Rivas, 2017). The digital news project was rooted in working *with* the local Latinx community instead of reporting *on* them, as journalists have historically done.

The inspiration for this project was simple. When I compared our demographic Census data against the existing media outlets in the community, I noticed an obvious disparity.

Although the county data showed nearly one quarter of the population identified as Hispanic, Spanish language or bilingual journalism was lacking. At the time, Univision's editorial desk was based eight hours away, so local news on Spanish-language television was often reduced to crime or big political stories. Spanish-language radio was made up mostly of entertainment, and the three local Spanish newspapers were published weekly, at best, and filled with business advertisements and AP newswire clips.

The project was funded by a micro-grant from the Online News Association called "The Challenge Fund for Innovation in Journalism" (University of Nevada, Reno, 2015).

With this grant, I wished to test three areas:

1. Were university journalism students interested in developing skills to become bilingual, Spanish-English reporters?
2. Was there an appetite from local media organizations to collaborate to diversify the kinds of stories they produced?
3. Was there a need for bilingual reporting in our community?

Each question resulted in an emphatic "yes."

The college students who worked on the project were enrolled in an upper division, three-credit course made up of both undergraduate and graduate students. Each semester, the group included some students who were Latinx, some Spanish-speaking, others with no experience in Latinx cultures, and inevitably, those who signed up for an "easy" three credits. The course was rigorous, and the students were treated as professional journalists who were expected to produce two to three complex, multimedia projects each semester in English and Spanish (see Figure 13.1).

During the first year of the project, the students worked on developing the brand; we worked with a local, Latinx designer to create the logo, the website and social media channels which included Facebook, Instagram and Twitter.

Our work focused on rich, feature stories ranging from an intimate look at the lives of local day laborers in a project titled *The Workers of La Piedra*, to a bilingual multimedia story about a local Guatemalan baker who fled his

FIGURE 13.1 College students enrolled in Noticiero Móvil were treated as professional journalists who were expected to produce two to three complex, multimedia projects each semester in English and Spanish. Here, Monica Gomez interviews local business owner Maria "Concha" Ramirez.

Photo Credit: Vanessa Vancour

home country seeking asylum. The comment sections for these pieces in particular highlighted the need for more content like this in our community as they sparked lively debate and conversation.

In the first two years of the program, we also invested heavily in community outreach to build meaningful relationships with local Hispanic business owners and their patrons. This directly contributed to the success of our in-person events, which we called "listening parties," during which we invited critical feedback on the stories we produced.

In 2017, KUNR Public Radio News Director Michelle Billman identified the opportunity to partner with *Noticiero Móvil* and pitched the idea of co-mentoring a paid, bilingual internship in both newsrooms. She sought funding through a university internship grant program, which *Noticiero* matched with additional funding to adequately pay the student reporter. Initially the reporter focused on in-depth feature stories centered on sports, business, health disparities, immigration and art. Over time, the position evolved to include more daily news coverage as needed (KUNR, n.d.).

"We have been able to have consistency with the interns so that they're building on their knowledge and becoming actual beat reporters - that's been huge. The ability to extend the experience beyond one semester is also critical. To see the interns building contacts and relationships in the community has also contributed to the evolution and depth of their story ideas," said Billman in a conversation with me in March 2018, during which we reflected on our program.

Our collaborative model earned national recognition, including two national Murrow awards, one PMJA award, and a Gracie Award. The first national Murrow was earned by our inaugural bilingual intern Stephanie Serrano for best sports reporting for her story on the local professional soccer league (Serrano, 2017) (see Figure 13.2). As Billman wrote in an article for RTNDA, the story was about much more than sports (Billman, 2019).

In under five minutes, Stephanie was able to tell a story that resonates far beyond any soccer team or sporting event. She gave voice to a struggle many children and their families are experiencing in this country by doing what the best reporters do—cultivating understanding and empathy through personal storytelling.

FIGURE 13.2 Bilingual reporter Stephanie Serrano earned a national Murrow Award for best sports reporting in small market radio. The story highlights Reno's professional soccer team, Reno 1868 FC. Serrano earned the award as a student intern at KUNR Public Radio.

Photo Credit: Aaron Serrano, 2017

The best stories our team produced were centered around vulnerable experiences, sometimes rooted in heavy topics such as immigration and mental health; those stories in particular took months to put together.

And the work didn't end once the audio piece was produced; the reporter was responsible for repackaging it for two newsrooms and in different mediums – two websites, two Facebooks, two Instagrams and in two languages. It's a labor-intensive process for both the reporter and the editors.

In early January 2019, our bilingual intern Karina Gonzalez published a story titled "Roughly 4,400 TPS Holders Await their Fate" (Gonzalez, 2019). Gonzalez localized a national issue by centering the narrative around a local woman from Nicaragua.

In a KUNR digital analytics report, the English version of the story held the number one position for most viewed on the KUNR website. The most astounding data point, though, was that 97% of the readers were new visitors to the site. It was also one of the highest performing stories on the station's Facebook page at the time.

The Spanish content on KUNR's website typically saw the least amount of views and engagement. The process was always iterative and experimental as we attempted to understand how to best reach the local bilingual audience via what had historically been an English-only news station.

We also frequently debated how much time we should spend "explaining" concepts or Spanish words to a primarily Anglo audience, as well as how long we should let a Spanish soundbite run on air. The public radio model generally only allows non-English soundbites to appear for a few seconds on air, quickly covered by voice over, but we felt doing that could affect the integrity of the story, and over time extended the length of the Spanish soundbite.

Adrián Florido is a national correspondent for NPR who covers race and identity in the United States, and inevitably, much of his coverage on natural disasters included a number of interviews in Spanish. In an interview with Holly Pretsky for NPR in 2017, he said, "The thing we love about radio is how intimate it is, right? But that removes a lot of the intimacy if you have someone translating or interpreting for someone" (Pretsky, 2017).

What we learned in our endeavor is community-centered, bilingual audio production is a time consuming process, and it is truly a grassroots effort, which is why strategic partnerships like ours are critical (see Figure 13.3). While journalistic style guides have evolved over the years to include guidance on how to approach certain themes or marginalized communities, little exists on how to produce bilingual journalism. (Thus the catalyst for this book.)

We eventually refined a workflow that worked for our newsrooms, and I hope it may be useful to you as well.

FIGURE 13.3 Noticiero Móvil hosted a series of "listening parties" aimed at seeking critical feedback on the program's reporting, from the community, via in person events. This event was hosted over dinner at a local Mexican restaurant.

Photo Credit: David Calvert, 2016

Workflow

- Ideation process – I would work with the reporter first in forming the story pitch, and if necessary, connecting them with data, contacts and context related to the local Latinx community.
- Story pitch – Billman, as the station's news director, would approve the pitch and provide mentorship for script, audio and web edits in English.
- Translation and voicing support – I would collaborate with our paid, professional translator on the Spanish elements which included voice coaching for the Spanish script.
- English edit – Ultimately, the story would air on KUNR and be published in English online. The Spanish version was distributed digitally and via social media. The reporter took the lead on posting to the numerous social media accounts in both languages.

For the work samples below, I provided editorial direction, specifically in working with the reporter to develop the story as well as post production edits and translation.

- Noticiero Móvil program overview - https://www.facebook.com/928922053836139/videos/2142817202490353/?__so__=channel_tab&__rv__=all_videos_card

- https://www.facebook.com/Noticiero Móvil/videos/2275625676038320/
- https://www.kunr.org/post/roughly-4400-tps-holders-nevada-await-their-fate#stream/0
    - https://www.kunr.org/post/aproximadamente-4400-beneficiarios-de-tps-en-nevada-esperan-su-destino#stream/0
- https://www.kunr.org/post/prevention-programs-address-mental-health-washoe-youth#stream/0
- https://www.kunr.org/post/keeping-language-interpretation-demand#stream/0
- https://www.kunr.org/post/reno-1868-fcs-fan-base-growing-fast#stream/0

A Conversation with Felix Contreras, Founder and Host of NPR's Alt Latino

First and foremost, how do you identify?

Contreras: I identify as Chicano, and I define Chicano as a politicized Mexican-American. I've identified as Chicano since I was in high school, probably just a little bit before I graduated from high school in 1976. So it was not that long after the Chicano movement was very active in the early 1970s; I was a benefit of things that happened during that time. I was a La Raza studies major at Cal State University, Fresno. It's strictly a Southwest thing, and Chicano is a tricky term because not all Mexican-Americans are comfortable with that. Like my parents, my dad does not consider himself a Chicano because during his generation it was a negative term, but that is the result of the 1970s young activists reclaiming the word for themselves and their identity.

Can you remember the first time you saw or heard yourself in the media?

Contreras: I started high school in 1973, and by then I was reading Rolling Stone Magazine, which at that time was much more political. They were covering the Vietnam War extensively. They were covering alternative leftist politics extensively. There were a few writers dealing with Latino or Chicano politics at the time, specifically Chicano politics. I was reading some of that stuff. There was a writer, he wrote a book called "The Autobiography of a Brown Buffalo," Oscar Zeta Acosta, and so I was reading his stuff, his books, he eventually wrote some stuff for Rolling Stone and was a very controversial political figure. So I was reading things that were out there already.

Personal History – Who are you and what was your start in radio or podcasting?

Contreras: I was recently reminded by an old high school friend of mine and something I completely forgot, I had petitioned our high school to allow us to play records over the school P.A. during lunch time. The vice principal, who was a Mexican-American, he gave me a shot. "OK, we're going to buy you a turntable." And the guy's people hooked it up into the little P.A. system, and I was playing mostly like rock and roll, Allman Brothers, Jeff Beck, stuff like that. So people could sit in the little quad area and they could hear the music.

Since the seventh grade, I knew I wanted to do journalism. I was a radio TV major at Fresno State, and they had a little TV production studio. I started college in the fall of 1976 and by October of 1978 I was fortunate to get a 20-hour-a-week minimum wage paid internship at the local NBC affiliate in Fresno, which at the time was KMG TV and eventually they changed their call letters to KSEE.

Then it was 1980 when Hugo Morales, who was one of my La Raza studies teachers, said, "hey, I'm starting this radio station," a listener-supported, local radio station. At that point, I didn't know what NPR was. What I *was* listening to was the listener supported radio station out of Berkeley, California, KPFA. So, I volunteered and I was one of the first five volunteers at Radio Bilingue when they started.

I'd like to discuss the history of Alt Latino – walk us through the journey/timeline of how and why you started this podcast.

Contreras: I started working for NPR in 2001, and I got hired to do jazz programming. Eventually I got absorbed into the news department. So then I started doing stories about Latino arts and culture for the Arts Desk at NPR with NPR News. So I was in the news department up until I started doing the program Alt Latino in 2010, but from 2001 to 2010 I was doing stories about jazz profiles on Latino artists. I did a series on this new Latin alternative Rock en Español sound that was coming from Mexico and Latin America. I did stuff like that, always looking to present something that wasn't there.

My desk in the old NPR building was right next to the little room where they had candy machines, potato chips and soda. So people were walking by my desk constantly, and I got to know this young woman who was working for the Michel Martin show, "Tell Me More," Jasmine Garsd. She was in her early part of her career as a journalist. She's originally from Argentina and spent some time in the Bay Area, went to UC Berkeley.

One day she was walking by and I said, "who are you and what do you do?" And she said, "I'm from Argentina." I said, "Oh, you know Fabulosos Cadillacs?" She says, "Oh, my God, I love that band!" So we bonded over this love for this music. And then one day she said, wouldn't it be cool if we could do a show about the music? And I said, "yeah, good luck," because my feeling at the time was that the public radio system didn't have space for it, and wouldn't consider it because it can be a pretty conservative programing approach.

And then NPR got a grant for some RFPs for new podcasts. This is 2008, 2009 maybe. You know, the first wave of podcasting. We pitched the idea first to a guy who was working at NPR just before the RFP. He was heading up podcasting, whatever that was going to be. He said, "you have put a pilot together and let's run up the flagpole."

So Jasmine and I went in, I remember very distinctly, we went in after work, into the production studio. We met for a long time with what would it sound like? How are we going to do this? We patterned it after an NPR newsmagazine – an intro headline, what we are going to talk about, and then different segments.

Jasmine and I submitted our pilot, and there were like 150 people who submitted podcast ideas, and Jasmine and I were one of three projects that were selected. The other two didn't survive, their ideas just didn't work for a whole bunch of reasons. But ours kept going. Ours had life, and we pitched it and NPR Music was just getting started.

The first show, I think, was like 12 minutes or so, and was during the World Cup 2010. The first show was about soccer songs. Jasmine had gathered soccer songs from Latin America, Europe, Britain, Ireland, and then we interviewed Juanes backstage at the World Cup about his favorite soccer songs. So that sort of set the tone for what we wanted to do.

The curious thing, and it goes back to presenting a podcast like this within, you know, mainstream culture; we know who Juanes is and Juanes was a huge star, but the majority of NPR listeners probably didn't know who he was or how big of a deal he was, so by us presenting this within the structure of NPR Music and NPR proper, we're introducing artists to them that may they may not have heard of before, even though he was extremely popular among Latino communities, here in the states and beyond. That's always been sort of the rubric. The framework that we work with is that we're doing music discovery.

Attempting to capture 20 years of experience, what key lessons or takeaways are salient?

Contreras: I'm a music fan. I'm a music geek. I play music. I'm curious about all kinds of music. So, I'm able to indulge my passion for music and combine it with my passion for journalism, storytelling, fact finding, sharing, you know, curating this stuff. I think, above all, find something that you love to do and then make that your job, your career, your thing.

Why is language so important to this kind of work?

Contreras: One of the first shows we did, we did a Spanish interview and we had a voiceover underneath or over the entire thing. We found a woman to voice over the interview and listening back, it's like fingernails on a chalkboard. You know, it didn't really work.

We assumed that people who don't speak Spanish are listening to the show because they want to become familiar with Spanish or they're trying to learn Spanish or they appreciate something in a different language, they're not going to shut us off. They're not going to press the stop button on the podcast because they hear Spanish, because all of our music's in Spanish, our talking's in English.

Spanish is not my native language, I'm an English speaker, born and raised in the United States. So I will read some intro, usually start the show, "hey, this is going to be a Spanish show. This is the last you're going to hear in English, OK." Because it comes across people's podcast feed and if they start hearing the Spanish, at least I give them a warning.

The Spanish interviews allow people to express themselves in a way that they're comfortable with. Just about every Spanish interview involves some kind of Spanglish. We go back and forth.

For radio, I'll run shorter Spanish cuts, but I'll leave it what we call "up." I won't dip it under, I won't do a translation. Sometimes I'll dip it under and say, "well, what she said was blah, blah, blah." Paraphrase. But for the most part, I'll leave it out. People are listening to NPR on the radio. If they're listening to our show, they have some affinity or some connection to listening to things in Spanish.

A resounding theme in both your project and mine is the value of experimentation. What advice can you give to others trying to create something new or "different" in connecting with Latinx communities?

Contreras: I think the first lesson or advice is that nature abhors a vacuum. Look for what's not there, and then find a way to fill that spot, which is what we did with Alt Latino. Maria Hinojosa and Latino USA … Maria is a friend of mine and she's a colleague, and I respect her immensely because she is absolutely a pioneer in journalism and in radio in particular. Latino USA was already on the air, so they were already doing news magazine, touching on crucial news issues of the day, and they do the best job doing that.

We found a niche talking specifically about culture every week; they will touch on culture occasionally, maybe seven-minute segments. We'll do a whole 45 minutes on it. So, find what's not being done and then figure out a way.

And then know when it comes time to present your ideas, know who you're pitching to. If it's a mainstream media organization, one of the many podcast companies, even radio stations, college universities; try to understand the internal politics and where these groups are with their DEI efforts, and how your show or idea can help them achieve their overall goals.

Find your niche and stick to it.

Just keep refining the ideas; nothing's ever going to be golden 100% right out of the gate. It's a process of learning, about building and getting better, but at the same time being able to pivot whenever things change.

What advice would you give to students on getting a meaningful internship?

Contreras: It's an interesting time right now since DEI has become a thing. I've been at NPR for 20 years, I've been on every single diversity panel and group and, you know, very rarely did it take off, very rarely did managers take it seriously and were in it beyond just having lip service. I'm not speaking out of turn. I'm not saying anything in public that I haven't said elsewhere in other times. We're in a position at NPR right now where I think that the new CEO has made DEI our North Star, and so there are lots of things going on within the building that are reflecting that. So, again, how can your project or your journalism or cultural skills, your language skills, how can that advance the cause of inclusion? What can you do to help that? Because, again, it's not just because it's a good thing to do. It's the right thing to do. It's a solid business proposition. You're going to be successful if you can do that, if you can find a way to reach that market, what the general market calls "the buying power."

What tips can you offer to newsroom leaders for designing a more inclusive mentorship/internship experience?

Contreras: People are at NPR because they want to be there, not because it's a stepping stone. So we believe in the mission. A part of that is that we want to make NPR better, and be more inclusive. It's not always easy, but you just have to be consistent.

And the other advice is, get a buddy. Find somebody so that when you say, "oh, my God, I can't take this anymore." Your buddy will say, "OK, don't do anything, I'm here. I'll go to the meeting, I'll raise the ruckus. I'll make the point." Because it's hard to be the diversity cop every single day. You also need to be able to survive mentally, intellectually, emotionally to be effective.

Trade Tools and Tips

What You Need to Start a Podcast

1. **Your big ideas**

   My project was inspired by demographic data, which can often be a great place to draw inspiration. Where might you identify a gap and fill it? What's geographically relevant in your community? Where does your target audience currently engage, and what are they discussing? What do you bring to the table that's different from other podcasts in this space?

2. **Format and structure**

   I like to start creative endeavors with inspirational research. If you're interested in producing NPR-style feature stories, listen to NPR feature stories! Similarly, scan the abundant podcast sphere to find styles you may want to borrow for your own production.

   This article from NPR's training forum offers great questions to consider before starting your story (MacAdam, 2016).

3. **Equipment**

   One of the great things about producing audio content is it's accessible! You can start a podcast using your smartphone. There are lots of phone based podcast recording apps on the market, including Anchor.fm or Spreaker Studio. Keep in mind these only allow for minor edits.

   If you'd like to use more professional equipment, there are USB digital mics, which are easy to use, to dynamic mics. Always be sure to record using sound cancelling headphones, *not* earbuds.

   For sound editing software, you can explore and choose from Adobe Audition, Reaper, Garageband, Hindenburg, or Audacity. If you're new to audio mixing, know it is time consuming, but there are tons of great training programs online, including this one from NPR (Byers, 2018).

4. **Distribution**

   In addition to uploading your show to Soundcloud, iTunes, Spotify, Google Play, etc., I'd like to offer other ideas for building your audience:

   - Consider traditional advertising, especially in community publications or spaces where your audience exists.
   - Design strategic partnerships with other media organizations or content creators.
   - Facebook groups can allow listeners to submit ideas or ask questions about episodes.
   - Consider videotaping your show and distributing it via IGTV or YouTube. You can also host Facebook or IG Live events to create exclusive interactions with your fans.
   - WhatsApp is a text-based way to engage with people and build personal interactions and connections. "Documented," a non-profit news outlet in New York, uses WhatsApp to connect with the local immigrant community (Castellano & Loker, 2020).
   - Don't discount analog engagement! Put up flyers in communal areas and consider hosting in person events. KUNR used virtual events in Spanish to connect folks with resources during the pandemic (Van Hoozer, 2021).

Be a Mentor

If you're a decision-maker, hopefully you already know that having a successful and mutually beneficial internship experience is an organizational responsibility, and it requires a real investment of both time and money.

Invest in a team and resources to support bilingual reporters, like a professional translator, a bilingual mentor and be selective and mindful during the recruitment process as well. The goal is to find and nurture strong writers and communicators in both languages. The Latinx community presents a different set of access challenges; it takes longer to build trust and relationships and contacts.

Advice

- Spend more time in the key places where people meet and talk.
- Embed people and issues from minority communities into "mainstream" stories about politics, business, economics, health and other topics.
- Understand the history and context of your community. Humanize your neighborhoods; you must be willing to devote the time to truly diversify your sources.
- Identify community partners, like universities, with resources to help.
- Hire a translator. Many newsrooms are not investing in translators or tools to help bilingual journalists with their language skills.
- Be willing to feel uncomfortable. Create a safe space to have uncomfortable and honest conversations. It cannot be ignored.
- Understand the difference between reporting *on* versus *with* a community, and know when to adopt different models.
- Invest in professional development for your team, like Next Generation Radio.
- Listen to podcasts and audio narratives – lots of them – and experiment with your format.
- Establish a feedback loop with your audience; be willing to accept critical feedback and be willing to pivot or iterate as needed.

Discussion Questions

In my experience as a faculty member, I had several students throughout the years tell me I was the first person to explicitly tell them their second or native language was an asset, beyond their Spanish classes. It stopped me every time.

At the start of each semester, I would lead my students in an exercise about our identities.

Our experiences and assumptions inevitably influence our behaviors and decisions, and certainly how we approach our stories. We are cultural beings, and our identities evolve and transform over time.

As you ideate and create bilingual content, remember – if your identity isn't static, neither is your audience. How can you lean into your own lived experiences to create compelling or relatable content in either English or Spanish?

Five Discussion Questions to Ask

1. What keeps you listening to a podcast?
2. How do other podcasts use narrative, natural sound, music and interviews?
3. What subjects do Latinx podcasters cover that may be overlooked by mainstream media?
4. How many podcasts are bilingual and how do they create a fusion of English and Spanish?
5. Language and word choice is important in developing an environment of cultural inclusivity – in the newsroom and in your coverage. Why do we have standards of language? Can you provide an example of good or poor word choice?
6. How do we avoid pigeonholing our reporters of color? And how do we encourage all reporters to report in communities that are different from their own?

Assignments

1. Make a list of formal and informal institutions within your community that provide jobs, essential services or space for Latinx community members to talk and resolve problems. Compare that against your existing contact list and identify key people you should or can develop a relationship with.
2. Food is a great entryway to understanding culture and its people. For this assignment, I want you to visit a panaderia or mercado in a neighborhood you don't frequent or have never visited. You can go in pairs, but you must each submit a unique, individual assignment.

   I want you to find a product you've never seen before and/or are unfamiliar with. You must find someone in that store – an employee or patron – who can explain what it is as well as its uses. What did you learn about the Latinx culture through this item? What surprised you about the conversations you had? Journal and critically reflect on your experience, and address any assumptions you encountered. Tell me about people you met with as much detail as possible. What were they wearing? How did they respond to your approach? Where did you meet? What preconceived notions did you have about them prior to engaging in a conversation? What surprised you about the person and/or the conversation? What will you take away from this experience/what can you apply to your future work as a journalist?

Be sure to take a least three (3) photos total, one of the location, one of the person you interviewed and one more establishing shot that captures the character of the place.

3. Data exploration + immigration studies: Choose one of the 12 studies cited in this report https://journalistsresource.org/studies/government/immigration/mexico-immigration-economy-crime-research and read it critically. How might you localize this study? What local data can you find from reputable sources to help you do this?

References

Barber, K. (2020, January 7). *USA Today tests bilingual content with new series.* Digiday. Retrieved September 30, 2021, from https://digiday.com/media/usa-today-tests-bilingual-content-new-series/?utm_source=Daily%2BLab%2Bemail%2Blist&utm_campaign=696e3ce5aa-dailylabemail3&utm_medium=email&utm_term=0_d68264fd5e-696e3ce5aa-396104397

Billman, M. (2019, January 14). *National Murrow winner uses bilingual skills to tell new stories while still in college.* RTDNA. Retrieved September 30, 2021, from https://www.rtdna.org/article/national_murrow_winner_uses_bilingual_skills_to_tell_new_stories_while_still_in_college

Byers, R. (2018, October 31). *The producer's handbook to mixing audio stories.* NPR. Retrieved September 30, 2021, from https://training.npr.org/2018/10/31/mixing/

Casillas, D. I., & De La Torre, M. (2019, July 11). *Looking back on the lesser-known histories of 'Chicano Public Radio'.* Current. Retrieved September 30, 2021, from https://current.org/2019/07/looking-back-on-the-lesser-known-histories-of-chicano-public-radio/?wallit_nosession=1

Castellano, S., & Loker, K. (2020, April 22). *How documented uses WhatsApp to reach local immigrant communities.* American Press Institute. Retrieved September 30, 2021, from https://www.americanpressinstitute.org/publications/articles/how-documented-uses-whatsapp-to-reach-local-immigrant-communities/

Gerson, D., & Rodriguez, C. (2018, July 18). *Going forward: How ethnic and mainstream media can collaborate in changing communities.* American Press Institute. Retrieved September 30, 2021, from https://www.americanpressinstitute.org/publications/reports/strategy-studies/ethnic-and-mainstream-media-collaborations-in-changing-communities/

Gonzalez, K. (2019, January 3). *Roughly 4,400 TPS holders in Nevada await their fate.* KUNR. Retrieved September 30, 2021, from https://www.kunr.org/post/roughly-4400-tps-holders-nevada-await-their-fate#stream/0

Guerrero, C. (2018). *Radio Ambulante - distribution, audience, community. CUNY Latino media summit: Lightning Talks.* CUNY Craig Newmark Graduate School ofJournalism. https://www.youtube.com/watch?v=9ygsvAoXvOk&t=1903s

KUNR. (n.d.). *KUNR Noticiero Movil Stream.* KUNR. Retrieved September 30, 2021, from https://www.kunr.org/search/google/noticiero%20movil#stream/0

MacAdam, A. (2016, December 13). *Beyond the 5 W's: What should you ask before starting a story?* NPR. Retrieved September 30, 2021, from https://training.npr.org/2016/12/13/beyond-the-5ws-what-should-you-ask-before-starting-a-story/

Martin, M. (2019, November 17). *The state of Spanish-language media in U.S.* NPR. Retrieved September 30, 2021, from https://www.npr.org/2019/11/17/780312543/the-state-of-spanish-language-media-in-u-s

Pretsky, H. (2017, December 14). *NPR in Spanish: Approaching content for a bilingual audience.* NPR. Retrieved September 30, 2021, from https://www.npr.org/sections/publiceditor/2017/12/14/570848670/npr-in-spanish-approaching-content-for-a-bilingual-audience

Reynolds School wins $35,000 Online News Association Challenge Fund grant. University of Nevada. (2015, April 24). Retrieved September 30, 2021, from https://www.unr.edu/nevada-today/news/2015/ona-journalism-grant

Rivas, 2017. *Bilingual emphasis introduced at Reynolds School of Journalism.* Retrieved September 30, 2021 from http://nevadasagebrush.com/blog/2017/10/24/bilingual-emphasis-introduced-at-reynolds-school-of-journalism/

Serrano, S. (2017, May 12). *Reno 1868 FC's fan base is growing fast.* KUNR. Retrieved September 30, 2021, from https://www.kunr.org/post/reno-1868-fcs-fan-base-growing-fast#stream/0

Soto, G., & Castro, M. (2020, June). Edison Research. Retrieved September 30, 2021, from http://www.edisonresearch.com/wp-content/uploads/2014/06/edison-logo-300x137.jpg

Tameez, H. (2021, March 11). *Fully bilingual, no voiceovers: How one podcast centers the Puerto Rican experience.* Nieman Lab. Retrieved September 30, 2021, from https://www.niemanlab.org/2021/03/fully-bilingual-no-voiceovers-how-one-podcast-centers-the-puerto-rican-experience/

Univision: The Data reveals a growing opportunity for Spanish-language podcasts. Insideradio.com. (2019, March 22). Retrieved September 30, 2021, from http://www.insideradio.com/podcastnewsdaily/univision-the-data-reveals-a-growing-opportunity-for-spanish-language-podcasts/article_c300ba8a-4cc4-11e9-9f0f-a77d9e54d196.html

Van Hoozer, N. (2021, March 3). *KUNR's virtual events in Spanish connect the northern Nevada community to Pandemic Resources.* RTDNA. Retrieved September 30, 2021, from https://www.rtdna.org/article/kunr_s_virtual_events_in_spanish_connect_the_northern_nevada_community_to_pandemic_resources

14

Social Media and the Digital Landscape

Amara Aguilar

The days of watching Spanish language news in the evenings on television with parents or grandparents settling in on the couch as the sun goes down have slowly come to pass. While television still remains a popular form of news consumption among older generations of Hispanics, the internet, social media and mobile devices have created a new media frontier that has brought news and information into the palms of people's hands. For Hispanic millennials, it represents a unique shift in the way they consume news compared to the generations before them (Flores & Lopez, 2018).

They are the force behind growing news consumption on the internet, according to a 2016 study by Pew Research Center (Flores & Lopez, 2018). The use of social media and mobile apps to get news was also a trend among Hispanics overall. "The growth of the internet as a news source on a typical weekday among Hispanics mirrors the trend in the overall U.S. population. As Pew Research Center previously reported, the internet is closing in on TV as the top source for news among all Americans," according to Pew Research Center (Flores & Lopez, 2018).

Hispanic millennials also tend to rely more on English-language news sources. Some of these factors have weighed heavily on Univision and Telemundo, two of the most popular Spanish-language television networks in the United States. Despite generational differences in media consumption, Univision and Telemundo's audiences have grown overall, according to Pew. Univision and Telemundo have tried to adapt to digital and social media trends, while newer startups and verticals have specifically targeted younger Latinos who have come to expect very visual, shorter and more engaging information formats (Pew Research Center, 2021).

DOI: 10.4324/9781003212331-14

Fusion, a cable network and news website targeted at English-speaking Hispanics in the United States, was launched in 2013 by ABC and Univision. Broadcast journalist and legendary news anchor Jorge Ramos served as host of Fusion's "AMERICA with Jorge Ramos" (Kim, 2013). Later he would host "Real America with Jorge Ramos," which premiered on Facebook Watch in 2018.

In 2016, Univision launched Univision Beta, a project that aimed to increase innovation, audience reach and exploration and implementation of emerging technology.

One year later, Univision launched local editions of Edición Digital, which aired on television and digital platforms simultaneously (Marszalek, 2017).

"As our audiences needs and habits change, we must evolve with them. Edición Digital allows us to experiment and be more engaging and creative with how we present news, content and information to our viewers," Chris Peña said in Next|TV, Univision's senior VP of news, local media. "The new midday shows allow our stations to make headline topics more accessible and personal to our audience, giving our communities what they demand and delivering content how and where they want to consume it" (Marszalek, 2017).

FMG became a leading digital publisher, but as it grew, there were challenges (Weprin, 2016). Layoffs and reorganization were announced in 2016. "Despite our size, what we have today are just the building blocks that will allow us to go after larger audiences and advertisers on multiple platforms, something we must do aggressively in these rapidly shifting and challenging digital landscapes. We need to constantly make sure we have the right mix and level of talent for this journey that we are on, making sure we are being efficient and streamlined in how we manage and use all our resources and talents," Univision chief news, digital and entertainment officer Isaac Lee said in a memo to staff. Fusion was never the same (Weprin, 2016).

A few years later, Univision tried more new initiatives and restructured its television group as part of a multi-platform media company strategy taking into consideration streaming and other media platforms. It announced it was launching a global streaming service in 2022 with two options: Free and subscription-based services (Business Wire, 2021).

Telemundo also announced it was going to create dozens of projects in 2022 through a new division focused on creating content for Peacock and NBCUniversal's other streaming platforms.

While streaming is seemingly the trend of the moment, some digital-startups have focused on exclusive content on websites and social media focused specifically on Latinx/a/o audiences.

In 2016, BuzzFeed launched Pero Like, targeted at English-speaking Latinx audiences. Pero Like took a distributed content strategy approach, focusing on content on Facebook and YouTube at first. Creators Alex Alvarez and Norberto

Briceño said in a Twitter announcement that it was "an exciting initiative celebrating Latinx/a/o voices, experiences, and viewpoints across multiple platforms, and a trailblazing collaboration between Editorial and BFMP [BuzzFeed Motion Pictures]." The brand explored identities, intersectionalities, and hoped to reach groups that were historically "under- and misrepresented in media." Pero Like's Twitter profile states, "Doing it for la cultura."

Remezcla, BESE and other digitally focused companies all have made their mark in the landscape of media companies targeting Latinx audiences, but it was mitú that helped make history when it came to showing a digital media company solely focused on Latinx/a/o audiences could thrive. The Los-Angeles based company states on its website:

> mitú is the leading digital media company representing the Latino point of view among consumers 18-44. Through our multiple touch points in video, editorial, social media and commerce, we connect brands, content buyers, and creators to the massive community of Latino consumers in America. Our audience is the 200% — 100% American and 100% Latino – who inspire us to create authentic, culturally relevant stories. We reach a massive, cross-cultural audience across a variety of social and O&O platforms. (mitú, 2021)

Mitú combined memes, gifs, social videos and web content focused on Latinx/a/o culture that made people laugh, kept them informed and resonated with audiences who saw their culture, habits and values reflected in their digital news feeds and timelines. Headlines and videos have included stories that focus on the Flamin' Hot Cheetos salad trend, 10 Queer Latine Influencers You Have to Follow, Cholas talk Chola Fashion – all along side stories about politics and entertainment focused on issues Latinx/a/o audiences care about. The company hired journalists, entertainers such as actors and comedians, documentary filmmakers and more to develop content that was not only diverse in storytelling, but included a variety of formats from video to text.

A study entitled, "We are the 200%": How Mitú constructs Latino American identity through discourse" found that "as a part of the company's strategy to engage audiences, on social media they are able to create news, comedy, animations and even nostalgia with multimedia content through a Latino point-of-view. Intertextual cues from popular American and Latin American cultural references, as well as an emphasis on the diversity of Latinos, contributes to the notions of intersectionality and simultaneity – that multiple characteristics can define identity, and that these characteristics can work at the same time to create plurality in how identities are articulated" (Wallace, 2020).

Merchandize, sponsored partnerships and new advertising models also helped the company grow. The mitú online shop features sweatshirts that say, "cool mami," stuffed plush Guacardo and friends figures, and accessories and decor that feature conchas, tacos and lotería, among other items.

Regarding Guacardo, a study focused on mitú stated, "As an anthropomorphic representation of one of the United States' most notable imports from Latin America, mitú's clever mascot Guacardo is far more than a naughty avocado. Videos of the cartoon character emerged through the publication's social media accounts in early 2017, and since then he has become a symbol not only for the publication, but also for its audience. Created by Danna Galeano, a Colombian Latina and one of mitú's animators, Guacardo is an awkward and comedic character who can often be found dancing or fumbling his way through situations. And although this animation is not directly a part of mitú's journalistic discourse, his character contributes largely to the publication's construction of a Latino American identity" (Wallace, 2020).

A Closer Look: Dímelo

Mitú inspired others to launch verticals and Latinx-focused media projects, including student newsrooms. At the University of Southern California Annenberg School for Communication and Journalism, students created the school's first Latinx-focused student media outlet, Dímelo, starting out on Facebook and evolving to launch on YouTube, Spotify and TikTok as the growth of digital platforms and social media usage among Generation Z and Millenials expanded (See Figure 14.1). Stories on COVID-19 and the Latinx community, celebrating Latinx women, asylum seekers, food, culture and more resonated with audiences on Snapchat Discover, helping the USC Dímelo account grow to more than 150,000 subscribers on the platform. Dímelo also collaborated with Fusion to cover stories near the California-Mexico border, Azteca America and mitú to produce and publish journalistic content and social media videos.

Dímelo's mission statement says:

> Dímelo means "tell me" in Spanish. The aim of Dímelo, a student-run media brand created at USC Annenberg School for Communication and Journalism, is to reach young Latinx and Hispanic adults with stories and content experiences that matter to them. Dímelo covers community stories, including those in Los Angeles, but also focuses on content that goes beyond boundaries — beyond geographic borders, beyond cultural borders, beyond stereotypes and beyond the surface of important issues that affect our world. Dímelo was born out of USC Annenberg and it is run by students who stand for: Strength. Resilience. Family. Identity. Reflection. Motivation. Culture. Diversity. Dímelo publishes in English and Spanish and aims to amplify unheard voices, engage audiences, create community

> and focus on issues that diverse audiences care about. Topics we focus on include politics, family, culture, diversity, food, sports, education, entertainment, humor, lifestyles, empowerment and more. "Dimelo" seeks to hear your voices and stories.

What were some keys to success for Dímelo and similar Latinx focused media outlets? A 2017 report by researchers at USC Annenberg entitled, "We're More Than That: Latinx Millennials, Media Reception, and the Role of Spanish-Language Media in Their Lives," found a variety of factors that influence millennial news consumption in Los Angeles (Luna-Peña, 2017).

FIGURE 14.1 Dímelo. Annenberg Media Dímelo, based at the University of Southern California, has grown its audience on Snapchat Discover to more than 100,000 subscribers as of 2021

Key findings from the report include:

- **Family is Central, Focus on the Tone.**
- **Latinx Millennials are Busy, their Media Consumption Reflects this.** Traditional television, in their opinion, is too time consuming. As such, they opt for a more non-linear mode of television watching. In other words, they seek out media in ways which fits around their busy schedules.
- **Latinx Millennials are Loyal, but not to Networks**. Instead, they are loyal to the personalities and celebrities they enjoy, are familiar with, and trust.
- **Music is Still in Spanish.** While nearly all of the respondents we spoke with characterized their television and streaming content as English-dominant, there was one area of media which many respondents admitted was still dominated by Spanish: music. Respondents in our study talked about listening to music in both languages, but enjoying music in Spanish more than English.
- **Social Justice is important to Latinx Millennials.** Latinx millennials care deeply about their community and the issues which impact them. ms which educated them or made them more aware of issues.
- **Latinx Millennials are Tired of Stereotypes.** Many of our research participants identified stereotypical portrayals—especially of women—as one of the main reasons they no longer consume Spanish-language television at the level they once had when they were younger. Latinx millennials want to see the Latinx community represented in media in a variety of ways. They are no longer satisfied with Latinxs playing the same roles. Instead, they want to expand the idea of what it means to be Latinx.
- **Everyday stories of Latinxs are important.** Latinx millennials are looking for more nuanced and diverse storylines from Spanish-language television.
- **Latinx Millennials want a greater variety of genre choices from Spanish-language television.**
- **Latinx millennial content is relevant across generations.**

—(Luna-Peña, 2017)

Using many of these concepts, Annenberg Media Dímelo and other Latinx-focused media have found some formulas for success in digital and social media. Producing authentic content, capturing and elevating voices that represent Latinx culture, and stories related to family, social justice and that resonate across generations have worked well for some in targeting Latinx audiences. A focus on audience trends and habits, innovation, authenticity and culture are essential as the media landscape continues to evolve.

Trade Tools and Tips

Dos

- Be authentic
- Bring unique perspectives
- Study your audience, including demographics, habits, values
- Focus on where your audiences are engaging
- Examine analytics and use tools that help you measure engagement
- Reflect diverse viewpoints
- Create visual and engaging content
- Think about distributed content
- Reflect on sustainability and growth
- Focus on stories that reflect family and a variety of cultures
- Create merch!
- Remember stories on social justice are important to young, Latinx audiences

Don'ts

- Focus on stereotypes
- Invest in only one platform
- Create repetitive content
- Limit creativity or pitches
- Lump Latino/a/x into one group
- Don't forget about sustainability

A Conversation with Beatriz Acevedo, Co-Founder of Mitú

When it comes to digital media targeted at Latino/a/x, mitú helped set the standard. At the helm, was co-founder Beatriz Acevedo, who spoke about the challenges and successes of her journey and career in media and entertainment (See Figure 14.2). The following are excerpts from an interview with Acevedo. Interview has been edited for length and clarity.

I am a very proud immigrant entrepreneur. I was born in the border between Mexico and the United States. I was born in Tijuana in Baja, California and my dad was a very proud Mexican man. So although my parents had a house in San Diego he rushed my mother across the border so I could be born in Mexico and be President of my country, one day … So I am an immigrant by default, could've been U.S. born. But anyway, I am a dual citizen today … I started in media when I was very young at 8 years old. I had a radio show.

And then, in my early teens I wrote, hosted and produced a TV show that won the first three Emmys for the network that I worked for which was Televisa.

FIGURE 14.2 Beatriz Acevedo. Beatriz Acevedo co-founded mitú, a digital media company focused on serving young Latinos in the United States. (Image courtesy of Beatriz Acevedo)

I always wanted to portray, whether it was in my home country at the time of Mexico, and now very active here, portray our community, in a very different light. So even though I was a teenager, I wanted the content that I produce to be aspirational and that people saw themselves represented in a way that they could dream bigger and aspire to be more. I think media till this day does a horrible job instilling that in our younger generation. I have been pretty obsessed with that from a young age…

I moved here in my early 20s after I had won my Emmys and an MTV Award for directing a music video.

I was definitely someone who spoke my mind … I have made it my life's mission to open as many doors as I can.

Hollywood is tough, you know Hollywood's a tough place to open doors, even if you are the executive producer. I could not for the love of God bring in anybody from my community into my own shows.

So when I discovered digital a few years back, I was enamored with digital … I just love digital. I thought this is amazing. I get to hire anybody I want. I get to incubate ideas and talent and build franchises with digital audiences that can make something big before a network exec decides if it's good or bad—already it's big before they even see it.

So I was just obsessed with digital media and that's where my husband and I co-founded mitú, which was the digital media brand for young Latinos who English dominant and U.S. born, etc. with a double goal. One was to be that incubator, playground place for the next generation of Latino storytellers. And on the other hand, to really super serve this very young and massively growing demographic of kids in our community that you know Spanish language media just is not them. They grow up watching it in the background, with a mom or abuelas whether it's a soap or a game show, but it doesn't really quite reflect their own experiences as U.S. born, just younger Latinos.

So you know, I was excited to build a brand that had that and that really sent that message to our community that you know they belong, that they were seen.

And that was super powerful and I'm super, super proud that that continues to thrive. I'm not involved in the company anymore. We sold it a few years back, but still very excited of what that mission was at the time.

That's how my involvement early on in entertainment happened as a young child in Mexico. I moved here to try to do some more. I was lucky that I was fortunate enough to be in the system and very frustrated with the fact that I couldn't break in and digital media at least gave me a place where I could do a little of that. Did I change Hollywood for the better? Did I move the numbers on representation? No. Do I continue to fight that fight every day? Yes, but that's where I am today…

My hope for the future is that we start being a little bit more vocal and aware that not being represented has a massive implication of erasure in our community, has massive implication on how our own children don't see themselves belonging in their own country, massive implications on how like I was saying in the beginning, how big you could dream of who you can become.

Discussion Questions

1. What content focused on Latinx audiences do you consume and why?
2. How does your news and information habits differ from your parents or someone your parents' age?
3. Reflect on the platforms and devices you use to consume news. How have you seen those habits change over the last year, five years, ten years.

Assignments

1. Keep a log of your news and information consumption for one week. Then interview someone outside of your generation about their news and information habits. Write a two-page paper or create a two-minute video about your findings. Use other formats if you wish (TikTok, Instagram Stories, etc.)
2. Create a story pitch for a local news organization that focuses on Latinx millennials or Gen Z. What would the headline be? Write a few paragraphs about what the story would be about, sources you might contact, who the audience would be, and what platform you'd produce the story for and why.
3. Do some research on social media consumption by ethnicity. What trends do you notice among Hispanics and Latinx audiences in the United States. Visualize your findings with paper and pencil or a digital chart.
4. Create a TikTok, Instagram Story or other news or feature story of your choice on the platform of your choice that you think would resonate with Latinx audiences in your community. Be creative!
5. Interview a Latinx journalist of your choice. Come up with at least 7-10 questions to ask. Include: What are your biggest challenges? What tips do you have for journalists when it comes to succeeding in journalism? What are you most proud of? You may conduct the interview in any media of your choice. Share it on social media if you wish or on your blog.

References

Business Wire, 2021. "Univision Announces New Structure of its Television Networks Group as Latest Step in Global and Multi-Platform Transformation. Retrieved on Sept. 30, 2021 from: https://www.businesswire.com/news/home/20210719005647/en/Univision-Announces-New-Structure-of-its-Television-Networks-Group-as-Latest-Step-in-Global-and-Multi-Platform-Transformation

Flores, A. & Lopez, H., 2018. *Among U.S. Latinos, The Internet Now Rivals Television As A Source For News.* Pew Research Center. Retrieved on Sept. 30, 2021 from https://www.pewresearch.org/fact-tank/2018/01/11/among-u-s-latinos-the-internet-now-rivals-television-as-a-source-for-news/

Kim, S., 2013. *ABC and Univision Announce New Cable Network 'Fusion' Will Launch Later in 2013.* ABC News. Retrieved on Sept. 20, 2021 from https://abcnews.go.com/Business/abc-news-univision-announce-cable-network-called-fusion/story?id=18468776

Luna-Peña, G., 2017. *We're More Than That: Latinx Millennials, Media Reception, and the Role of Spanish-Language Media in Their Lives." Media Activism and Participatory Politics/Civic Paths.* USC Annenberg Final Report.

Marszalek, D., 2017. Univision Launching Local Newscasts for Cross-Platform Broadcast. Retrieved on Sept. 20, 2021 from https://www.nexttv.com/news/univision-launching-local-newscasts-cross-platform-broadcast-164878

Mitú, 2021. About us. Retrieved on Sept. 30, 2021 from: https://wearemitu.com/about-mitu/

Pew Research Center, 2021. *Hispanic and Black Media Fact Sheet.* Pew Research Center. Retrieved on Sept. 30, 2021 from https://www.pewresearch.org/journalism/fact-sheet/hispanic-and-black-news-media/

Wallace, R., 2020. "We are the 200%": How Mitú Constructs Latino American Identity Through Discourse. Retrieved on Sept. 30, 2021 from: https://isoj.org/research/we-are-the-200-how-mitu-constructs-latino-american-identity-through-discourse/

15

Writing and Reporting Bilingually

Teresa Puente

Bilingual journalist Patricia Guadalupe recalled doing a radio interview with a U.S. Congressman from New York in Spanish. The radio interview was for a radio station in Mexico.

He was complaining about how some other Congress members were not taking him seriously on an issue.

He said, in Spanish: "Yo no sé por qué no me están cogiendo en serio".

"In Mexico the word 'coger' means a whole different thing than in the rest of the whole Spanish speaking world. It means I don't know why they're screwing me – in a real literal way," Guadalupe explained.

She told the Congressman that the interview was for a radio station in Mexico City. "I can't use this if you keep saying coger. And he started laughing."

He asked for another word and he redid the interview with: "No me están tomando en serio".

Translation: "I don't know why they are not taking me seriously."

This demonstrates just one of the challenges faced by bilingual journalists interviewing sources.

There are regional and country differences in the Spanish-language and bilingual journalists must be aware of these nuances so they can communicate effectively and also not offend their audiences.

Latinos in the United States have different experiences when it comes to language.

Around 36% are bilingual, 25% mainly use English and 38% mainly use Spanish, and among those who speak English, 59% are bilingual (Krogstad & Gonzalez-Barrera, 2015).

DOI: 10.4324/9781003212331-15

As a journalist, you can't assume what language a person speaks. You can ask an interview subject in which language they feel more comfortable and proceed with the interview in that language.

If you don't speak Spanish or the language of the interviewee, you could seek a translator. Careful to use a professional translator and avoid relying on people who don't have the experience translating as they might miscommunicate what is said.

Also, it's important to note that some people from Latin America may speak indigenous languages. There are an estimated 560 indigenous languages spoken in Latin America today (World Bank Group, 2015). Among the most spoken indigenous languages are Mayan, Nahuatl, Quechua and Guarani.

Whether you are reporting for an English-language or a Spanish-language media outlet, you will have an advantage if you are bilingual. It will allow you to interview more people and earn more income by publishing and producing work in two or more languages.

Case Study – Overview of the Style Guides

When writing in English, most U.S. journalists use the Associated Press Style guide. There was a Spanish-language edition but it has been discontinued.

Several Spanish-language media outlets have published their own style guides, including El País (Aguilar, 2014), the leading newspaper in Spain, Proceso, a leading news magazine in Mexico (Loya, 2009) and *La Nación*, a leading newspaper in Argentina (Hornos & Nacinovich, 1999).

There also is a guide "Manual de Periodismo" or "Journalism Manual" published in Mexico City (Marin, 2019). The National Association of Hispanic Journalists published a style guide (NAHJ, 2003) to create guidelines for writing in Spanish for U.S. audiences. It has not been recently updated.

There is not a single style guide in Spanish that is used as universally as the AP Style Guide.

That said, there are some guidelines one should follow when writing in Spanish. These are adapted from a style sheet created by journalism students for a bilingual magazine course taught at California State University, Long Beach. Bilingual journalism students at CSULB publish Díg en Español, the first Spanish-language news magazine in Long Beach, California.

The course has been taught as a blend of journalism history with facilitation of discussion of the failure of mainstream media to adequately report on the U.S. Latino community, the role and importance of Spanish-language and ethic media in covering the Latino community. The class produces a magazine once a semester as well as publishes weekly content online at digenespanol.com and on social media platforms @digenespanol on Instagram, TikTok and Twitter. The students created a style sheet in Spanish used by student reporters and copy editors. Here is a sample of the style sheet:

FIGURE 15.1 Style Guide

Accent Marks

Always include the accents even on your names.

Acronyms

Keep the acronym in the English letters, then explain what the acronym is and then you can keep using the acronym in the story instead of having to explain it each time.

Example: ICE, según sus letras en inglés, la agencia de inmigración y de seguridad. When possible, translate the name of the organization from English into Spanish.

Check to see if there is an official translation from a government entity or NGO.

Capitalization

In English all days of the week and months of the year are capitalized. In Spanish, they are all lowercase.

In English, the name of a county and the people of that country are capitalized. In Spanish, the name of the country is capitalized but the references to the people are lowercase.

Countries

Use Estados Unidos, not América. Avoid EE.UU. or E.U. (E.U. also can be used for the European Union.)

Use México, Perú and other countries that require an accent.

Numbers

Use period instead of commas when referring to big numbers

Instead of 10,000 use 10.000 or 1.000

Billions is not billones, it's mil millones. Billones is actually trillions.

Percentages

For percentages, use the symbol %, for example: 70%.

Quoting Style

When quoting in Spanish the periods and commas always go outside the quotation marks.

Here is a quote in Spanish:

> "Nuestra población es mucho más multirracial diversa y multicultural que lo que habíamos medido antes", señaló Nicholas Jones, Director de la División de Investigación Racial y Étnica de la Oficina del Censo (EFE, 2021).

Here is the same quote in English:

> "Our population is much more multiracially diverse and multicultural than we had measured before," signaled Nicholas Jones, director of the Division of Investigation of Race and Ethnicity of the Office of the Census.

Tildes

N and ñ: They are distinct letters of the alphabet. Both make different sounds so be careful when using them in stories. Also if you omit a tilde on a word such as año, it changes the meaning of the word. Leaving off tildes could cause errors or embarrassment.

Verbs

In English, generally one uses said or says when writing news articles. In Spanish, one can use as many verbs as possible to convey the same meaning. They are called sinónimos. You can use online references to seek for help, like: Wordreference https://www.wordreference.com/es/translation.asp, Real Academia de la Lengua https://www.rae.es/, among others.

Verbs other than said (dijo):

- proclamó
- reclamó
- gritó
- alegó
- discutío
- declaró
- comentó
- habló
- explicó
- interpretó
- testificó

Y

When to include "y" or "e" depending on what words or used

- Use "y" when you mention two things and the second word doesn't begin with the letter "i"
- Example: Estela y Carlos
- Use "e" when the second thing you mention begins with the letter "I"
- Example: Mirar e iniciar

In Conversation with Patricia Guadalupe

Patricia Guadalupe, is the Washington correspondent, Latino magazine, a contributing writer to NBC Latino, and an adjunct professor at American University.

FIGURE 15.2 Patricia Guadalupe

What were some of your first jobs in journalism?

I was writing and reporting in Spanish for Radio Bilingüe, writing and reporting in English for Hispanic Link News Service and I was writing and reporting in English for Latino USA. I was the first Washington correspondent for Radio Bilingüe, the first Washington correspondent for Latino USA and first Washington correspondent for WKAQ radio in Puerto Rico.

How long have you covered politics in Washington D.C.?

I've been in D.C. since covering the Clinton Administration, the Bush Administration, the Obama Administration and a little bit of the Trump Administration.

Although the White House is considered a plum assignment. I consider it extremely boring. Congressional coverage is much more interesting. You have (more than 500) members that you can talk to. Even if each office has just one person, that's more people. You have literally thousands of people that you can speak with and that will give you the kind of information you want. You can go to hearings at the Capitol that are open to the public. You can try to track down members in the (hallways) You can't really move around in the White House as easily especially after 9/11.

What is your approach to working in two languages?

I've managed two languages ever since I could talk. I've been bilingual my entire life. I grew up in Puerto Rico. We spoke Spanish and English at home. My father is Irish American from New York and we speak English to him. My mother is from Puerto Rico and to this day we speak Spanish to her.

She was very adamant from the very beginning that we would not lose our (Spanish) language. We went to a bilingual school in Puerto Rico.

I know that there are many Latinos who were discouraged even by their own families from speaking the language. You can be completely assimilated and keep your own languages.

I always tell people my favorite foods are rice and beans and cheeseburger and fries, just not together. You can be in both places without forgetting where you're from. Even though Puerto Rico is politically part of the United States, in our hearts and minds we are Latin American.

What are some tips for reporting and writing in Spanish?

I make sure that when I am interviewing someone that I don't use Spanglish.

The same sorts of nuances that you run into in English, we do the same in Spanish. I look at the different dictionaries that are out there online like the Real Academia, the Royal Academy of the Spanish language (rae.es). You can put in the little idioms in there and they can tell you where they are most popular and whether they are acceptable or not. Wordreference.com you can put in the chat, "Does this phrase make sense to people from Mexico?"

How do you approach interviewing Latino politicians in Washington, D.C.?

The Latino members of Congress have gotten so used to the Spanish-speaking press here that a lot of times when you run into them they ask: Do you want me to do the interview in English or Spanish? I say let's do both.

Ileana Ros-Lehtinen was the first Cuban American in Congress (before she retired). She came into the Capitol and looked around at the beginning of a press conference, and she said "It looks like pretty much everybody here is from the Spanish-speaking press so let me go ahead and start speaking in Spanish and then I'll say a few words in English." And this was live on C-Span ...You see more and more of that with the Latino members of Congress. They'll actually go on the floor of the House and speak in Spanish.

One of the biggest pet peeves I have is reporters and legislators alike saying they are fluent when they are not. Sometimes they come out sounding incredibly ridiculous when they say a few phrases. You don't have to be fluent in a particular language to be part of that community. I'm not saying to be Hispanic, to be

Latino or Latina that you even have to speak one word of Spanish. But if you are claiming to be fluent then be fluent.

Don't say "troca" and "lonchera" (Spanglish for truck and lunch) and things like that when you are doing a formal interview. People say the language is evolving. Well we don't have the same criteria in English. You wouldn't be using double negatives in English. You wouldn't say ain't in English and say it's ok because it's evolving.

What do you recommend for those who aren't fully bilingual to improve their Spanish?

Watch the Spanish "novela" with the captions on. You can get a bit more conversational. The Spanish language cartoons on Saturday mornings on Univision and Telemundo. Netflix and all the streaming services have a ton of Spanish-language content. Watch Univision and Telemundo newscasts. Watch as much as possible and another excellent resource is your local library, your school library, your neighborhood library. Go and check out a book or a movie, and all that stuff is free. Also, Voice of America has a service available online when they have all their languages in slow. They give you the news at a much slower pace so you can hear how they enunciate the words.

One of the reasons to watch the soap operas is you can hear the different nuances and inflections. Someone from Colombia speaks a lot different than someone from Mexico. The Argentinian accent is well known to be very different because it's closer to Italian. So their Spanish is more sing-songy. The Cuban, Puerto Rican and the Dominican Spanish is very, very fast. The Mexican Spanish is slower and more formal. People in Mexico use a lot more Ud (you formal) than they do in the Caribbean.

If it's available, pick up a copy of a Spanish-language newspaper, or read it online.

If you do an interview in Spanish and write the story in English, do you disclose the language the interview was done in originally?

Yes. You just say told me in Spanish. Or commented in Spanish. Or you can even say at the beginning. This interview was originally conducted in Spanish. You want to be as honest and open as possible and as transparent as possible. One thing that you don't ever want to do is write a story that has been translated and not say that it's been translated.

If I don't mention anywhere that the interview was in Spanish, then I'm not being truthful.

And I'm doing a disservice not to my readers or viewers or listeners but also to (my source.)

Some Spanish-language news outlets have unfortunately not been forthright. They'll take an article that was clearly written in English, translate it and then not say it was translated. That also does a disservice to the translator.

What advice do you have for bilingual journalism students?

Don't let them take advantage of the skills that you have. If you're bilingual, you need to get paid more.

While the whole multimedia category ... you're getting paid one salary for doing the job of four or five different people. And that is especially egregious if you're doing it in two languages.

If I'm writing something in English and then I'm doing it in Spanish. I'm basically doing two jobs. There is no reason for you not to pay me more. Tell them "I want and I'm not asking for but I want more money." Or you can negotiate and say give me an extra day or give me some more vacation time.

You are in charge of your own destiny. You have to be your best advocate. It's always a good idea to have a mentor.

Don't be afraid of where you're from and what your name is and what you represent.

Trade Tools and Tips

- If you did an interview in Spanish and translated the quotes to English, be sure to indicate that in the text with a phrase such as said in an interview in Spanish. The same applies if you did an interview in English and translated it into Spanish.
- Write in a universal Spanish to reach the widest Spanish-speaking audience.
- It's ok to ask a source to restate a phrase if it doesn't make sense or may confuse or offend a Spanish-speaking audience.
- Read Spanish news outlets from around Latin America and Spain.
- Watch as much Spanish-language television as you can.
- For broadcast, it's ok to use the Spanish-language pronunciation for your name.
- Do not omit tildes. This changes the meaning of the word.
- Avoid using words that may be specific to one Spanish-speaking country.
- Don't forget the accent marks.

Assignments

- Find articles from three Spanish-language media outlets on the same topic. Identify if there is a universal style and differences in the writing from acronyms to titles.
- Come up with a list of verbs or different ways to say said in Spanish.
- Come up with a list in Spanish of the 10 most common acronyms used in government.

- Complete an interview in Spanish or in English. Translate three of the quotes using proper quoting style in English and Spanish.
- Create a vocabulary list of ten nouns in Spanish and these words have different meanings depending on the country of origin.

Discussion Questions

- What are the major Spanish-language outlets in your community? What are their strengths and weaknesses? What audience are they trying to reach?
- What are some of the media outlets that use Spanglish? What are their strengths and weaknesses? What audience are they trying to reach?
- What are some of the English Latinx news sites? What are their strengths and weaknesses? What audience are they trying to reach?
- What are some of the differences in accents in spoken Spanish? Is there a universal Spanish?

References

El País, *Libro de Estilo*. AGUILAR, Mexico City, 2014.

Hispanos y otras minorías impulsan el crecimiento demográfico en EEUU. (2021 August 12) EFE. https://www.latimes.com/espanol/eeuu/articulo/2021-08-12/censo-muestra-creciente-diversidad-de-la-poblacion-de-eeuu-incluyendo-latinos

Hornos, P.O., & Nacinovich, N. *La Nación: Manual de Estilo y Ética Periodística*, ESPASA, Buenos Aires, 1999 (fourth edition).

Krogstad, J.A., & Gonzalez-Barrera, A. *A majority of English-speaking Hispanic in the U.S. are bilingual*, Pew Research Center, March 24, 2015. https://www.pewresearch.org/fact-tank/2015/03/24/a-majority-of-english-speaking-hispanics-in-the-u-s-are-bilingual/

Loya, S. *Manual de estilo de Proceso*. Random House: Mexico City, 2009, (second edition).

Marin, C. *Manual de Periodismo*. Penguin Random House, Grupo Editorial, Mexico City, 2019 (second edition).

National Association of Hispanic Journalists (NAHJ), *Manual de estilo*, Washington, D.C. 2003.

World Bank Group, Indigenous Latin America in the Twenty-First Century, 2015. https://documents1.worldbank.org/curated/en/145891467991974540/pdf/Indigenous-Latin-America-in-the-twenty-first-century-the-first-decade.pdf

16

A Glimpse Into the Future: Digital-Native Latinx News Media

Lourdes M. Cueva Chacón and Jessica Retis

When Maritza Félix was studying Communications in Mexico more than 15 years ago, she was one of the few students who actually did reporting work. Most of her classmates were pursuing careers in corporate communication or public relations. She, instead, rode on buses and walked on dirt roads and relentlessly searched for sources for her stories.

Little did Félix know that all that hard work would prepare her for the news service she would provide through Conecta Arizona where she reaches a transnational audience from Phoenix, Arizona to Sonora, Mexico and beyond.

Félix's experience, which we discuss in depth below, is not uncommon among Latinx journalists. You might be familiar with famous reporters and anchors, such as Jorge Ramos (Mexico) and Ilia Calderón (Colombia) who started their careers in their native countries, came to the United States and had to work hard to make a name for themselves. What is different about Félix is that she is among the leaders of a group of entrepreneurial Latinx journalists who are creating and leading a new wave of digital-native Latinx news organizations that are listening and engaging with Latinx communities where they are and, many times, in Spanish.

But, What Are Digital-Native Latinx News Media?

In a 2021 study (Retis & Cueva Chacón, 2021), digital-native Latinx news media were defined as "journalistic ventures launched, developed, and maintained online to gather, assess, present, and disseminate news and information about, or relevant to, Latinx communities." These ventures produce news in Spanish, English, bilingually and sometimes even in Spanglish.

DOI: 10.4324/9781003212331-16

Many traditional media: newspapers, TV and radio have an important online presence and are also innovating in news media. But the digital-native news media are media that have emerged solely in the digital world. Most of these news organizations are four years old or younger. Because of their youth and their technological savviness, these digital enterprises are increasingly producing original content beyond the web. Some of them might not even have a web presence and instead, distribute their content through social media or messaging applications.

The coronavirus pandemic and the changes in the advertisement models that sustained traditional media have tested the resilience of publishers and news organizations. However, experts agreed that there were important shifts in news media business models happening for some time already (Glasser, 2020a, 2020b). Among these shifts are: (1) news outlets are being created as non-profit organizations in larger numbers than in the past; (2) local news outlets are joining efforts to improve the coverage of their communities and (3) coverage is focusing more on underserved communities.

Latinx media, as part of the U.S. media landscape, are impacted by these trends and others that are more particular to the audiences they serve. Among the most important ones are the following.

Non-Profit Organizations

Latinx news organizations are increasingly being created as non-profits. In the study mentioned previously, which included 103 digital-native Latinx news organizations, 21.4% were identified as non-profit. Well-established organizations such as Radio Ambulante and the Futuro Media Group – producers of Latino USA and In The Thick – are independent non-profit organizations that support their operations through grants, donations, events and by partnering with public media.

Latino USA, originally a radio show and now a fully digital media enterprise, was distributed by National Public Radio (NPR) for more than a decade. Recently, in 2020, they partnered with PRX securing distribution of their podcast in more than 220 public radio stations as well as on their on-demand audio service. "(As) The longest-running Latino-centered public media program, the show is essential for U.S. audiences. PRX is thrilled to bring Latino USA to stations across the country and to podcast listeners everywhere" said Shona Koester, Chief Strategy Officer at PRX (Latino USA, 2020), when the partnership was announced recognizing the importance of covering Latinx audiences.

Another example of national reach, Radio Ambulante, a podcast in Spanish that tells stories about the under-served Latin American and Latinx communities, similarly partnered with NPR in 2016 for the distribution of the podcast (NPR, 2016). But there are Latinx non-profit media of all sizes and ranges. *The*

Nevada Independent, a non-profit newspaper for the state of Nevada, serves the Nevada Latinx community with *The Nevada Independent En Español*. The online newspaper also produces a Spanish-language newsletter *¿Qué Pasó en la Semana?* and a podcast – Cafecito con Luz y Michelle – to discuss important issues in the community.

A smaller effort but not for that less important is Cicero Independiente, a bilingual news site that focuses on what is happening in Cicero, a western suburb in Chicago, Illinois, with more than 80,000 residents who are mostly immigrants. The news site was founded by three young community members who realized that their suburb was neither being covered by mainstream news media nor by alternative media and decided to talk with residents to learn about their information needs. In July 2020, they launched the site which covers schools, city council and local entrepreneurs among other hyperlocal issues (Nelson, 2021).

Another group of non-profit digital Latinx news media that is growing is college media. These digital outlets are exploring new technology affordances and are innovating in ways to deliver news. Among the most notable are bilingual online magazine Borderzine.com (The University of Texas at El Paso), bilingual news site Noticiero Móvil (University of Nevada, Reno) and the Spanish-language outlets Dímelo (University of Southern California), Al Día (California State University Fullerton) and DÍG (California State University Long Beach). These outlets have won multiple awards and grants and produce content for multiple platforms including social media (Cal State Fullerton, 2019; Mizgata, 2012; Noticiero Móvil, 2021).

Amplifying the Latinx Community in Spanish, English or Both

In the past, Hispanic or Latino media would clearly differentiate in the U.S. media landscape because they produced news almost exclusively in Spanish. However, because new generations of U.S.-born Latinos/as use English-language news sources more than older generations, Latinx media are shifting to offer these audiences the news in the language and culture they appreciate. In a study on digital-native Latinx news media (Retis & Cueva Chacón, 2021), the authors found that just a little over half of the organizations analyzed delivered news in Spanish. A growing group delivered the news in English (28%) or bilingually (15.5%).

Similarly, Latinx media are changing with the new generations and getting more vocal at clearly stating their objectives and mission as covering the Latinx community for the community's benefit. These outlets pay more attention to their communities' needs by holding events where they invite residents to share their information needs. For instance, El Tímpano held events where hundreds of Oakland residents shared what news they would like to have (Bair, 2018a), Cicero Independiente interviewed residents before launching (Nelson, 2021), and Conecta Arizona held weekly La Hora del Cafecito where they directly connected with people in their WhatsApp group (Félix, 2021).

Latinx media are listening more and getting more engaged with the Latinx communities they serve. As they do so, they are changing their discourse and talking about amplifying and elevating the voices of under-represented Latinx communities. These news organizations say that they would correct past errors of under reporting or ignoring the Latinx community. They also express the need for correcting stereotypes, avoiding false and inaccurate media narratives and "elevating … the status of and the discourse about Latinos" (Retis & Cueva Chacón, 2021, p. 49).

Creating Transnational Spaces

Latinx media in the United States often covered Latin American issues as their audiences continued their connections with their places of origin. However, more recently, technological affordances and the COVID-19 pandemic have boosted their ability for creating transnational spaces for their teams as well as their audiences. In the previous research mentioned above (Retis & Cueva Chacón, 2021), the authors found that close to 20% of digital-native Latinx media would have part of their staff located outside of the United States, reported from both sides of the U.S.-Mexico border, or were refugees from Latin America who reported about their countries of origin creating "complex and multifaceted geographical synergies instead of excluding each other" (p. 50).

Spanish-language podcasts such as El Washington Post and El Hilo – which are produced in Washington D.C. and New York respectively – have hosts located in Washington D.C., Madrid, Spain, Bogotá, Colombia, London, United Kingdom and Mexico City. They report on world or Latin American issues as well as the most important U.S. events for Spanish-speaking audiences in the United States and the world.

The bilingual online magazine Borderzine, created in 2008, is the oldest digital native doing this at El Paso-Ciudad Juárez border. Many students in their staff are Ciudad Juárez residents who attend The University of Texas at El Paso and cross the border every day. The Spanish-language newsletter El Migrante, a project by Internews, covers the San Diego-Tijuana and El Paso-Ciudad Juárez borders with reporters crossing the border on a regular basis. Another case is Conecta Arizona (see interview below) conceived from its origins as a transnational project intended to serve audiences in Arizona, United States and Sonora, Mexico.

Digital But Non-Traditional

One of the most important trends emerging among digital Latinx news organizations is their efforts to exploit the affordances of new platforms and digital applications. A sign of this trend is that only 20% of digital-native outlets produced original content exclusively for a website (Retis & Cueva Chacón, 2021). Almost half of the outlets in the study produced original content for more than one platform. In other words, they would not simply repurpose content and distribute it on social media, for instance. These outlets understood the different audiences they reached using different platforms and applications and produced content accordingly.

Digital media focused on millennial Latinas and the Latinx community is a good example of this trend. They understand that Instagram is one of Latinas preferred social media and produce content for them. News sites such as BESE, Be Latina and Hip Latina are among these news outlets. These media organizations produce traditional multimedia news about entertainment, culture, gender and general Latinx issues for their websites. Their Instagram accounts are a different story. BESE has BESE Chats sometimes hosted by actor Zoe Saldaña, its founder. Be Latina produces news recaps, chats or conversations with influencers and artists, and they also reproduce TikToks from comedians. Similarly, Hip Latinas hosts Charlas with HL where they interview Latinx artists and celebrities to discuss Latinx issues.

Another group of Latinx media, focused on serving Spanish-speaking new immigrants, are producing newsletters and audiocasts for messaging apps, especially WhatsApp. These news organizations understand that WhatsApp is a well-established messaging app in Latin America because users can place voice calls over Wi-Fi and because many mobile providers do not charge for its use on data plans (Ariano, 2020), and communities in the United States use it to get in contact with their relatives. Documented, a news site covering New York's immigrant communities, is recorded as the first using WhatsApp to distribute news to Spanish-speaking communities. Conecta Arizona, El Migrante, Qué Hay De Nuevo NH? and Tu Voz KUNR also have daily, weekly and monthly news services through the messaging app (see Figure 16.1). Their news services were especially important during the worst part of the coronavirus pandemic as they provided vital information about safety measures, lockdowns, access to government help, vaccines, among other issues.

As the analysis of these trends reveals, digital-native Latinx news media are taking advantage of technology to reach audiences where they are. They continue listening and procuring the news that their communities need. Latinx news entrepreneurs are also taking advantage of changes in the media landscape and are venturing to start smaller but very focused news enterprises sometimes as non-profit organizations.

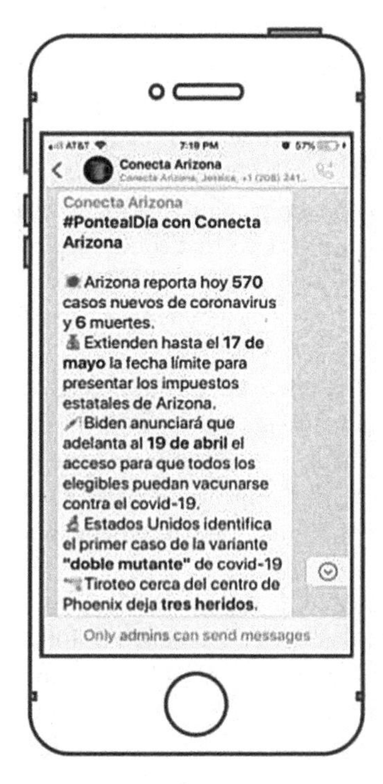

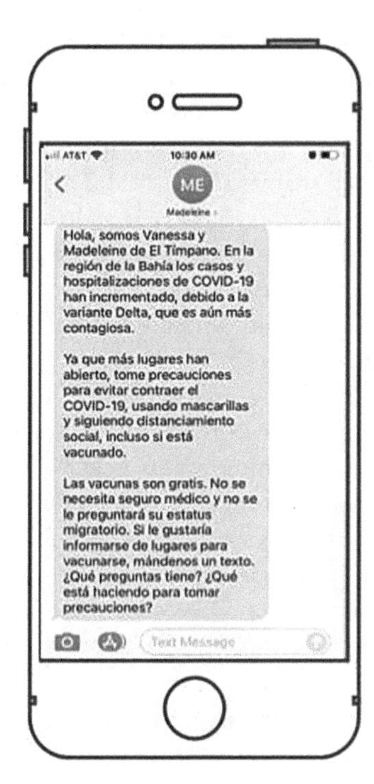

FIGURE 16.1 Examples of news services by Conecta Arizona and El Tímpano

A Closer Look: El Tímpano

El Tímpano – Spanish for eardrum – is a Latinx news media that seeks to provide "Equitable and impactful local news, information, and civic engagement" (El Tímpano, 2021, p. 5) to Spanish – and Mayan-speaking communities in Oakland, California.

El Tímpano started in 2018 when founder and director Madeleine Bair decided to talk with the Latinx community about the high cost of housing in the San Francisco area. Following a model designed and tested by the Listening Post Collective for mapping communities' information needs, Bair interviewed and met with dozens of community leaders and hundreds of Fruitvale residents (Bair, 2018b).

Fruitvale community members shared with her that they didn't have access to local news or to information that could help them get access to resources. Bair was familiar with the media landscape in the area and asked them about traditional sources of news and information for Spanish-speaking communities.

Bair was surprised to learn that even though the majority of residents watched Univision and Telemundo, they considered them too negative and sensationalist. Bair also found that only half of the residents accessed Spanish-language radio and very few read newspapers in Spanish and had a hard time recalling the newspapers' names (Bair, 2018b).

All of this made Bair realize that the Spanish-speaking communities in what is known as "Deep East Oakland" were in dire need of news that could improve their quality of life. Based on this information, she founded El Tímpano, a community oriented, local journalism and civic engagement non-profit media.

The most innovative service provided by El Tímpano is their Spanish-language SMS reporting platform. Oakland residents sign up for their service at the listening events held by El Tímpano's staff or get El Tímpano's phone number through word of mouth. Twice a week, El Tímpano's reporters send text messages with relevant information for the community and ask them about their main concerns.

In the period between March 2020 and March 2021, the worst of the coronavirus pandemic, El Tímpano grew their SMS subscribers base from 400 to 1,400. It has also reported that "46% of SMS subscribers texted El Tímpano at least once in the past year" (El Tímpano, 2021, p. 8). As El Tímpano has made it their objective to answer every question they receive, they claim to be breaking the cycle of neglecting information to Spanish- and Mayan-speaking communities in the area (see Figure 16.2).

El Tímpano's sustainability model relies mostly on donations and grants. Subscriptions or other forms of payment from their audience are not an option because El Tímpano serves mostly low-income communities. However, recently, El Tímpano has started innovating in finding new revenue sources as it has developed a revenue stream through civic partnerships. Their first partnership was with the U.S. Census. Census officials found valuable El Tímpano's access to a segment of the community that they had difficulty counting and awarded them a contract. El Tímpano informed their subscribers about the census, why it was important to be counted and how it would happen (Dejarnette, 2021). The experience with that partnership has led to another one with the local health department to inform the subscribers about COVID-19 safety and vaccine access.

Non-profit news organizations such as El Tímpano often struggle finding revenue sources because they serve non-traditional and marginalized communities. It is also difficult to measure their impact using traditional metrics (i.e. clicks, likes) or to sell advertisements as their audiences are mostly low income and the platforms they use (SMS, WhatsApp, social media) might not be able to host them. Nevertheless, Latinx media continue to innovate to serve their communities, creating opportunities for new organizations.

FIGURE 16.2 El Timpano constantly asks East Oakland residents about their needs

In Conversation with Maritza Félix, Founder of Conecta Arizona

Maritza Félix (see Figure 16.3), an award-winning journalist turned journalism entrepreneur, has 15 years of experience reporting border communities. Félix started her career reporting for Televisa and newspapers in Sonora, Mexico.

FIGURE 16.3 Journalist and news entrepreneur Maritza Felix

In Arizona, she has worked for Prensa Hispana and Telemundo. In 2018, she decided to become an independent journalist and produced and wrote for Discovery Channel, BBC Channel 4 and Al Jazeera, among others.

Félix was freelancing and working on a documentary when lockdowns were put in place because of the pandemic. Soon, she created Conecta Arizona, a transborder community journalism project that delivers news in Spanish through WhatsApp, Facebook and other social media to residents in Arizona, United States and Sonora, México. In an interview, Félix talks about why she thought a journalism project such as Conecta Arizona was needed and how much she has accomplished. (The authors translated the interview from Spanish and edited it for brevity and clarity.)

How Did You Get the Idea of Conecta Arizona?

When the pandemic hit, all my projects were postponed or canceled. I had to reinvent myself and started writing in English. I realized that my creative process happens in Spanish. I think, search and write in Spanish and then translate to English. So, as I was covering the pandemic in English, I realized that there was no information in Spanish about the COVID-19 in Arizona. I started translating (into Spanish) a few things here and there and I would post them on my Twitter and Facebook accounts. People reacted and asked me lots of questions.

That made me think that we had to do something (to cover the pandemic) in Arizona. John Rudolph from Feet in Two Worlds, a non-profit that empowers migrant journalists, and Jesse Hardman from The Listening Post Collective, a non-profit that supports the revitalization of local news, offered me a fellowship to start my project and that is how it started.

How Did You Decide WhatsApp Was the Best Platform?

When we started planning the project, our sponsors suggested using text messaging (SMS) because the Listening Post Collective had already supported a similar idea in Louisiana. And I said, no, it won't work because my community, my raza, doesn't use text messages. It costs money. It is even more expensive for transborder Mexicans. We use WhatsApp.

My mom, without planning it, reassured me that WhatsApp was the right platform. She stayed over in Sonora during the pandemic and she communicated with me through WhatsApp. She would send greetings, gifs and prayers and all of that several times a day. She would also send me misinformation. I would tell her to check first with me, her journalist daughter, before sending misinformation. But that made me think, we had to use the same platform where the community was sharing misinformation.

It didn't matter if we were few at the beginning. I thought, we will start a small WhatsApp group and will grow from there. The group started with family and friends and then we grew organically. By mid-summer 2020, we had reached the max number of participants in a WhatsApp group, 257. (WhatsApp groups allow 256 members and the manager of the group.)

The next step was creating a Facebook page. Conecta Arizona had to grow even though it was going to be more work for me. Now we have a daily radio show and a newsletter as well.

Was Conecta Arizona Originally Thought of as a Transborder Journalism Project?

Yes, it was a transborder project from the start. My mom stayed on the Mexican side because of border restrictions. And a big part of my audience, people who follow me on Facebook, people I serve and who read me are on the Mexican side.

To me it is odd to speak about Arizona and Sonora as if they were two separate entities. This is a border region. We have grown together. Even though we are divided by the wall, we always have had a life on both sides. For instance, when I was a child living in Sonora, my mom would say "Ay, necesito ir al súper," and she would go to the "Kmart" in Nogales, Arizona. And many of my friends in Arizona would spend their weekends in Sonora.

The lack of fact-checked information in Spanish is not only an Arizona problem. The Mexican authorities are lagging in terms of information. The United States is leading with resources and research and the Mexican government is playing catch up.

How Is Conecta Arizona Being Financed?

So far, it has been through grants. I first got a small grant to create Conecta Arizona and to test which was the best format for it. But I cannot think small. I don't know if it's good or not, but when they give me a seed, I start thinking about the tree and a hammock and the ocean. It is how I am.

Then, I was named a JSK Community Impact Fellow from Stanford University which covered my expenses and allowed me to continue the work. After that, I got another larger grant which I used to hire a producer for the radio show and got merchandising to promote our brand.

I will continue applying for grants. Meanwhile, I am also part of the Executive Program in News Innovation and Leadership at the Craig Newmark Graduate School of Journalism where I am learning as much as I can so I can make Conecta Arizona sustainable.

In general, it is complicated to measure the success of an innovative and experimental project like this. Because WhatsApp doesn't record metrics, it is difficult to show impact to potential donors who haven't made a decision about supporting us yet. They don't know what impact their dollars will make. I keep track of group members' participation, number of guests we have hosted, the number of questions our members have asked and so on, but it is all because I decided to do it. I can tell you stories about our group members; how people are using our information, how we have helped people and I use those stories in my grant applications, but I think we all need better training.

Universities and journalism teachers who are preparing you to get to the world, they are not teaching you how to deal with this, how to assess impact. They do not understand how the dynamics of news media use is changing and news production and delivery as well. Especially in places like Arizona, where there is a mix of more tech savvy residents and new immigrants.

What Changes Do You Think Are Needed in Journalism Education?

When I was attending college, I was the only one who would go out and do reporting. I was the odd one. Here (in the United States), journalism students are better prepared in technology, in how to produce multimedia, how to deliver a news package, how to write a web story, how to dance for a TikTok and much more. But they (the universities) never teach you how to do it for yourself, for your own news media. You are taught to do more for the people who hire you. And sometimes, our employers do not look like us, do not talk like us; they do not have the same cultural baggage; they do not have our immigration experience. Then is when culture clashes start to happen and resentment emerges. And many talented people end up leaving the profession, don't you think?

Trade Tools and Tips

1. In the post-digital era, seeking a job in the newsrooms is not the only option for journalism graduates. There are several organizations that provide funds for innovative news projects. Check out, for example, this list from American Press Institute https://www.americanpressinstitute.org/about/sources-of-funding/, or this other from the Society of Professional Journalists https://www.spj.org/foundation-grants.asp
2. Get into the practice of seeking funding for your projects. Start by applying to the ones that your own school must be offering on a yearly basis. You can also apply to the ones offered by the National Association of Hispanic Journalists https://nahj.org/2020/12/16/2021-nahj-scholarships/
3. In the era of information disorder, there are many ways to fact check your stories. Bookmark sites where you can find advice on how to confirm the accuracy of information like the one from Poynter International Fact Checking Network: https://www.poynter.org/ifcn/

Assignments

1. Search information about Latino digital-native media in the United States. Review and compare where they are located and what type of media they are. You can use the Google Advanced Search (https://www.google.com/advanced_search) and seek for the boolean "Latino Media," or any available mapping of Latino digital media available like the one produced by CUNY (https://thelatinomediareport.journalism.cuny.edu/)
2. Search information about Latinx digital-native media in the Americas. Review and compare their locations, investigate what type of funding they have, what issues they focus on, what types of content they offer. You can use the Google Advanced Search (https://www.google.com/advanced_search) or any available mapping of Latino digital media like the one produced by Sembramedia (https://www.sembramedia.org/sembramedia-directory-2/)
3. Review the Listening Post Collective Playbook (https://www.listeningpostcollective.org/playbook). Their toolbox includes guides and templates you'll need when creating your own project as well as resources to help you keep organized and learn from your work. Follow their guide to analyze the stages to understand the needs of your community. Where in the community do you think you could find people to listen to? Walmart, food banks, Latinx centers, etc. What information needs can you identify?
4. Plan and write a newsletter. But, first check out some good examples like these ones (a) Migratory Notes; (b) The Los Angeles Times' LatinX Files; (c) The New York Times' El Times and (d) Documented Community.
5. Explore the pros and cons of these tools: Substack (https://substack.com/), Twitter newsletter or Medium.
6. How to pitch an audio project. Review Radio Ambulante instructions on how to pitch a story idea and work on yours: https://radioambulante.org/escuela-radio-ambulante/el-arte-del-pitch
7. Once you created your audio piece, seek ways to publish it. For example, check SoundCloud, an online audio distribution platform. You can also check Spotify for Podcasters.
8. Let's talk about free content on the web. Creative Commons is a nonprofit organization that helps overcome legal obstacles to the sharing of knowledge and creativity to address the world's pressing challenges. Check their website and select some available content for your multimedia project: https://creativecommons.org/
9. Social Media strategies for your projects. Once you have your project, you can explore ways to publish and promote it via social media. Check out Facebook for Journalists, Google's Journalists Studio, or Google News Lab, for example.

10. Let's approach our story ideas not from the conflict but the solutions perspective. The Solutions Journalism Network is a nonprofit organization dedicated to supporting newsrooms and journalists who are sharing solutions stories. Check out their learning lab and try to rethink your multimedia story from a solutions perspective.

Discussion Questions

1. After reading this chapter and learning about digital-native Latinx media, what have you learned about the current state and future of news media in the post-digital era?
2. How would you differentiate news stories about and for Latinx audiences from those directed to mainstream audiences in the era of post-truth?
3. If you were planning on launching a digital-native news outlet, would you produce it in English? Why? In Spanish? Why? Bilingual? Why?
4. Would you consider digital-native Latinx media local, hyperlocal, translocal or transnational? Elaborate your answer.
5. After reviewing diverse types of digital-native Latinx media, what types of content do you think are most covered? Why?

References

Ariano, R. (2020). 'How does WhatsApp work internationally?': How to use WhatsApp internationally for free with Wi-Fi. *Insider.* https://www.businessinsider.com/how-does-whatsapp-work-internationally

Bair, M. (2018a). Deep listening to map a community's information needs. *El Tímpano.* https://medium.com/el-t%C3%ADmpano/deep-listening-to-map-a-communitys-information-needs-17da9daffc8a

Bair, M. (2018b). "Más Información" An Information Needs Assessment of Latino Immigrants in Oakland California. https://internews.org/wp-content/uploads/2021/02/INA_Oakland-California_7.11.18_for-web.pdf

Cal State Fullerton. (2019). *Titans Win Prestigious College Television Award.* [*Press Release*]. https://news.fullerton.edu/2019/12/al-dia-emmy/

Dejarnette, B. (2021). What happens to that reader revenue strategy when your readers can't spare it? Lion Publishers. https://www.lionpublishers.com/news-guest-madeleine-bair/

El Tímpano. (2021). *Impact report: March 2020 to March 2021.* https://static1.squarespace.com/static/5a577957bff200d963b549df/t/606a9c55fb09410062464a14/1617599607273/ElTi%CC%81mpanoImpactReport2020-2021.pdf

Félix, M. (2021). We are on air! *JSK.* https://medium.com/jsk-class-of-2021/we-are-on-air-939363775087

Glasser, M. (2020a). 5 business models for local news to watch in 2020. *Trust, Media and Democracy.* https://medium.com/trust-media-and-democracy/5-business-models-for-local-news-to-watch-in-2020-82223d856896

Glasser, M. (2020b). 5 business model shifts for local news in 2021 and beyond. *Trust, Media and Democracy*. https://medium.com/trust-media-and-democracy/5-business-model-shifts-for-local-news-in-2021-and-beyond-997207650d38

Latino USA. (2020). *Latino USA and PRX announce a new partnership*. [Press release]. https://www.latinousa.org/2020/06/30/latinousaprx/

Mizgata, J. (2012, August 29). *2012 Online Journalism Awards finalists announced*. [Press release]. https://journalists.org/2012/08/29/2012-online-journalism-awards-finalists-announced/

Nelson, M. (2021, February 28). Three residents launched an online bilingual news publication in Cicero. 14 East. http://fourteeneastmag.com/index.php/2020/02/28/three-residents-launched-an-online-bilingual-news-publication-in-cicero/

Noticiero Móvil. (2021). *Noticiero Móvil receives National Murrow Award for its joint bilingual pandemic coverage*. [Press release]. https://noticieromovil.com/noticiero-movil-national-murrow-award-2021-bilingual-pandemic-journalism/

NPR. (2016, November 22). *NPR adds Radio Ambulante to its podcast lineup*. [Press release]. https://www.npr.org/about-npr/501768246/npr-radio-ambulante-release

Retis, J., & Cueva Chacón, L. M. (2021). Mapping digital-native U.S. Latinx news: Beyond geographical boundaries, language barriers, and hyper-fragmentation of audiences. #ISOJ. https://isoj.org/research/mapping-digital-native-u-s-latinx-news-beyond-geographical-boundaries-language-barriers-and-hyper-fragmentation-of-audiences/

INDEX

Note: Bold page numbers refer to tables and *italic* page numbers refer to figures